11·11·77

CHURCH AND STATE
IN REVOLUTIONARY VIRGINIA, 1776-1787

Church and State

in Revolutionary Virginia, 1776–1787

Thomas E. Buckley, S.J.

University Press of Virginia

Charlottesville

THE UNIVERSITY PRESS OF VIRGINIA
Copyright © 1977 by the Rector and Visitors
of the University of Virginia

First published 1977

Library of Congress Cataloging in Publication Data

Buckley, Thomas E.   1939-
    Church and state in Revolutionary Virginia, 1776-1787.

    Bibliography: p. 201
    Includes index.
    1. Church and state in Virginia—History. 2. Religious
liberty—Virginia—History. I. Title.
BR555.V8B8   261.7'09755   77-4283
ISBN 0-8139-0692-X

Printed in the United States of America

For My Mother and Father

Contents

Maps

Preface

Shortly after the outbreak of the American Revolution, the newly independent commonwealth of Virginia began a lengthy reexamination of the formal relationship which had bound its colonial government to the established Church of England. The process moved forward in fits and starts, provoked debates which at times threatened to convulse the state, and culminated in a series of heated legislative battles and the passage of Thomas Jefferson's bill establishing religious freedom in 1786. Ultimately the Old Dominion separated church and state in a way substantially identifiable with later American law and practice, for in its articulation of the issues and their ultimate resolution, Virginia provided the rationale and the preliminary draft for the First Amendment and its later interpretation. As Justice Rutledge of the Supreme Court wrote in 1947, "the great instruments of the Virginia struggle . . . became warp and woof of our constitutional tradition."[1]

This is a study of the controversy over religion in Revolutionary Virginia. In particular I have focused on the evolution of religious legislation in the General Assembly, the shifting strengths and interaction of the major churches in the commonwealth, the development of both rationalist and evangelical thought on church and state, and the various positions taken not only by political and religious leaders but also by the average citizens of the state. Their petitions are especially significant, for no other single issue of the time genuinely aroused so many ordinary people to address their

[1] *Everson* v. *Board of Education,* 330 U.S. 1, 39 (1947). The Supreme Court has consistently drawn upon the Virginia experience to interpret the meaning of both the free exercise and no establishment clauses of the First Amendment. See, for example, *Reynolds* v. *United States,* 98 U.S. 145 (1878), *McCollum* v. *Board of Education,* 333 U.S. 203 (1948), and *Engel* v. *Vitale,* 370 U.S. 421 (1962) (Richard E. Morgan, *The Supreme Court and Religion* [New York, 1972], passim).

legislators. It is perhaps useful to realize that in exercising their right to make their voices heard, they ensured that the views of the majority would prevail. In describing and enumerating the opposing forces in this contest, I have not attempted a quantitative analysis, either of the legislature or the petitioners, in terms of other partisan issues. As Jackson Turner Main has already shown, the religious questions in Virginia cut across factional party lines.[2] Often men who were intimate friends and in complete agreement on other political measures clashed on the advisability of governmental involvement in religion and the best means for forming Virginians into a virtuous people. Finally, the entire process which resulted in the passage of Jefferson's bill provides an opportunity to study the theories of religious liberty and the church-state relationship among both the pietists and the rationalists. The latter have often received a disproportionate amount of attention. The evangelicals had ideas also, and their support for the final settlement was not simply the product of vested interests but the result of a committed vision of the role of religion in society which would prove enormously significant in the next century.

In view of its importance, it is surprising that the history of this settlement has not received more careful attention in recent years. Denominational historians have understandably portrayed the controversy with special reference to their own religious traditions, but frequently their accounts have been flawed by limited data and an apologetic bias.[3] The only substantial work by a

[2] Jackson Turner Main, *Political Parties before the Constitution* (Chapel Hill, N.C., 1973), pp. 259-60.

[3] For a Baptist interpretation, see Charles F. James, *Documentary History of the Struggle for Religious Liberty in Virginia* (Lunchburg, Va., 1900), and in a more summary fashion, Garnett Ryland, *The Baptists in Virginia, 1699-1926* (Richmond, 1926). The traditional Presbyterian interpretation was stated by William Henry Foote, *Sketches of Virginia, Historical and Biographical, First Series* (Richmond, 1850). See also Thomas Cary Johnson, *Virginia Presbyterianism and Religious Liberty in Colonial and Revolutionary Times* (Richmond, 1907). An extremely important article, revising substantially the position of Foote, is Fred J. Hood, "Revolution and Religious Liberty: The Conservation of the Theocratic Concept in Virginia," *Church History* 40 (1971): 170-81. Finally, the second volume of George MacLaren Brydon, *Virginia's Mother Church and the Political Conditions under Which It Grew* (Philadelphia, 1952), is the most recent account from an Episcopalian viewpoint.

secular writer dates from the first decade of this century when Hamilton James Eckenrode, the archivist at the Virginia State Library, assembled many of the relevant documents into chronological order, together with a commentary. Although useful for its printed sources, his book is incomplete and at times inaccurate. Moreover, Eckenrode's interpretations, particularly his viewpoint that the entire controversy developed within a liberal-conservative framework and ended in a radical triumph, need revision.[4] More recent historians have dealt with one or more aspects of the Virginia religious settlement, but without the full-scale treatment it deserves.[5]

This study began as a doctoral dissertation under the direction of Morton Borden at the University of California at Santa Barbara, and for his patient assistance and wise counsel both as a teacher and friend, I am immensely grateful. I have also profited from the advice of Robert Michaelsen and Carl V. Harris, both of whom served on the doctoral committee. William M. E. Rachal, W. Harrison Daniel, and James H. Smylie read the entire manuscript in its later stages and, along with liberal doses of encouragement, offered a number of useful suggestions for its revision. Any errors or shortcomings are, of course, entirely the fault of the author.

Grants from the University of California at Santa Barbara and the Jesuit Community at Loyola Marymount University financed the research trips on which the book depended. The library staffs of a large number of institutions were invaluable in their assistance,

[4]Hamilton James Eckenrode, *Separation of Church and State in Virginia: A Study in the Development of the Revolution* (rept. New York, 1971).

[5]For example: Freeman H. Hart, *The Valley of Virginia in the American Revolution, 1763-1789* (New York, 1942), pp. 137-48; Robert E. and B. Katherine Brown, *Virginia, 1705-1786: Democracy or Aristocracy?* (East Lansing, Mich., 1964), pp. 295-301; Marvin K. Singleton, "Colonial Virginia as First Amendment Matrix: Henry, Madison, and Assessment Establishment," *Journal of Church and State* 8 (1966): 344-64; Elwyn A. Smith, *Religious Liberty in the United States: The Development of Church-State Thought since the Revolutionary Era* (Philadelphia, 1972), pp. 27-67; Cushing Strout, *The New Heavens and New Earth: Political Religion in America* (New York, 1974), pp. 77-90. Finally, there are two recent dissertations in this subject area: Miryam Neulander Kay, "Separation of Church and State in Jeffersonian Virginia" (Ph.D. diss., University of Kentucky, 1967), and Mary Elizabeth Quinlivan, "Ideological Controversy over Religious Establishment in Revolutionary America" (Ph.D. diss., University of Wisconsin, 1971).

but in particular I wish to acknowledge the Virginia Historical Society, the Virginia State Library, and Margaret Cook of the manuscripts division of the Earl Gregg Swem Library at the College of William and Mary. The following libraries have graciously extended permission to quote from materials in their possession: the Earl Gregg Swem Library at the College of William and Mary in Virginia, the Virginia Historical Society, the Virginia State Library, the Library of Congress, the University of Virginia, Duke University, the University of North Carolina, the Union Theological Seminary in Richmond, the Houghton Library at Harvard University, the Pierpont Morgan Library in New York City, and the Historical Society of the Episcopal Church at Austin, Texas. The *Journal of Presbyterian History* has granted permission to publish portions of my article "Church-State Settlement in Virginia: The Presbyterian Contribution," which appeared in its bicentennial edition (54 [Spring, 1976] : 105-19).

Finally I wish to express my appreciation to my colleagues in the History Department at Loyola Marymount University and to my brother Jesuits for their support and encouragement throughout this project.

Los Angeles, California
February 1977

CHURCH AND STATE

IN REVOLUTIONARY VIRGINIA, 1776-1787

Introduction

WRITING to an old college friend shortly before the outbreak of the Revolution, James Madison posed the problem of the relationship between religion and the state. "Is an Ecclesiastical Establishment," he asked, "absolutely necessary to support civil society?"[1] At that early stage of his intellectual and political development, Madison was unsure of the correct position to assume in Virginia's increasingly bitter struggle between the established Church of England and the dissenting sects. During the ensuing years, he and the other men who formed the leadership of the nascent United States would be forced to wrestle with the complex issues of religious establishment, freedom of conscience, and the need for moral virtue in a republic. Their frequent and sometimes acrimonious conflicts stemmed not only from the difficulties inherent in a precise delineation of the relationship which ought to exist between civil government and the churches but, on a more fundamental level, from their philosophical, political, and religious differences.

But Madison was articulating an issue which was much older than the emerging American republic. The alternatives only appeared to be clear. Some asserted that the church was imperative to the welfare of the state either because of the order and stability which it contributed to the body politic or because it was essential to maintain a virtuous citizenry. Others reversed the proposition by declaring the state imperative to the church for the church's continued existence in society and the influence of religion upon human development. The history of Western civilization displayed the complicated interaction of these persuasions

[1]William T. Hutchinson and William M. E. Rachal, eds. (after vol. 7, Robert A. Rutland and William M. E. Rachal, eds.), *The Papers of James Madison* (Chicago, 1962–), 1: 101.

and values. In the Middle Ages civil society was ultimately legitimized by the church and in the Christian synthesis the Roman Empire was reconstituted as Holy. The Treaty of Westphalia reversed this dependence, and the maxim which distinguished the peculiar national character of the ecclesiastical establishment was the axiom *cujus regio, ejus religio.* The Enlightenment attempted to end the discussion by isolating the participants like a mother placing quarrelsome children in different rooms marked public weal and private conscience.

This sketch of the issues, of course, grossly oversimplifies its tangled reality, for the nature of civil society, the reality of the church, and the structures which constitute political stability, human virtue, and religious development are not stable and fixed. These terms are not constants either in their definitions or their applications; they are historical variables rather than inflexible and immutable ideas. These variables realize a historical existence with different values, and the history of their realization is not the progressive elaboration of a single problem but the constantly changing variations upon a single ambiguous theme: church and state.

To treat this theme as if it were a single thesis is to fail to account for the divergent meanings and the different accommodations which religion and politics have attempted. It is to read history dogmatically and falsely. Each significant settlement was reached within its own historically conditioned persuasions. Each reduced the abstract theme to a particular definition and precision, but in this reduction distinguished it from similar settlements in different circumstances. The historian must follow suit. As each major accommodation between church and state has its own uniqueness, so it must be treated on its own terms. This is not to deny the influence of one moment in history upon another, but simply to deny that they are the same.

And influence there certainly is. Church and state, howsoever ambiguously understood, continually embody the major concerns of man, his destiny, and human possibilities. They are communities which assert a character to the life of man with man and the life of man with God, and any resolution of their respective claims is bound to color all the textures of man's life. Any successful resolution is bound to influence profoundly all subsequent discussions and attempts at new settlements.

For Americans of the Revolutionary period the experience of their British parent over the previous two and a half centuries was particularly crucial. The catholicity of religion in England had been shattered by the middle of the sixteenth century. Attempting to unite the nation behind the state and unwilling "to make windows into men's souls," Elizabeth had sought to maintain a broad Erastian settlement of religion with toleration for dissenters willing to accept its terms. Those who rejected it were punished for civil offense, not matters of conscience. Despite the subsequent conflict between the high church party of Archbishop Laud and the Puritans, the general movement toward toleration was only retarded, not checked; and the persecutions of Restoration England were but aftershocks of the civil wars. New and powerful forces were at work, exemplified in the writings of Milton and Locke and the growth of religious indifference, skepticism, and anticlericalism. Thought shifted from a defense of orthodoxy toward rationalism with its cardinal belief in the need for free inquiry in the pursuit of truth. Paralleling this development of secularism was the growth of a new religious perspective, particularly among sects such as the Baptists, which argued that religious liberty was essential for man to respond to God's will and urged the separation of church from state so that the church might fulfill its mission uncontaminated by civil government. Most important of all, the rapid multiplication of churches and sects made religious uniformity an impossibility. In granting Protestant dissenters the freedom to worship in peace, the Toleration Act of 1688, albeit grudgingly, recognized reality. Men agreed that a limited measure of religious liberty was imperative, not simply for the preservation of religion, but for the well-being of society.[2]

Nevertheless, throughout the eighteenth century the preferred position of the Church of England was carefully guarded by the state, and toleration was severely circumscribed. Nonconformists and, even more, Jews and Roman Catholics were subjected to a

[2]W. K. Jordan, *The Development of Religious Toleration in England* (Cambridge, 1936-40), 4:466-88.

number of civil disabilities which hampered their freedom of
action and effectively cut them off from the traditional avenues of
preferment. Services such as baptism and marriage were not recognized in law unless performed by Anglican clergy. Dissenters were
refused admission to municipal and business corporations, dis-
qualified from holding civil and military offices under the crown,
and excluded from the universities. Although the enforcement of
the Test and Corporation Acts varied with time and place, the
government remained unmoved by pleas to alter or eliminate
them. On the eve of the American Revolution, petitions for relief
were presented by both the liberal element of the Anglican clergy
and the London dissenting ministers, but it was not until 1779
that dissenting ministers were no longer required to subscribe to
the Thirty-nine Articles of the Elizabethan Settlement. William
Blackstone stated it succinctly a decade earlier: "There is always a
difference to be made between toleration and establishment."[3]
The distinguished jurist considered nonconformity to be a crime,
the penalties for which had only been suspended by the Toleration Act. For England the national church was the dominant
expression of religious faith. Those whose consciences rebelled
might worship as they wished, but only by paying the price of
civil and political disability. So it would remain until well into the
nineteenth century.

While Parliament beat back the assault on the structure of the
church-state arrangement in England, Revolutionary America broke
with the past, for the transformation of the political system taking
place there provided both an opportunity to test new ideas and a
willingness to listen to dissenting voices. Blackstone's viewpoint of
toleration had its defenders, but the scathing criticisms of liberal
thinkers such as Joseph Priestley, Richard Price, and Philip
Furneaux were published across the Atlantic and met a favorable
reception in certain intellectual circles. Both Madison and Jeffer-

---

[3]W[illiam] Blackstone, *Commentaries on the Laws of England* (London, 1769), 4:
52; see also Ursula Henriques, *Religious Toleration in England, 1787-1833* (Toronto,
1961), pp. 1-57 passim.

son, for example, were conversant with Priestley's theory of progress and Price's elaboration of natural rights.[4] Ironically, these English apologists for toleration would achieve more success in the former colonies than in their homeland. In America the situation was ripe for change, as the events of 1776 and the release of Revolutionary ideology inherent in the condition of independence forced a redefinition of the function and place of religion in society.

Amid the turmoil of the years that followed, arrangements had to be settled in the new states. The solutions varied widely. Even before the Revolution the pattern of religious toleration and the relationship between the churches and civil government in the various colonies had differed considerably. Only a few, most notably the royal colonies such as Virginia where the Church of England was established, had followed the English model closely. Now those states which previously had a single established church tended to move toward a multiple system with state support for at least the major religious groups. Massachusetts, for example, opted for a system of "public Protestant teachers of piety, religion, and morality" who would contribute to the happiness of the people and the stability of the state by inculcating virtue in the citizenry.[5] South Carolina established the "Christian Protestant religion," and Maryland toyed with the idea of religious taxation for nine years before finally rejecting it.[6] Other states such as Rhode Island and Pennsylvania, where religious pluralism was already a fact of life, simply allowed the existing conditions of freedom of worship and voluntary church support to continue.

---

[4]Hutchinson, *Papers of Madison* 1: 145, 150, 158, 160-61, 6: 88-89; Julian P. Boyd, ed., *The Papers of Thomas Jefferson* (Princeton, N.J., 1950–), 1: 471, 477. For an excellent treatment of the relationship between European and American ideas during this period, see Henry F. May, *The Enlightenment in America* (New York, 1976).

[5]Francis Newton Thorpe, ed., *The Federal and State Constitutions* (Washington, D.C., 1909), 3: 1890; see also John D. Cushing, "Notes on Disestablishment in Massachusetts, 1780-1833," *William and Mary Quarterly*, 3d ser., 26 (1969): 169-90; and C. Conrad Wright, "Piety, Morality, and the Commonwealth," *Crane Review* 9 (1967): 90-106.

[6]Thorpe, *Constitutions* 3: 1689-90, 6: 3255-57.

But almost every state instituted some form of religious test or qualification for full citizenship rights.[7]

Virginia was unique. In its religious settlement and the process by which it was determined, the Old Dominion broke sharply with the pattern set by the other states and its own colonial past. At the same time, it provided the most critical experiment of the Revolutionary era, for Virginia served as a politicoreligious microcosm in which the whole nation could study the alternatives for a church-state relationship and then choose from among them. As John Adams wrote Patrick Henry in 1776, "We all look up to Virginia for examples."[8] From Chesapeake Bay across the mountains to the Shenandoah Valley there existed both a church established by law and a religiously diverse society. In this largest and most populous of the new states with a leadership noted for its intellectual and political talent, all sides of the church-state controversy were ably represented: the traditional religionists who clung to the establishment ideal and insisted upon civil support for religion; the rationalists who believed religion to be an entirely personal affair and fought for an absolute separation of church and state; and dissenters of every stripe who, despite their own differences in polity and theory, wanted equal religious rights and a church freed from state control. For over a decade these Virginians developed the full range of arguments over the various alternatives presented for consideration: the retention of a single establishment, its replacement by a multiple system with state aid for all churches, the removal of religion from any relationship with civil authority, and the equality of religious groups without governmental assistance but free to influence society's morals and values.

In the heat of this intense political discussion and experimentation lies the larger significance of what transpired, for the American definition of religious liberty and the relationship between church and state is not the unreflective product of colonial pluralism or Revolutionary idealism. Rather, it depends in large

---

[7] Anson Phelps Stokes, *Church and State in the United States* (New York, 1950), 1: 438-39, 442-44; Robert Allen Rutland, *The Birth of the Bill of Rights, 1776-1791* (Chapel Hill, N.C., 1955), pp. 41-105 passim.

[8] Charles F. Adams, ed., *The Works of John Adams* (Boston, 1850-56), 9: 387.

measure on what developed in Virginia during the Confederation period. By the end of this time the majority of Virginians had imprinted upon their commonwealth the church-state settlement that the nation as a whole would eventually assume.

Chapter One

Prologue to Conflict
The Religious Situation, 1776

"I FIND our session will be a long one, and indeed the importance of our business requires it and we must sweat it out with Fortitude."[1] So a sagacious Edmund Pendleton informed his friend Thomas Jefferson from Williamsburg. There in early May 1776 a special convention had already assembled in the capital to modify the political structure of Virginia in accordance with the Revolutionary situation. Within the space of two months the delegates issued a call to the Continental Congress for a declaration of independence, drafted and promulgated their own statement of individual liberties and a Virginia constitution, and passed a series of bills to solve problems ranging from military defense to the lack of salt.[2] By no means were their efforts uniformly successful. One major issue which they confronted but failed to resolve dealt with the religious situation in the commonwealth. The question of religious toleration and the place of the established church had been debated before, and it is not surprising that in a frantic summer of formal revolution the delegates did not succeed where other assemblies and conventions had foundered. For the dispute over religion resulted from a particular and long-standing church-state relationship.

The Church of England had enjoyed a legal supremacy in Virginia since the beginning of the colonial period, but by the time of the Revolution its adherents numbered at best a bare majority

[1]David John Mays, ed., *The Letters and Papers of Edmund Pendleton, 1734-1803* (Charlottesville, 1967), 1: 180.

[2]William Waller Hening, ed., *The Statutes at Large: Being a Collection of All the Laws of Virginia from the First Session of the Legislature in the Year 1619* (Richmond, 1809-23), 9: 109-51.

of the white population.[3] Bypassed by the Great Awakening, without a resident bishop to ensure ecclesiastical discipline and a supply of competent clergy, and dependent upon the legislature and lay vestries for religious as well as temporal order, the church was in a sad state of disarray. Thirty years earlier massive revivals had swept the American colonies; and though their prime catalyst, George Whitefield, was an Anglican divine, his church alone among the principal denominations in the colonies solidly opposed the movement. To the established clergy of Virginia as well as their brethren up and down the Atlantic seacoast, the revivals contradicted all valid norms for religious truth and expression. The revivalists preached a faith far removed from the security of episcopal government and the orderly worship of the Book of Common Prayer. Their sermons were riddled with Calvinistic heresies. Even worse, they encouraged "enthusiasm," that bane of true religion which exalted the imaginative powers and sensible feelings over reason, doctrine, and the traditional religious order. The Great Awakening offended and provoked the ministry of the establishment, and its very success hardened their opposition. As the revivalists siphoned off masses of common folk to their own religious groups, the Anglican church cut itself off from participating in the definitive movement of American religion in the eighteenth century.[4]

It is ironic that the established clergy should have criticized the revivalists' lack of respect for proper church government, for the Church of England in the colonies was at best a faulty imitation of its British parent. For over one hundred fifty years the Virginia church functioned without a resident bishop to provide the sacraments of orders and confirmation or to supervise the clergy. In

---

[3]Jefferson estimated that two-thirds of the people were dissenters in 1776 (*Notes on the State of Virginia*, ed. William Peden [Chapel Hill, N.C., 1955], p. 150). However, this may reflect only the population in his native Albemarle County and environs. It is extremely difficult to estimate religious membership at this time, but judging by the number of clergy available for the various churches, it would seem that at least half of the people could well have been nominal Anglicans. For a more complete discussion, see Katherine L. Brown, "The Role of Presbyterian Dissent in Colonial and Revolutionary Virginia, 1740-1785" (Ph.D. diss., Johns Hopkins University, 1969), pp. 332-33.

[4]Gerald J. Goodwin, "The Anglican Reaction to the Great Awakening," *Historical Magazine of the Protestant Episcopal Church* 35 (1966): 343-45, 352-57.

church polity it had become more congregational than episcopal. The local religious unit was the parish, which, due to the absence of towns and a scattered population, was often coextensive with the county. Parish affairs were controlled by a vestry, a self-perpetuating body of twelve men selected from the economic and political elite of the county. Its authority extended to the hiring and firing of the clergy, the payment of clerical salaries, and the general supervision of all parish matters both temporal and religious. The vestry decided whether to induct a clergyman into the parish; that is, to offer him tenure as rector. But it was not required to do so, and the practice of renewing a minister's contract for a year at a time was commonly accepted. Although the Book of Common Prayer and the Canons of the Church of England governed religious worship, the vestry administered the ordinary affairs of the parish. The House of Burgesses legislated in cases of major decisions involving either individual parishes or the Virginia church in general. In disputes between the rector and his vestry, the minister might appeal to the commissary, the nominal representative in Virginia of the bishop of London, but this usually availed him little. More often he petitioned the legislature, but here also he faced problems, for the House of Burgesses was but a vestry on a larger scale; and if he should seek the intervention of the governor, he ran the risk of permanently alienating his parishioners. In short, the Virginia clergy were effectively controlled by lay administrators and deprived of religious leadership.[5]

Given this situation it is little wonder that the life of the ministry did not attract an abundance of promising candidates. However, by 1776 the chronic shortage of clergy which had plagued the church throughout the colonial period had somewhat abated. On the eve of the definitive break with Great Britain, there were approximately 105 clergymen of the established church in Virginia serving the 95 parishes, all but 5 of which had resident

[5]George MacLaren Brydon, *Virginia's Mother Church and the Political Conditions under Which It Grew* (Richmond and Philadelphia, 1947-52), 1: 98-102, 2: 334-35; Arthur Pierce Middleton, "The Colonial Virginia Parish," *Historical Magazine of the Protestant Episcopal Church* 40 (1971): 431-46. For a new perspective on the role of the vestry, see Joan Regner Gundersen, "The Myth of the Independent Virginia Vestry," ibid., 44 (1975): 133-41.

ministers.[6] They were a mixed lot. Native vocations were infrequent and necessitated a trip to England to obtain ordination, while the clergy who came out from the mother country as missionaries sometimes proved deficient in knowledge or morals or both. The church in Virginia was not served by members of the Society for the Propagation of the Gospel, and the men who did choose to exercise their ministry in the colony sometimes did more harm than good. But for every clergyman who rode to the hounds or swilled a bit too much madeira, there was also a devout, hardworking minister genuinely concerned with the cure of souls. Even the most caustic critics of the church during the Revolution had to admit that some ministers were outstanding models of virtue and piety as well as solid preachers of the word.[7]

Yet it was a ministry totally dependent upon the state for its financial support. Laws passed by the government during the colonial period made it possible for a clergyman in Virginia at the time of the Revolution to make a respectable living. Each parish was required to furnish its minister with a rectory and a glebe of at least two hundred acres of suitable farmland together with all necessary farm buildings and dependencies. If the parish did not own such property, then the vestry had to provide a sufficient allowance for the minister to rent a residence and farm. In addition, his regular salary was sixteen thousand pounds of tobacco a year plus the cost of preparing it for export and a small override to replace any that was unsuitable for sale. The vestry collected this salary by assessing every head of a household who lived within the parish boundaries on the basis of his tithables. Finally, the minister could augment his income by fees for performing marriages and preaching funerals and perhaps teaching a small school.[8] The net

[6]Brydon, *Virginia's Mother Church* 2: 415, 433.

[7]*Virginia Gazette* (Dixon & Hunter), Oct. 11, 1776. A recent study of the clergy of all the churches during this period concludes that the ministers of the establishment at the opening of the Revolution were perhaps the best which either the Church of England or the Episcopal church produced in Virginia before the nineteenth century. The major problem was with the clergy after the Revolution (Otto Lohrenz, "The Virginia Clergy and the American Revolution, 1774-1799" [Ph.D. diss., University of Kansas, 1970], pp. 219-20).

[8]Brydon, *Virginia's Mother Church* 2: 239; Arthur Pierce Middleton, "The Colonial Virginia Parson," *William and Mary Quarterly,* 3d ser., 26 (1969): 426-29.

income from all these resources varied greatly, depending upon the size of the parish, the quality of the glebe land, the kind of tobacco grown, and the value of the crop in a given year; but in this financial instability the minister was sharing the ordinary lot of his parishioners. This the clergy were not always willing to do; and the salary issue was a major factor in the growing anti-clericalism of the people in the years immediately before the Revolution.[9]

Another, even more fertile source of discontent and resentment against the Anglican church came from those who were not members of the church yet suffered discrimination and even persecution for their failure to conform. The earliest group of dissenters from the Virginia establishment were the Quakers. During the second half of the seventeenth century they formed meetings in the counties along the coast, suffered and survived through intermittent and occasionally harsh persecutions, and developed into solid communities under the leadership and encouragement of itinerant Friends, including George Fox himself. During the next century emigrants from Pennsylvania and other northern colonies started meetings in northern Virginia and the Shenandoah Valley, so that by the time of the Revolution there were Quakers scattered throughout the colony.[10]

After 1730 the few Quaker settlements in the Valley were overwhelmed by a tidal wave of Scotch-Irish Presbyterian immigration. The Great Awakening created a temporary split in the ranks of this religious body, and for a time both Old and New Side preachers ministered to congregations scattered throughout the western counties. Generally the Old Side ministers were most successful in the Valley while New Side congregations were established in the Tidewater. During the ministry of Samuel Davies and under the impetus of the revivals, Presbyterians penetrated into

---

[9]Richard Lee Morton, *Colonial Virginia* (Chapel Hill, N.C., 1960), 2: 751-819; Rhys Isaac, "Religion and Authority: Problems of the Anglican Establishment in Virginia in the Era of the Great Awakening and the Parsons' Cause," *William and Mary Quarterly,* 3d ser., 30 (1973): 3-36.

[10]Rufus Jones, *The Quakers in the American Colonies* (new ed., New York, 1966), pp. 268-96; Freeman H. Hart, *The Valley of Virginia in the American Revolution, 1763-1789* (New York, 1942), p. 38.

the settled areas around the fall line which divided the Tidewater from the Piedmont and won converts from among established families. This rapid period of growth led to the formation of the New Side Presbytery of Hanover in 1755, and after the reunion of the two sides this Presbytery encompassed all the ministers working in Virginia. In 1776 the Presbyterians claimed the religious allegiance of a large majority of the settlers beyond the Blue Ridge Mountains and dominated that region's political and social life. After the Anglican church, they formed the most influential religious group in Virginia.[11]

Fast approaching the Presbyterians in political clout and perhaps already outstripping them in numbers, the Baptists were the most rapidly developing body of dissenters in the colony on the eve of the Revolution. Most of their growth had occurred during the preceding decade. They actually formed two distinct groups. The Regular Baptists were Calvinists in theology and adhered to the London Confession of 1677 which in turn was based upon the Westminister Confession of Faith. They developed from the influx of Particular Baptists from Maryland into the northern counties in the years after the Great Awakening. These immigrants had swallowed up the remnants of the older General Baptists in the colony and together had formed the Ketocton Association. The Regulars were concentrated in the Northern Neck, that region of Virginia between the Potomac and Rappahannock rivers which formed the original land grant to the Fairfax family. After 1770 they spread out across the Allegheny Mountains to the west and south.[12]

They were called Regular Baptists to distinguish them from the "irregular" and more numerous Separate Baptists who had flooded into the colony after the middle of the eighteenth century. Coming from New England, the Separates had first passed through Virginia and settled in North Carolina. Later they returned to

[11]Ernest Trice Thompson, *The Presbyterians in the South* (Richmond, 1963), 1: 43-46, 54-59; Brown, "The Role of Presbyterian Dissent," pp. 225-26, 239-49; Hart, *Valley of Virginia,* pp. 34-36 and passim; James G. Leyburn, *The Scotch-Irish: A Social History* (Chapel Hill, N.C., 1962), 200-210, 278-83.

[12]David Benedict, *A General History of the Baptist Denomination in America, and Other Parts of the World* (Boston, 1813), 2: 24-26, 33-36.

Southside Virginia, those counties located south of the James River. As "new light" advocates of enthusiastic, evangelical religion, they were the "swarms of separatists" about whom the Reverend Jonathan Boucher complained so bitterly. In a sermon preached in 1771, this distinguished Anglican divine compared them to gnats: "though they can neither give pleasure nor do any good, they do not want either the disposition or the ability [of] those little insignificant animals to tease, to sting, and to torment."[13] The combination of unbridled enthusiasm and extensive itinerancy not only irritated members of the established clergy, it also was responsible for the phenomenal spread of Baptists between 1770 and 1776. The Separates had also formed an association, the Rapidan or General Association of Separate Baptists; and by 1773 this loose confederation already numbered thirty-four congregations distributed throughout the Tidewater and Piedmont.[14]

The primary purpose of this cooperation was the defense of their religious views, for the Separates were more subject to persecution than the Regulars or any other group of dissenters. In conformity to the toleration laws in force in the colony, the Regular Baptists, Presbyterians, Quakers, and the other, smaller religious groups such as Lutherans, Dunkers, and Mennonites had applied for and received both permits for meetinghouses and licenses to preach. This the Separates refused to do, and their itinerant preachers with their harsh invectives against the established church drew down upon themselves the wrath of many a local magistrate. During the years immediately before the Revolution, the Separate Baptists furnished the preachers who were most subject to fines, whippings, and imprisonment.[15] This in turn won

[13]Jonathan Boucher, *A View of the Causes and Consequences of the American Revolution: In Thirteen Discourses, Preached in North America between the Years 1763 and 1775* (rept. New York, 1967), p. 100.

[14]Benedict, *History of the Baptist Denomination* 2: 53-58; Robert B. Howell, *The Early Baptists of Virginia* (rev. ed., Philadelphia, 1864), p. 139.

[15]Lewis P. Little, *Imprisoned Preachers and Religious Liberty in Virginia* (Lynchburg, Va., 1938), is a full account of the persecution of the Baptists.

for them the notice and sometimes the sympathy of more liberal members of Virginia society, including the young James Madison.

Commenting upon the religious situation in Virginia in 1774, Madison confided in a friend:

I . . . have nothing to brag of as to the State and Liberty of my Country. Poverty and Luxury prevail among all sorts: Pride ignorance and Knavery among the Priesthood and Vice and Wickedness among the Laity. This is bad enough But It is not the worst I have to tell you. That diabolical Hell conceived principle of persecution rages among some and to their eternal Infamy the Clergy can furnish their Quota of Imps for such business. This vexes me the most of any thing whatever. There are at this [time?] in the adjacent County not less than 5 or 6 well meaning men in close Goal for publishing their religious Sentiments which in the main are very orthodox. . . . pray for Liberty of Conscience [to revive among us.][16]

Madison's interest in religious freedom was not the product of a sudden conversion, the result of one exposure to the effects of persecution. Rather it was a combination of education, experience, and much personal reflection. While a student at the College of New Jersey, he had come under the influence of John Witherspoon; and the learned Scottish Presbyterian minister had a profound effect on the development of Madison's views on theology, politics, and the rights of conscience. Upon his return to Virginia, he investigated the religious establishment in the colony and came to the conclusion that it produced both ignorance and corruption.[17] As the movement toward political independence quickened, Madison's interest in religious freedom grew apace. "Religious bondage shackles and debilitates the mind and unfits it for

[16]Hutchinson, *Papers of Madison* 1: 106.

[17]Ibid., 1: 101. Irving Brant, *James Madison* (Indianapolis, 1941-61), 1: 111-18, is a good treatment of the young Madison's attitudes toward religion. But see also Ralph L. Ketcham, "James Madison and Religion—A New Hypothesis," *Journal of the Presbyterian Historical Society* 38 (1960): 65-90. For Madison and Witherspoon, see James H. Smylie, "Madison and Witherspoon, Theological Roots of American Political Thought," *Princeton University Library Chronicle* 22 (1961): 118-32; Ralph L. Ketcham, "James Madison at Princeton," ibid., 28 (1966): 24-54. For a summary of Witherspoon's thought on religious freedom, see James Hastings Nichols, "John Witherspoon on Church and State," *Journal of the Presbyterian Historical Society* 42 (1964): 166-74.

every noble enterprise[,] every expanded prospect," he wrote in April 1774. In the same letter he offered his opinion of the character of the legislature and the influence of the clerical order:

That liberal catholic and equitable way of thinking as to the rights of Conscience, which is one of the Characteristics of a free people ... is but little known among the Zealous adherents to our Hierarchy. We have it is true some persons in the Legislature of generous Principles both in Religion and Politicks but number not merit you know is necessary to carry points there. Besides[,] the Clergy are a numerous and powerful body[,] have great influence at home by reason of their connection with and dependence on the Bishops and Crown and will naturally employ all their art and Interest to depress their rising Adversaries; for such they must consider dissenters who rob them of the good will of the people and may in time endanger their livings and security.[18]

Madison overestimated the power of the clergy, as well as their dependence upon overseas authority. Only a few years earlier during a controversy over the introduction of a bishop into Virginia, the vast majority of established church ministers were either uninterested or opposed to the measure.[19] Scattered across the commonwealth in isolated rectories, the clergy had no regular means of communicating with one another. As the Revolution waxed, the problems inherent in their lack of internal unity and organization as well as their total dependence upon the secular government became apparent. In addition, their quality as well as their popularity with the people varied greatly from parish to parish. Madison himself did not care for either his own local rector or the one in neighboring Culpeper County. The latter was expelled from his ministry in 1775 for his tory sentiments, and Madison had suggested that if he did not conform, he should "get ducked in a coat of Tar and surplice of feathers" to serve as his "new Canonicals."[20]

[18] Hutchinson, *Papers of Madison* 1: 112-13.

[19] Carl Bridenbaugh, *Mitre and Sceptre: Transatlantic Faiths, Ideas, Personalities, and Politics, 1689-1775* (New York, 1962), pp. 316-32, is a recent though brief treatment of the crisis over a Virginia episcopate. More extensive coverage is given in Arthur L. Cross, *The Anglican Episcopate and the American Colonies* (New York, 1902), pp. 226-40; and in Brydon, *Virginia's Mother Church* 2: 347-59.

[20] Hutchinson, *Papers of Madison* 1: 161.

With these warm feelings against an established church and some of its ministers, Madison became a part of the Virginia government in May 1776, taking his seat as a delegate to the convention. The first serious business confronting that body was the proposal of independence; and on May 15, less than ten days after the session had begun, the convention passed a resolution instructing the Virginia delegates in Congress to make the motion formally severing the colonies from Great Britain.[21] After an extended weekend for the appropriate celebrations and a fast day "observed with all due solemnity," the convention reassembled and Edmund Pendleton, the president, appointed a committee to draw up a Declaration of Rights and a constitution for the independent commonwealth. The chairman was Archibald Cary and its membership included Robert Carter Nicholas, Patrick Henry, Edmund Randolph, and eventually James Madison; but its prime mover was George Mason. "The Political Cooks are busy in preparing the dish," Pendleton wrote to Jefferson in Philadelphia, "and as Colonel Mason seems to have the Ascendancy in the great work, I have sanguine hopes it will be framed so as to Answer it's end."[22]

The initial draft of the Declaration of Rights was published in the *Virginia Gazette* on June 1; it was thoroughly debated and amended by the convention before its final passage two weeks later. "Prosperity to the Community and Security to Individuals," Pendleton had stated as its goals; and the resulting statement of sixteen articles enunciated in clean, simple prose the basic liberties of men in society. The Declaration opened with the assertion that "all men are by nature equally free and independent" and in succeeding paragraphs elaborated some of the implications of that philosophy.[23]

The final article, the sixteenth, pertained to religion; and it became one of the most controversial in the discussions of the

[21] For the text of this statement, see Mays, *Letters of Pendleton* 1: 178-79.

[22] Thomas Ludwell Lee to Richard Henry Lee, May 18, 1776, "Selections and Excerpts from the Lee Papers," *Southern Literary Messenger* 27 (1858): 325; Brant, *James Madison* 1: 204; Mays, *Letters of Pendleton* 1: 180.

[23] *Va. Gaz.* (Dixon & Hunter), June 1, 1776; Mays, *Letters of Pendleton* 1: 180; Hening, *Statutes at Large* 9: 109.

convention. Mason's original draft as amended in committee and
presented to the convention stated that "all men should enjoy the
fullest toleration in the exercise of religion." But this failed to
satisfy young Madison; and with Edmund Pendleton, one of the
staunchest churchmen in the assemblage, offering his amendment,
he was able to have the crucial wording changed to read that "all
men are equally entitled to the free exercise of religion."[24]
Madison perceived the difference between toleration and freedom.
Toleration, given or withheld at the pleasure of the legislature,
implied the ultimate power of government over the exercise of
conscience. But freedom of belief was a natural right, not subject
to the demands or will of a majority. The convention was willing
to make the alteration in wording, but failed to grasp its implications.

This was readily apparent when it refused to extend the concept
of free exercise to the existing situation of an established church.
Genuine free exercise, at least in the minds of some, was inconsistent with the continuation of an establishment, for the very nature
of that institution demanded that civil government grant preferential consideration and attention to one church over all others. The
obvious implication was that those who did not adhere to the state
church were second-class citizens, inherently unequal before the
law precisely because of their religious beliefs. For both rationalists and dissenters, the pressure to conform to the "approved"
faith created an intolerable violation of man's freedom; and they
would spend the coming years elaborating and publicizing their
arguments against it. But this situation also discriminated against
the free exercise of the members of the established church. Since
the state was involved in the direction of their church's worship
and polity, they were not at liberty to regulate their own Christian
community. Although few members of the church seem to have
appreciated the dimensions of this problem, it would prove
extremely detrimental to their interests during the next decade.

Madison realized the inconsistency. In an earlier amendment
which he had drafted and prevailed upon Patrick Henry to sponsor

[24]Hutchinson, *Papers of Madison* 1: 173, 175; Brant, *James Madison* 1: 257.

before the convention, he had proposed a statement which would have effectively disestablished the Church of England in Virginia. After the sentence on free exercise, he wished the addition "and therefore that no man or class of men ought on account of religion to be invested with peculiar emoluments or privileges; nor sub-jected to any penalties or disabilities."[25] Then the watchdogs for the establishment had roused themselves and someone asked if by this statement a movement for disestablishment was afoot. Henry denied that intention—it was Madison's, not Henry's—but the amendment failed nonetheless. The approved article stated: "That religion or the duty which we owe to our CREATOR, and the manner of discharging it, can be directed only by reason and conviction, not by force or violence, and therefore all men are equally entitled to the free exercise of religion, according to the dictates of conscience; and that it is the mutual duty of all to practice Christian forbearance, love, and charity, toward each other."[26] The Revolutionary convention could accept the concept of freedom of conscience, but it would not sever the special relationship which bound Virginians to the church of their fathers.

With the Declaration of Rights approved, the convention directed its attention to the form of government. "It is a work of the most interesting nature," Jefferson wrote, "and such as every individual would wish to have his voice in."[27] Although his congressional obligations kept him in Philadelphia, Jefferson com-posed three successive drafts of a state constitution, the last of which he sent down to the convention in the middle of June. George Wythe wrote him later that his plan had arrived too late to receive the full attention it deserved, but some small portions were incorporated in what was fundamentally Mason's work.[28] None of

[25]Hutchinson, *Papers of Madison* 1: 174: Edmund Randolph, *History of Virginia*, ed. Arthur H. Shaffer (Charlottesville, 1970), p. 254. It was altogether in character that Madison should have asked another member to introduce his amendment, and it was advantageous to have it done by one of Henry's prestige.

[26]Randolph, *History of Virginia*, p. 254; Hening, *Statutes at Large* 9: 111-12.

[27]Boyd, *Papers of Jefferson* 1: 292.

[28]Ibid., 1: 476-77.

his suggestions pertaining to religion were included, but they are an important indication of Jefferson's thoughts on freedom of conscience and the relationship of church and state in 1776. In his section on "Rights Public and Private," he proposed the statement that "all persons shall have full and free liberty of religious opinion; nor shall any be compelled to frequent or maintain any religious institutions."[29] The first part of this draft was already contained in Madison's amendment to the sixteenth article of the Declaration of Rights. But the second half of his proposal would have eliminated taxation for the established church and introduced the voluntary system of church support, thus precluding the possibility of an assessment for religion in general or any religious group in particular.

Jefferson would not, however, have completely disestablished the church or freed it from state control. For the establishment and the church-state relationship in Virginia meant much more than just support from the public purse. In a great variety of ways, the government determined the operation of the churches, and particularly the established church. There is no hint in Jefferson's writings on the constitution that he planned any alteration to this system. In the section on the judiciary, for example, Jefferson provided that cases under ecclesiastical law should be settled by jury trial, just as those arising under common, chancery, or maritime law. There is no indication that he considered church matters to be part of a separate system, separately administered. Further, his constitution would have required all officials whether civil, military, or ecclesiastical (though he placed the last category in brackets) to take an oath of fidelity to the state and swear they had not obtained their office by bribe. There was no question of treating clergymen as private citizens in the eyes of the state; rather, he would have made them in some ambiguous way dependent upon the government. Jefferson's anticlerical sentiments were already well developed, and he was certainly more skeptical than Madison in his attitude toward organized religion. Perhaps this explains the proposals he formulated. At least in the summer of

[29]Ibid., 1: 363.

1776, although advocating freedom of conscience and the voluntary system of church support, Jefferson did not envision a truly free church, separated from state control.[30]

In this respect he was not unlike the majority of men who composed the convention. One of their last resolutions before adjournment in early July ordered certain changes in the liturgy of the established church. All references to George III and the royal family were to be eliminated from the litany, the morning and evening prayers, and the communion service; and in their place were to be substituted prayers for the magistrates.[31] No clearer indication is needed that these men continued to regard themselves as the legislative body for the church.

The new government opened its first session of the legislature in early October. The lower house, now called the House of Delegates, possessed the lion's share of authority in the constitution. It had been constituted from the members of the summer convention; but there were some notable additions, the most significant being Jefferson. His service in the Continental Congress had been completed, and he now resumed his seat as the senior delegate from Albemarle County. The most significant absence was that of Patrick Henry. Elected to the prestigious but powerless position of governor, Henry had been removed from the scene just as the battle over the relationship of church and state was about to reach a new intensity. In a similar situation eight years later, he would again be promoted out of the House.

On October 11, Edmund Pendleton, the newly elected Speaker of the House, assigned members to the committee for religion. Some eighteen were appointed, including Robert Carter Nicholas and Thomas Jefferson, and Carter Braxton was selected to serve as chairman.[32] The dissenters had been primed for the session. From Prince Edward County, the heart of Presbyterian strength in the

---

[30]Ibid., 1: 362, 364; Dumas Malone, *Jefferson and His Time* (Boston, 1948–), 1: 109; Ketcham, "Madison and Religion," pp. 86-87.

[31] *Va. Gaz.* (Dixon & Hunter), July 20, 1776.

[32]*Journals of the House of Delegates of Virginia* (Richmond, 1827-28; hereafter cited as *JHD*), Oct. 11, 1776, p. 7.

Piedmont, came a statement of esteem for the sixteenth article of the Declaration of Rights as "the rising sun of Religious Liberty to relieve them from a long night of Ecclesiastical bondage." The petition pointed out that now Virginia had the opportunity of becoming "an asylum for free inquiry, knowledge, and the virtuous of every denomination," by abolishing both the establishment and religious taxation.[33]

Also on that day both Williamsburg *Virginia Gazettes*, signaling a press war which would last throughout the session, published articles against the establishment. A letter from Augusta County quoted the free exercise clause from the sixteenth article and asked that it be carried into effect immediately by placing all religious groups on the same basis "without preference or preeminence" given to any one church.[34] This was to prove a common theme, particularly on the part of the Presbyterian petitions and those from the counties in which they were dominant. Although the convention had deliberately differentiated between free exercise of religion and disestablishment of the church, approving the one and rejecting the other, the dissenting religious groups both in the press and in their petitions viewed the two as necessarily linked. Their primary objectives were the disestablishment of the Church of England and the cessation of all taxation for religious purposes. A self-styled "county poet," most probably a Baptist preacher, put the latter request to rhyme:

> Tax all things, water, air, and light,
> If need there is, yea tax the night
> But let our brave heroic minds
> Move freely, like celestial winds.
> Make vice and folly feel your rod,
> But leave our consciences to GOD [35]

"Vice and folly" were a concern commonly voiced. Reflecting

---

[33] Ibid. The ordinary procedure was for the House to receive a petition and then assign it to the appropriate committee for investigation and recommendation.

[34] *Va. Gaz.* (Purdie), Oct. 11, 1776.

[35] *Va. Gaz.* (Dixon & Hunter), Oct. 11, 1776. Lohrenz, "Virginia Clergy," pp. 263-64, ascribed this verse to the Baptist preacher David Thomas.

upon the ruins of Norfolk, burned and destroyed by the British, one writer lamented the sins of Virginia which had visited upon them this sign of the divine wrath: "open impiety and profaneness have long been practised among us, vice reigns triumphant, and the seeds of virtue seem to be almost eradicated."[36] Dissenters as well as churchmen might agree, at least in part, with this judgment— certainly it was echoed from both pulpit and stump—but the opposing camps saw contradictory causes and solutions. The award for the most vitriolic statement of the press campaign that winter would have gone to "A Preacher of the Gospel." Denouncing the clergy of the established church as "dumb dogs" and "drones, who have long lived on the sweets of the land, unprofitable to, and a heavy charge on the public," he suggested that they be made useful to society by sending them off to fight the British, while other preachers, men like himself who were possessed of the Spirit and commissioned by Christ rather than by *carnal bishops,*" should assume the care of their churches and congregations.[37]

The establishment also had its apologists, and they were not slow to respond. "A Plain Dealer," answering the attack on the clergy, condemned the attempt "to bring an odium upon a religious society" and in measured tones insisted that those who truly believed in religious freedom and the equality of sects would not traffic in such insults.[38] "Philoepiscopus" countered "A Preacher" in even stronger terms. After emphasizing the need for an educated clergy, he attacked the "nonsense and blasphemy" of those who presumed to be called by God but freely attacked the established church and subverted its doctrines and discipline. Those who carried on in this fashion were "cheats and enthusiasts, a scandal to religion, and dangerous to the commonwealth; they break violently into the sheepfold, and stand upon record in the book of God as hirelings, thieves, and robbers." Having completed the exchange of insults, he concluded his article with the warning that if these dissenting bodies were placed on a level of equality

---

[36] *Va. Gaz.* (Dixon & Hunter), Oct. 11, 1776.

[37] Ibid.

[38] Ibid., Oct. 18, 1776.

with the established church, it would produce not only the complete destruction of genuine religion but also "a civil war among
ourselves," which considering the present situation might be
thought "a little unseasonable."[39]

The welfare of the state, as well as the dangers that would ensue
if the religious conflict was not properly resolved, was an argument
used by both sides. The dissenting protagonists stressed the need
for unanimity in confronting the crisis of revolution. They insisted
that it could only be achieved by giving all citizens an equal stake
in the outcome. To give justice to all immediately by eliminating
religious taxation and the establishment would be the most prudent thing for the legislature to do, for it would increase the self-
interest of all who had suffered discrimination under the old
system.[40] The establishment supporters countered with the assertion that unanimity had already been achieved by the toleration
granted to the dissenters, that the present threats being made
against the establishment were the work of "bullies," and that the
Assembly should "carefully avoid a measure by which the greater
and more orderly part of the state will be aggrieved and may be
sickened" of the Revolution. The good of the state and society in
general required that religion be supported by the government; and
taxation for the established church would guarantee that men of
genuine abilities and real learning would enter the ministry, men
who would be capable of preaching "sensible discourses" and
avoid the enthusiastic harangues of fanatics. Although this "Member of the Establishment" claimed to appreciate the difficulties
imposed upon men forced to pay for the support of a church to
which they did not belong, nevertheless, he pointed out, since it
was for the good of the commonwealth, they should quietly comply and take comfort in the fact that they were still free to maintain their own religious beliefs and worship.[41]

In the final blast of the season's newspaper war, the establishment received a measure of support from an unlikely quarter. In

[39]Ibid., Dec. 13, 1776.

[40]*Va. Gaz.* (Purdie), Oct. 11, Nov. 8, 1776.

[41]Ibid., Nov. 1, 1776.

an article dripping with sarcasm and filled with left-handed compliments to the church, the writer scorned the "fantastick mode of worship that has been displayed for seventeen centuries" and found all religions equally absurd. However, he noted that some of the doctrines preached by the dissenters were dangerous to the state, especially those which forbade military service or introduced a leveling spirit incompatible with subservience to proper authority. Therefore, the established church was "expedient," for while it received support from the state, it also obeyed the government and helped restrain, at least to some degree, the more annoying among the dissenters. The latter were mistaken, he concluded, if they believed they were required to support a church; in reality they were contributing their mite to stable government.[42]

While the religious controversy raged in the press, the masthead of Purdie's *Virginia Gazette* proclaimed: "High HEAVEN to Gracious ends directs the STORM!" Though obviously intended as a reference to the Revolution, it applied equally well to the activities of the Assembly. During the session at least ten major petitions for relief from religious taxation and against the establishment were referred to the committee for religion. Jefferson later wrote that these petitions "brought on the severest contests in which I have ever engaged."[43]

In the first full week of its meetings, the committee received a startling portent of the proportions which the struggle over religion would assume. Claiming inspiration from the work of the summer convention, a petition asked that the pledge of equal liberty be fulfilled. The legislature should begin by ending an ecclesiastical system which had taken their property and handed it over "to those from whom they received no equivalent." It further noted that the virtues of forbearance, love, and charity of which the sixteenth article spoke would become a reality only when all religious groups were placed on an equal basis with the same privileges and protection from the state. The surprising aspect, however, was not the text of the petition but rather that almost

[42]Ibid., Dec. 13, 1776.

[43]Paul Leicester Ford, ed., *The Works of Thomas Jefferson* (New York, 1904-5), 1: 62.

ten thousand people had signed it. Nor did it exhaust the numbers
of those who wished to register their sentiments on the issue.
Through the rest of October and on into the early days of the
next month, other dissenting petitions flowed in: from the
counties of Albemarle, Amherst, and Buckingham, complaining of
the inequities created by the establishment and appealing to the
"Wisdom, Candour, and Integrity" of the delegates to grant them
relief; from the congregation of German Lutherans living in
Culpeper, pleading for freedom from religious taxation and equal
rights for their ministers; from the Presbyterians of Frederick
County, insisting that all laws incompatible with freedom of
conscience must be repealed; and from several other groups.[44]

In terms of content, the longest and most carefully worded
petition was submitted by the Hanover Presbytery, on behalf of
all its congregations in Virginia. Its principal objective was equality
for religious groups; and this goal could only be achieved by ending the Anglican establishment and its most pressing symbol,
religious taxation. Invoking the Declaration of Rights as the
"Magna Charta of our Commonwealth," the ministers and elders
expressed their confidence that that document and the "Justice"
of the lawmakers would result in complete religious liberty.
Although the Presbytery complained that any kind of religious
taxation violated its natural rights, the principal thrust of its
petition attacked the concept of church establishment. On religious grounds it was contrary to the Gospel, which needed no "civil
aid." On political grounds it was outside the scope of government
and inimical to the interests of the state. Therefore, the Presbytery
could not accept an establishment for itself, nor would it tolerate
one for any other church. In blunt terms the presbyters asked for
the repeal of all preferential laws for any religious group, the
adoption of a voluntary system of church support, and equal
protection for all religious bodies.[45]

The combined weight of these petitions from dissenters and

[44]Religious Petitions, 1774-1802, Presented to the General Assembly of Virginia
(hereafter cited as RP), Oct. 16 and Oct. 22-Nov. 9, 1776, passim, microfilm, Virginia
State Library, Richmond (hereafter VSL).

[45]Ibid., Oct. 24, 1776.

others opposed to the establishment placed the state church on the defensive. Sensing the imminent danger to their position, a number of the Anglican clergy submitted a lengthy memorial to the legislature. They pointed out, first of all, that they had undertaken their ministry in Virginia in good faith, fully expecting that under the laws of the colony they would be protected in their rights. They equated these rights with those of private property, now jeopardized by dissenters who wished to deprive them of their livings and the prospects they had been led to expect as ministers of the state church. The clergy noted that they had no desire to see dissenters deprived of religious freedom; but given the fact that mankind was most influenced by religious opinions and that Christianity was the best means to form those values and promote virtue in society, the government had an obligation to be concerned with its advancement. They insisted that this could best be achieved in the same manner in which it had been accomplished for the past one hundred fifty years, by the established church. And if these purposes were being achieved in Virginia, then the establishment should be continued; indeed, "the hardships which such a regulation might impose on individuals, or even bodies of men, ought not to be considered." The ministers reiterated the virtues of the establishment, its mildness toward dissenters, and the benefits it had produced during the colonial period. They strongly rejected the concept that with political changes should come an equality for all religious groups. Claiming that this would lead to a contest for superiority, they projected a picture of confusion and possible civil disorder. Finally, in what may be understood as a sign of either hope or desperation, the ministers requested that the whole matter of an establishment be deferred until the people of the state could be canvassed for their views.[46]

It was a bravado performance, since the supporters of the established church had evidently been unprepared for the onslaught from dissenters. Only one other petition sympathetic to the clergy's position was filed with the House that winter, and it came from a group for which most of the established divines had little liking. Although the church in Virginia was definitely antirevivalist

[46]Ibid., Nov. 8, 1776.

and even rationalist in tone, a new movement originating under the leadership of John Wesley in England had recently spread to the American colonies. About ten days before the established clergy submitted their petition, another came from "the People Commonly called Methodists." The missionaries of this evangelical movement within the Church of England had concentrated most of their efforts in the middle colonies, but their greatest successes came in Maryland and Virginia. In the latter state they received the support of a few established clergymen, the most enthusiastic being Devereux Jarratt.

Jarratt had experienced conversion while living in a Presbyterian household, and it was this influence which gave his preaching and ministry an evangelical style. Although the settled rector of Bath Parish in Dinwiddie County, he carried out an extensive schedule of itinerant preaching which took him throughout Southside Virginia, and even into North Carolina. During the years immediately before the Revolution, his ministry met with substantial success; and for a brief time it seemed as if the established church, at least in those areas where Jarratt was at work, might be on the verge of an Awakening. There were "the many precious and reviving seasons," he later wrote, "when the spirit was poured out from on high, and such a number of souls was gathered into the fold."[47] Speaking of Jarratt's efforts, Francis Asbury, one of the foremost Methodist leaders of the century, testified: "I am persuaded there have been more souls convinced by his ministry, than by that of any other man in Virginia."[48]

Although the people responded to his type of preaching, the majority of the clergy did not. Jarratt's greatest opposition came from within the ranks of his own clerical brethren. Perhaps because of this lack of support and his own acute awareness of the

[47]Devereux Jarratt, *The Life of the Reverend Devereux Jarratt, Rector of Bath Parish, Virginia, Written by Himself in a Series of Letters Addressed to the Rev. John Coleman* (rept. New York, 1969), p. 95; Douglass Adair, "The Autobiography of the Reverend Devereux Jarratt, 1732-1763," *William and Mary Quarterly*, 3d ser., 9 (1952): 346-50; William Warren Sweet, *Methodism in American History* (rev. ed., New York, 1961), p. 66.

[48]Elmer T. Clark, J. Manning Potts, and Jacob S. Payton, eds., *The Journal and Letters of Francis Asbury* (Nashville, 1958), 1: 414.

need for reform in the Virginia church, Jarratt welcomed the advent of the Methodist preachers. Accepting as sincere their protestations of loyalty to the Church of England, he introduced them to communities of Anglicans throughout the regions of his preaching and provided them with the sacraments which they as nonordained preachers could not administer. The net effect was a rapid growth in their society; and when the religious conflict became pronounced in the fall of 1776, the Methodists rallied to the defense of the establishment. Noting that dissenters were busy petitioning to abolish the church-state relationship, the Methodists strove to clarify their own position. They were not dissenters, their petition proclaimed, but "a Religious Society in Communion with the Church of England," and they were prepared to do everything possible to assist that church. They did not want it to be disestablished.[49] After the Revolution they would adopt a very different position; but in October 1776 their statement, which purported to represent the views of almost three thousand members, must have comforted the establishment supporters in the committee for religion.[50]

Speaker Pendleton had appointed his old ally, Carter Braxton, to be the chairman of the committee. A wealthy Virginia aristocrat, Braxton had served in the House of Burgesses, the Revolutionary conventions, the Committee of Safety, and finally in the Continental Congress. Although he signed the Declaration of Independence, his conservative views on the state constitution were unacceptable to the political temper of the Virginia convention of 1776, and he was not reappointed to the congressional post. But Pendleton, anticipating the ensuing struggles in the Assembly, welcomed his friend's presence in Williamsburg, for he would be available "to assist in watching and breaking the Spirit of Party, that bane of all public Councils."[51] The Speaker was lining

---

[49] RP, Oct. 28, 1776.

[50] It certainly discomforted Jefferson. In some notes he prepared for the religious debates, he wrote that Methodists in Albemarle County had signed the petitions against the establishment and that George Shadford, who had signed the petition on behalf of the Methodists, had done so without authorization (Boyd, *Papers of Jefferson* 1: 557-58).

[51] Ibid., 1: 457, 472.

up his forces to form a conservative bulwark against the changes he knew were in the wind. Although he had given his support to the cause of independence, he did not agree with those who advocated wholesale reform of the social structure. Like Patrick Henry, with whom he often disagreed on details, Pendleton was a separatist, not a revolutionary. He was also a religious person, deeply devoted to the liturgy and traditions of the Church of England. In his concept of what the world should be, the old system had served well, and he was satisfied.[52] Robert Carter Nicholas completed the triumvirate of conservative leadership. The former treasurer of the colony, he had resigned from that position in order to be eligible for service in the legislature; and Pendleton had named him to the committee for religion. There he could be expected to use his considerable influence on behalf of the established church. As Jefferson later wrote of his struggles in the session, "Our great opponents were Mr. Pendleton and Robert Carter Nicholas; honest men, but zealous churchmen."[53]

Despite their positions of leadership, Pendleton, Nicholas, and Braxton were hard pressed that fall, for the dissenting petitions had armed the supporters of disestablishment with a powerful weapon. Two weeks of vigorous discussions in the committee for religion ended in deadlock, and the whole matter was transferred to the Committee of the Whole House. During these debates Jefferson drafted a series of resolutions as a basis for legislation. These proposals and the arguments which he elaborated in support of them represent his first extensive treatment of religious liberty and provide an important prelude to the bill establishing religious freedom which he formulated in the succeeding years. In his resolutions of 1776, Jefferson urged, first, that all laws passed either in Britain or Virginia during the colonial period which in any way restricted freedom of religious belief or worship be repealed. Second, he proposed that the dissenters' petitions for the disestablishment of the church and the equality of all religious

[52]David John Mays, *Edmund Pendleton, 1721-1803: A Biography* (Cambridge, Mass., 1952), 2: 129, 132-37.

[53]Ford, *Works of Jefferson* 1: 62. For Robert Carter Nicholas, see Hugh Blair Grigsby, *The Virginia Convention of 1776* (rept. New York, 1969), pp. 61-68.

denominations be found reasonable and, therefore, that all laws which established the church in Virginia, granted its ministers a privileged position in the state, and provided for their support by public taxes be revoked. At the same time, perhaps as a sop to the devotees of the establishment, he suggested that incumbent ministers be granted the use of their glebes during their lifetime and that all private donations given to the church be made part of its patrimony forever.

Jefferson's resolutions were clearly directed at guaranteeing complete liberty of conscience to each individual and placing all religious groups on an equal basis. Moreover, in contrast to his proposed state constitution of the previous summer, he also appeared to remove religion from the sphere of state control and regulation. None of his extensive writings or notes on religion for this session of the Assembly indicate that he thought civil government should maintain any formal contact with the various religious groups in Virginia. Indeed, in a preliminary draft of another resolution, he stated its purpose as "totally and eternally restraining the civil magistrate from all pretensions of interposing his authority or exercise in matters of religion." Thus Jefferson, in striking contrast to the majority of his fellow legislators, seems to have moved toward a position substantially identifiable with his later bill establishing religious freedom and his mature commitment to an absolute separation of church and state.[54]

In support of his resolutions, Jefferson drew up lists of data and notes to support his proposals. Most probably these formed the basis for one or more speeches which he delivered in committee. He enumerated, for example, all of the laws passed by Parliament or the House of Burgesses which inhibited religious freedom; it made an impressive summation. Writing about the debate that followed, Edmund Randolph commented: "the severest persecutions in England were ransacked for colors in which to paint the burdens and scourges of freedom in religion; and antiquated laws in England, against the exercise of which the people would even

---

[54]*JHD*, Nov. 5, 6, 9, 1776, pp. 41, 43, 48; Boyd, *Papers of Jefferson* 1: 530-31.

there have recoiled, were summoned up as so many demons hovering over every scrupulous conscience not bending to the church."[55] Jefferson's presentation may have been unduly harrowing, but his purpose was to illustrate to the delegates their ignorance of the extent of the persecution statutes. The legal status of rights of conscience was not commonly understood. Despite the prevalent mood of toleration, that was but the spirit of the age, not of its laws. In persuasive terms, Jefferson argued that men should not rely on feeling to protect their rights; the future was unpredictable, and to realize the injustice of the law but neglect to change it was injustice to the law itself.

Yet the brunt of his argument was a sweeping attack on religious establishments. The state, he insisted, had no authority to intrude into the area of religious conscience. Drawing upon the prevailing social contract theory, Jefferson argued that upon their entrance into society, men surrendered only those rights necessary to maintain civil government. Religious belief was not among them; in this dimension of their lives men were responsible to God alone. Therefore, for the magistrate to move into the realm of personal opinion and require conformity was a fundamental violation of human freedom. The uniformity which was the purpose of a state church was not justifiable. Nor was it to be desired, for it required the suppression of the free inquiry necessary for all growth in learning. Finally, as all the persecutions of history had shown, it was not attainable.

Never one to rest his case on a single line of attack, Jefferson also pointed out the advantages which would accrue to religious bodies if the church was disestablished. Religion would be strengthened, he argued, because its ministers would have to lead exemplary lives and be industrious in their work. Christianity had done quite well for its first three hundred years without any state assistance; to demand it now was to betray a lack of faith in its intrinsic excellence.[56]

The debates in the Committee of the Whole concluded on November 19 with a series of resolutions to the House. In some

[55]Randolph, *History of Virginia*, p. 264.

[56]Boyd, *Papers of Jefferson* 1: 536-39.

respects they followed the proposals made by Jefferson. All acts of the British Parliament which proscribed any religious opinions, styles of worship, or the refusal to attend services were to be declared invalid; and the act of Assembly of 1705 which applied certain features of these statutes to Virginia was to be repealed. Three of the resolutions pertained to finances and property. Dissenters were to be relieved of all taxation or forced contributions to the established church; nor were they to be required to contribute to their own ministers except upon a strictly voluntary basis. The acts of Assembly which provided for clerical salaries were to be repealed, though any arrears were to be paid. Finally, the established church was to keep forever its title to the glebes, churches, chapels, and all other material possessions it had received from either public or private sources. The net effect of these resolutions was to place all religious groups on a purely voluntary basis with respect to financial support, while giving the established church all the property and goods it possessed at the time.

In this last matter, the committee resolutions ran directly counter to those proposed by Jefferson. He had moved that only the incumbent ministers be allowed to retain their glebes for the rest of their tenure. The presumption was that at their death or the vacancy of the parish, all the material possessions which had been acquired from public sources would revert to the state. The delegates, however, went on record as favoring the retention by the church of all those properties it had accumulated during the colonial period. Involving as it did the question of property rights, it was an important point of distinction between Jefferson's view and that of the majority of the legislature. Before the church-state relationship was settled, it would reappear as a major subject of contention.

Finally, the delegates expressed their intention to maintain a firm control over the affairs of the churches. Another committee resolution declared: "That although the maintaining any matters of religion ought not to be regulated, yet that publick assemblies of societies for divine worship ought to be regulated, and that proper provision should be made for continuing the succession of the clergy, and superintending their conduct." The government might not set doctrine, but it would continue to license both the

meetinghouses and preachers of the dissenting sects. It would also
keep the parishes, clergy, and business of the established church
under its thumb, either directly or through the vestries. A committee of seventeen members, including Nicholas, Jefferson, and
Madison, was ordered to bring in a bill which would conform to
these resolutions.[57]

During the rest of November the conservative forces continued
to assert their strength, and on the last day of the month, the
House reversed its decision on several key issues. The committee
drawing up the bill was ordered to limit itself to those measures
which pertained to tax exemption for dissenters and the reservation of the church property to the use of the establishment and to
add provisions for the parish poor, the collection of the lists of
tithables, and clerical salaries. Actually, the committee had already
done this, for immediately after the resolutions calling for the new
provisions had been presented, a draft bill was submitted in complete accord with them. Gone were Jefferson's resolutions which
would have invalidated the parliamentary statutes and repealed
the Virginia act of 1705. Instead the draft opened with clauses
exempting the dissenters from any contributions or taxes for the
support of the established church. The vestries were to collect all
back salaries due to the ministers for past services and to make
assessments for the fulfillment of contracts already agreed upon
and for the continuing care of the poor. The glebes, churches, and
other property would "in all time coming be saved and reserved
to the Use of the Church by Law established."[58]

From this draft as well as from the amendments which were
later added, it is clear that the delegates had moved back into a
position which unmistakably affirmed the existence of an established church in Virginia. But while in the draft of the bill the
support of the church's ministry would have continued to be
provided by a tax on the membership of the church, Robert Carter
Nicholas proposed an amendment to suspend this tax until the end
of the next session, since "by the Exemptions allowed Dissenters
it may be too burthensome in some Parishes to the Members of the

[57]*JHD*, Nov. 19, 1776, p. 63.

[58]Boyd, *Papers of Jefferson* 1: 532; *JHD*, Nov. 30, 1776, p. 76.

established Church if they are still compel'd to support the Clergy by certain fixed Salaries."[59] Perhaps Nicholas feared that continued taxation of members of the church would drive them into the ranks of the dissenters. At any rate, the question of financial support for ministerial services proved itself to be at the end, as it had at the beginning, the most dominant point in the debates of the Assembly.

The final statement of the bill as approved by the legislature declared: 1985765

And whereas great Varieties of Opinions have arisen touching the Propriety of a general Assessment or whether every religious society should be left to voluntary Contributions for the support and maintenance of the several Ministers and Teachers of the Gospel who are of different Persuasions and Denominations, and this Difference of Sentiments cannot now be well accommodated, so that it is thought most prudent to defer this matter to the Discussion and final Determination of a future assembly when the Opinions of the Country in General may be better known. To the End therefore that so important a Subject may in no Sort be prejudged, Be it Enacted by the Authority aforesaid that nothing in this Act contained shall be construed to affect or influence the said Question of a general Assessment or voluntary Contribution in any respect whatever.[60]

Here was a new idea at work in the fertile minds of the legislators. The concept of a general assessment, of taxing everyone for the church or minister of his choice, had not been directly broached by any of the petitions or newspapers. Only the memorial from Hanover Presbytery had even touched on that possibility by asking for an exemption from taxation "for the support of any church whatsoever." The origin of the proposal is unknown. It may well have been sponsored as a compromise measure; more likely it was intended as a substitute for the old law which provided clerical salaries for members of the established clergy. The legislature of 1776 left the door open for this proposal—and it would remain so for almost a decade.

[59]Boyd, *Papers of Jefferson* 1: 534.

[60]Ibid., 1: 533. This passage, quoted here from the draft of the bill, was adopted by the House without alteration. For the full text of the final bill, see Hening, *Statutes at Large* 9: 164-67.

Jefferson was absent from the legislature when the old resolutions were truncated and the drafted bill was presented. While he rushed back to the session, George Mason stepped into the breach and successfully amended the bill to include Jefferson's clauses invalidating the British Parliament's statutes on religious matters. Other minor amendments were added, the bill quickly passed its three readings in the House, and the Senate concurred while adding a few amendments of its own. To these the exhausted delegates agreed, and the bill became law.[61] It had been a long, quarrelsome session. The members must have been anxious to return home to their plantations and farms by Christmas.

They left religion in Virginia and particularly the established church in an ambiguous situation. No longer were the dissenters taxed to support a state church; nor were they forced to contribute to their own religious groups. The laity of the established church were also freed, at least on a temporary basis, from any taxation to support their own ministry. Religion in Virginia had become voluntary, and a man could believe what he wished and contribute as much or as little as he thought fit to whichever church or minister pleased him. He could also worship when and as he chose, within certain limits; for the Assembly maintained a measure of control over the external operations of the churches. The legislators had not officially yielded their authorization to license meetinghouses and dissenting preachers. Local magistrates, if they wished, might still claim a legal basis for restricting freedom of worship. However, the Revolutionary situation and popular sentiment for the rights of conscience precluded any consistent or widespread enforcement of these laws, and they effectually lapsed.

Although the Assembly loosened its grip over the dissenters, it did not follow suit for the established church, and particularly for its clergy. Certain privileges, such as the exclusive right to perform marriages, were still retained by these ministers. Yet they were more completely dominated by the legislature than they had been before. With the commissary gone and the Revolution in process, the tenuous link to episcopacy and legitimate ecclesiastical author-

[61] *RP*, Oct. 24, 1776; Robert A. Rutland, ed., *The Papers of George Mason* (Chapel Hill, N.C., 1970), 1: 318-19; *JHD*, Dec. 9, 1776, pp. 89-90.

ity in England had been snapped. The Assembly was prepared to assume a universal jurisdiction over the clergy, but it would not make sure that they got paid. What had been the Church of England in Virginia gained nothing from the events of 1776, not even its own freedom.[62]

[62]Brydon, *Virginia's Mother Church* 2: 401-2, 425-26, suggested that the refusal to eliminate the establishment at one stroke was due in part to the fear that if the Revolution should fail, the action taken toward the church would be one more indictment against the rebels. He is more convincing in his argument that the Episcopal church would have fared better if completely separated from the government at the outset of the war. However, it should be remembered that the clergy petition asked not for an end to the establishment but for its continuance.

Chapter Two

Assault on the Establishment
1777–1783

DURING the Revolution the course of debate over the status of religion and the church-state relationship in Virginia followed the chart of a standard case of the flu. First came the aches and pains, resulting perhaps from an overly tired system; then the temperature rose, and the patient, acutely miserable, attempted various remedies. The antidotes eliminated some of the symptoms, gradually the body regained its equilibrium, and health seemed restored. In the case of this particular illness, however, the recovery was illusory; after the war, the patient caught pneumonia.

In 1777 the first audible moans were heard from the Baptists. Although in exempting dissenters from religious taxation, the legislature had eliminated a major source of their discontent, it had not disestablished the Church of England. At the same time, the Assembly had raised a new specter to haunt the foes of church-state alignment: the possibility of a general assessment. In broaching the subject of a general tax on all for the support of the church or minister of their choice, the act of 1776 had requested the opinion of the populace. The Baptists quickly accepted the invitation. On Christmas Day, 1776, representatives of the General Association of Separate Baptists met at Dover Church in Goochland, a central Piedmont county, and drew up a declaration calling the assessment proposal "pregnant with various Evils destructive to the Rights and Privileges of religious Society." Although their statement lacked the full elaboration of the Baptist view on church and state enunciated by Isaac Backus in New England, it was consistent with his position. Their primary concern was for the freedom of the church; and they cited the fourth article of the Virginia Declaration of Rights: "No man or set of Men are entitued [*sic*] to exclusive or separate Emoluments or Priveleges from the Community but in consideration of public Services." The acceptance of salaries raised by state taxation would undercut the relationship between the preacher and his congregation. It would transform the ministers into public servants, responsible and responsive to the government: "those whom the State employes in its Service, it has a Right to *regulate* and *dictate* to; it may judge and determine *who* shall preach; *when* and *where* they shall preach; and *what* they must preach." This was an intolerable intrusion in the affairs of religion. If the assessment should pass into law, the Baptist General Association declared that its preachers would return their portion of tax money to the people from whom it had been collected.[1]

The Presbyterians followed suit in the spring. At its April meeting held at Timber Ridge Church in the Valley, the Hanover Presbytery drew up a memorial to present to the next session of the legislature. Although the major portion of their argument against the assessment followed the direction taken by the Baptist declaration, the Presbyterian ministry added an ominous conclusion of their own: if the government controlled the churches through the power of taxation, it could also "revive the old Establishment in its former extent; or ordain a new one for any Sect they may think proper."[2] The assessment would unlock a Pandora's box of evil effects for the freedom of the religious groups in Virginia. Neither of the major dissenting denominations was willing to let that eventuality go unchallenged.

The Presbyterian clergy may well have formulated their petition with one eye cocked on the assessment proposal and the other on a newly published pamphlet defending the establishment. In March 1777 the *Virginia Gazette* had announced a publication entitled *The Necessity of an Established Church in Any State, or An Humble Address to the Legislators of the Commonwealth of*

---

[1]Boyd, *Papers of Jefferson* 1: 661. There is no mention of this petition in *JHD* or RP, but apparently Jefferson received a copy. It was also published in the *Va. Gaz.* (Dixon & Hunter), Mar. 28, 1777. For a succinct statement of Backus's position, see William G. McLoughlin, "Isaac Backus and the Separation of Church and State in America," *American Historical Review* 73 (1968): 1392-1413.

[2]RP, June 3, 1777. This is the date on which it was presented to the legislature. The document itself is dated April 25, 1777.

Virginia.[3] The anonymous author argued that the Assembly, for the good of the state and the preservation of civil concord and religious worship, should establish a system of religion in Virginia. With what proved to be an infelicitous analogy, he compared the relationship of church and state to the union of husband and wife. In a rejoinder published later that year, "A Freeman of Virginia" pointed out that marriages consummated between such disparate parties had never been successful. The church, holy and spiritual, could not mate with a wicked, carnal world, swimming "in flowing tides of sensuality." Moreover, the match was not only unsuitable but unnecessary; for as the example of Pennsylvania and New Jersey had proved, neither church nor state needed matrimony to survive. Equal religious freedom for all would preserve that unanimity of sentiment necessary for the peace of society. It would also prevent the historical corruption of religion produced by establishments which had turned the Church of Rome into the "mother of harlots" and transformed even the most chaste virgin among its "younger sisters" of the Reformation into a "common strumpet." In the same way, an established church corrupted the state and brought about its degradation. Like the tax which the colonials had been forced to pay for tea, the coin paid for an establishment was a "badge of slavery . . . SPIRITUAL SLAVERY." For his parting hyperbole, the author blamed all the evils of the world, including the necessity of revolution, on religious alignment of church and state: "I verily believe, had there never been an established Church in the British Empire, we should have been to this day, an united, peaceable, and happy people."[4]

Although the dissenters formed solid ranks against the proposed assessment, the members of the Church of England in Virginia did not reflect a similar unanimity of sentiment in its favor. During the Assembly sessions of 1777 and 1778, at least eight petitions were presented from various parts of the state on behalf of the

---

[3] *Va. Gaz.* (Dixon & Hunter), Mar. 28, 1777. This pamphlet has not been located. However, its general line of argumentation can be traced in the pamphlet written to refute it.

[4] "A Freeman of Virginia," *The Freeman's Remonstrance against an Ecclesiastical Establishment* (Williamsburg, 1777), pp. 7-8, 11, 13.

establishment. They clearly indicated a wide divergence of opinion.

One of the most significant was a printed broadside which circulated in the Southside counties of Mecklenburg and Lunenburg as well as in Westmoreland County in the Northern Neck. Although it did not betray any love for the dissenters and their efforts to topple the establishment, the petition did not insist upon the continuation of the church-state alliance. Though stating their personal belief that an established church was both scriptural in foundation and conducive to the welfare of society, the petitioners acknowledged that this was a disputed question. At the present time, they pointed out, a much more important issue was at stake in Virginia. For the sake of a united response to the challenge of the Revolution, they asked that the entire business of an establishment, including the specific problem of clerical salaries, be deferred by the Assembly until more pressing matters no longer intervened. There was no explicit rejection of an assessment, but the memorial noted: "If only withholding from a competent number of ministers of the gospel fixed salaries is the most likely means to make men unanimous in the defence of liberty, as had been urged, we should be very sorry indeed if there could be one found of that reverend order who would repine at the success of the measure."[5] More than one clergyman "would repine," but it would be in vain; union in the common cause was the order of the day. The position taken by this broadside reflected most accurately the course which the legislature would choose to follow until the war was concluded.

Other establishment petitions were more partisan. Generally a defense of the established church and its position in Virginia involved attacking other religious groups. For example, two very similar missives from Cumberland County denounced the subversive activities of the dissenters and enumerated the evil effects of their progress: the creation of family divisions, the night meetings of slaves held without the approval of their masters, and the general violence done to Christian truth and the peace of the community. The petitioners wailed that these sectaries were attempting "to pull down all the Barriers which the Wisdom of our

[5] RP, May 29, 1777.

Ancestors hath erected" to protect the church.[6] While the petitions did not object to a controlled and regulated toleration (i.e.,
something along the line of the colonial practice), they did insist
that the legal rights of the established church must be maintained
and its clergy properly supervised and disciplined.

The first group of petitions to request an assessment directly
was presented to the House in December 1777, from Caroline
County. The neighbors of Edmund Pendleton approved the tax
exemption from support of the established church granted to the
dissenters a year earlier, but they pointed out that the importance
of public worship required that it be regulated by the legislature.
They proposed a tax on all tithables for the support and maintenance of all church buildings and ministers, allowing each person
to allot his tax money to the religious society of his choice. Their
case for the assessment rested, first of all, on the need to free the
clergy from financial concerns so that they could devote their full
energies to the ministry and, second, upon the projected failure of
the voluntary subscription system. The petition claimed that the
latter method was inequitable, would produce discord between
clergy and people, would discourage capable men from entering
the service of the church, and perhaps in the end would bring
about the discredit of religion itself.[7]

In the following year, 1778, two more petitions were submitted
to the Assembly reiterating the call for financial support of the
clergy. One of these, from King William County in the Tidewater,
was the most violent statement of the early years. It insisted that
justice was not being done to the ministers who had lost their
salaries, lamented the "Confusion & Ill Effects arising from the
Want of a Law to regulate the Payment of the Clergy," and casti-
gated the Baptist meetings and their preachers for leading "immoral
& dissipated Lives."[8]

The strong tone of this petition may be indicative of the increasing difficulties experienced by the clergy of the established church.

[6]Ibid., Nov. 6, 1778.

[7]Ibid., Dec. 5, 1777.

[8]Ibid., Nov. 21, 1778.

As the Revolution continued, the ministers of the Church of England in Virginia were confronted by a critical situation. For them the revolt against the mother country meant not only a break in national allegiance but also the rupture of their ecclesiastical system. Unlike many of their laity, the clergy as a whole understood and were dedicated to the episcopal order. Their conflict derived from the constitution of an Erastian church, for at their ordinations the ministers had sworn fidelity to crown, bishop, and the English prayer book. The alteration in prayers ordered by the Revolutionary convention of 1776 and the newly required oath of allegiance to the commonwealth created for some a serious problem of conscience. It is not surprising, therefore, that at least one fifth of the clergy either left Virginia or retired from the active ministry after the definitive break with England. Among the tory clergy were the president and most of the faculty of the College of William and Mary, who had formed the intellectual elite of the Virginia church. The absence of this group deprived the remaining clergy of a recognizable center around which they might rally to confront the problems facing them in the years ahead.[9]

Those who stayed were the much larger and more significant group. They suppressed whatever scruples may have troubled them about their ordination oaths, accepted the verdict of independence, and attempted to survive in the ministry without benefit of state support. Some became fierce partisans of the American cause; others attempted to reorganize the church to meet the challenges of the new situation. During 1778 there was a flurry of activity. In April a "Friend to Equal Liberty" suggested in the *Virginia Gazette* that the most critical difficulty facing the church was the absence of a bishop. He proposed that this be remedied by a convention with each parish represented by two lay members and the rector, and that this convention assume the direction of

[9]Lohrenz, "Virginia Clergy," pp. 22-23, estimated that of the 129 ministers of the Anglican church in Virginia, 31 showed discontent with the Revolution in one way or another. He classified 74 clergymen as whigs in three categories: 22 were passive, 21 moderate, and 31 active. From a careful study of the backgrounds of all the clergy, he concluded that the closer the ties of the individual minister were to Virginia in terms of birth, family, position, and property holdings, the more likely he was to favor the Revolution (ibid., pp. 160-63, 216, 400).

the church and elect a bishop. He justified the suggestion by a lengthy appeal to Blackstone on the ancient method of choosing bishops.[10] Eight years later the church in Virginia would organize itself along the lines suggested by this writer, but in the early confusion of the Revolution his proposal was not taken up. However, two clergy meetings were called for 1778, one in May and the other in November. Whether they did in fact assemble is not known, but if they did meet, it apparently had no effect.[11]

As the years of revolution lengthened, the break with England, the absence of a bishop, and the suspension of the clerical salaries had a pronounced effect on the church. The supply of English recruits was cut off and the ordination of native vocations impossible. The ranks of the clergy were thinned by resignations and deaths. During a two-year period between 1777 and 1779, the Virginia newspapers advertised at least fourteen vacant parishes seeking ministers. These notices indicate a belief on the part of at least some of the vestries that, first of all, there were clergy available who might respond and, second, that the suspension of clerical salaries and the use of the subscription system might not greatly diminish the income of the rector. For example, Raleigh Parish in Amelia County had become vacant after its minister, John Brunskill, denounced the Revolution from the pulpit. He had been forcibly removed from his position in the church and retired to the glebe where he lived undisturbed throughout the war.[12] But he might have been evicted from his holdings there also if any minister had answered the advertisement that promised "the usual Salary" to any acceptable clergyman who applied for the post. Most of the notices promised that any minister who proved satisfactory to the vestry and belonged to the Church of England

---

[10] *Va. Gaz.* (Dixon & Hunter), April 24, 1778.

[11] The *Va. Gaz.* (ibid.) noted that the clergy was expected to meet in Williamsburg on May 16, 1778. On Oct. 30, 1778, the same paper printed a notice by "The committee appointed by the Clergy" calling for a general convention of the clergy on Nov. 12, 1778.

[12] William Meade, *Old Churches, Ministers, and Families of Virginia* (Philadelphia, 1891), 2: 21, called Brunskill "a dead weight upon the Church." But as there was no replacement, he resumed full charge of his parish after the Revolution (Brydon, *Virginia's Mother Church*, 2: 419).

would be granted "a genteel Provision," "a liberal salary," "a handsome subscription," or "good encouragement."[13]

The vestries themselves came under heavy attack during these years, primarily because of their nonrepresentative character; and a large number of petitions to the legislature asked that they be dissolved and reconstituted by new elections or that their secular functions, such as the care of the poor in the parish, be transferred to civil officials elected by all the freeholders.[14] The Assembly, engrossed in the problems of wartime supply and defense, generally handled only the minor vestry complaints which asked for new elections. The other church-related issues were left in abeyance.[15] Although the assessment and establishment petitions were duly handed over to the committee for religion, that body made no formal recommendations until almost the end of the second session of 1778, and then the House accepted the committee's proposal that these matters be deferred for another year.[16] During each of these sessions, however, the legislature did take the time to pass legislation continuing the suspension of clerical salaries.[17]

There were also subtle indications that the House was moving slowly in the direction of eventual disestablishment. Despite the postponement of a full-scale debate over assessment, the legislature rejected the Cumberland County petition to maintain the church in all its legal rights and supervise its clergy. In the same session of fall 1778, without the appearance of a single petition explicitly requesting the action, the House ordered the drafting of a bill which would remove from the established clergy their exclusive prerogative of performing all marriages within the commonwealth. The bill passed two readings before being rejected.[18]

---

[13]*Va. Gaz.* (Dixon & Hunter), May 9, Oct. 10, 1777; *Va. Gaz.* (Purdie), July 4, 1777, June 5, 1778; *Va. Gaz.* (Dixon & Nicholson), June 19, 1779. This is only a sample of the advertisements for clergy during this period.

[14]For these petitions, see RP, 1777-79, passim.

[15]A sample of the vestry legislation may be found in Hening, *Statutes at Large* 9: 317-19, 424, 430, 525, 527.

[16]*JHD*, Dec. 4, 1778, p. 99.

[17]Hening, *Statutes at Large* 9: 312, 387-88, 469, 578-79.

[18]*JHD*, Nov. 14, Dec. 4, Dec. 7, 1778, pp. 64, 99, 100-101.

An even more serious challenge to the establishment arose in June 1779 with the presentation of Jefferson's proposed statute on religious liberty. This measure was part of a general revision of the laws ordered by the legislature in 1776. The committee entrusted with the work was composed of Jefferson, Pendleton, Wythe, Mason, and Thomas Ludwell Lee. However, Mason and Lee did not participate in the drafting of any of the bills.[19] Jefferson, the chairman of the group, dominated the revision from the beginning. His fertile mind envisioned a sweeping reform of the Virginia legal system to remove from it the last vestiges of aristocracy and bring it into conformity with republican principles and spirit. In February 1779 he met with Wythe in Williamsburg for a final summation of their work before its presentation to the Assembly. Jefferson later recalled that during their meeting "we examined critically our several parts, sentence by sentence, scrutinizing and amending, until we had agreed on the whole." But, contrary to Jefferson's account written years after the meeting, Pendleton was not present.[20] Nor could he have agreed to the bill which Jefferson had drawn up to define the relationship between church and state in Virginia.

The Assembly which met that spring might have been firmly under Jefferson's control. Pendleton and Nicholas were gone from the legislature, having been elevated to the bench of the court of chancery; Braxton, though a delegate, was under a cloud and could no longer take a position of leadership; Madison was a member of the Virginia delegation to the Continental Congress in Philadelphia.[21] Jefferson was the most prominent delegate, but he fell victim to the same political fate which would render Patrick Henry impotent five years later. In the beginning of June, the legislature elected Jefferson to the governor's seat.[22] Despite his immense

---

[19]Boyd, *Papers of Jefferson* 2: 313-14. Lee died and Mason resigned from the committee.

[20]Ford, *Works of Jefferson* 1: 70. Boyd acknowledged this error on Jefferson's part (*Papers of Jefferson* 2: 317). See also Mays, *Letters of Pendleton* 1: 283.

[21]For Braxton's difficulties, see Mays, *Letters of Pendleton* 1: 278, 282. For Madison, see Brant, *Madison* 1: 360-61.

[22]*JHD*, June 1, 1779, p. 29. Jefferson defeated John Page by a vote of 67 to 61 on the second ballot. Although an intimate friend of Jefferson, Page was decidedly more

powers of persuasion, he had been effectively eliminated from any position of great influence in the legislative process. The stalemate over the religious question was predictable.

Jefferson had already left the Assembly when on June 4 the House ordered a committee "to bring in a bill 'concerning religious freedom,' " and eight days later it was John Harvie, not the author, who presented Bill number 82 of the revisal.[23] The enacting clause was brief: "that no man shall be compelled to frequent or support any religious Worship place or Ministry what-soever, nor shall be enforced, restrained, molested, or burthened in his body or goods, nor shall otherwise suffer on account of his religious opinions or belief, but that all men shall be free to profess, and by argument to maintain their opinions in matters of religion, and that the same shall in no wise diminish, enlarge, or affect their civil capacities."[24] The preamble to the bill was much longer. In sweeping phrases, it presented Jefferson's philosophical justification for the measure and reiterated the arguments which he had developed in the committee meetings of the Assembly in 1776. God had created the human mind free, and free it would remain; coercion in any fashion was productive only of "hypocrisy and meanness" and contrary to "the plan of the holy author of our religion," who wished it extended "by its influence on reason alone." Jefferson admitted no restrictions on the rational powers. "Truth is great and will prevail if left to herself," he insisted. But the heart of the preamble was its explicit rejection of any connec-tion between religious opinions and civil rights: "the opinions of men are not the object of civil government, nor under its juris-

---

conservative and a staunch supporter of the established church. The narrow margin of Jefferson's victory might be taken as a reflection of the conservative-liberal division in the House. If so, it helps explain the failure of both Jefferson's bill and the bill "concerning religion" proposed at the next session. For Page's embarrassment over his contest with Jefferson and the latter's reassurance of their friendship, see Boyd, *Papers of Jefferson* 2: 278-79.

[23] *JHD*, June 4, June 12, 1779, pp. 34, 44. Harvie, who served as chairman of this committee, was a close friend of Jefferson. See, for example, his letter to Jefferson in Boyd, *Papers of Jefferson* 2: 125-27.

[24] The quotations from the bill are taken from a broadside of the text published in 1779 and reproduced in Boyd, *Papers of Jefferson* 2: 305. It was listed as Bill number 82 in the Catalogue of Bills (ibid., 2: 329-35).

diction." Just as religious belief could not be a requirement for
the possession of civil rights, so the civil authority had no legitimate business in the area of conscience.

The preamble also denied the validity of requiring contributions
to any one church, as well as the concept of an assessment for the
support of religion in general. To require a man "to support this or
that teacher of his own religious persuasion, is depriving him of the
comfortable liberty of giving his contributions to the particular
pastor whose morals he would make his pattern, and whose powers
he feels most persuasive to righteousness." The proposed bill concluded with a forceful declaration that although the legislature
realized it had no authority to bind the decision of future assemblies, yet the rights elaborated in this statute belonged to "the
natural rights of mankind," and any future law which limited or
repealed the provisions of the enacting clause would violate those
rights.

The bill survived two readings before the House voted to postpone further consideration of the measure until August 1.[25] Since
on that date the legislators would be back on their farms and
plantations, the bill had been consigned to limbo. A similar fate
awaited the other new pieces of legislation pertaining to church
problems considered that session. Another bill of the revised code,
"for saving the property of the church heretofore by law established," was put off, along with a measure to dissolve and reconstitute all the vestries in the commonwealth. Finally, as had been
its custom since 1776, the Assembly voted once again to suspend
the salaries of the established clergy for another session.[26]

The interval between the two sessions of 1779 provided a
respite for the delegates while both advocates and opponents of
the bill took to the printing presses. A broadside of Jefferson's

[25]*JHD*, June 14, 1779, p. 46.

[26]Ibid. The bill on church property made more explicit the rights of the church
to the glebes, plate, buildings, etc., which had been granted by the act of 1776
exempting dissenters from taxation for the support of the establishment. For the text
of this bill proposed in 1779, see Boyd, *Papers of Jefferson* 2: 535-55. The bill concerning vestries had been ordered on May 17, 1779, with Jefferson one of the drafting
committee. It was postponed on June 19 (*JHD*, pp. 11, 59).

proposal, printed most probably at private expense, was circulated to various counties and interested persons.[27] But the opposition dominated the pages of the *Virginia Gazette*. In an article published in the middle of August, "An Eastern Layman" lambasted the naiveté of proposing norms for men living in organized society which were attainable only in a state of uncorrupted nature. The freedom present in the latter condition, he asserted, was different from and in contradiction to the responsibilities incumbent upon men once they formed a body politic. Although the author of this article accepted the major premise of the preamble that men's opinions did not come within the purview of civil government, he rejected the conclusion that men should therefore be free to profess and maintain those opinions without any control or supervision by the state. It was one thing to say that the government had no authority to dictate religious belief, but quite another to assert that men were therefore beyond regulation in the external manifestations of those beliefs. The demands of "social tranquility" required that the state should set the times and places of religious worship, so that the citizenry were protected from the effects of "an over pious or misguided enthusiasm."[28]

Although this writer appeared more nervous over the possible license granted to evangelical religion, another attacked Jefferson's preamble for containing "the principles of a Deist" and decried the lack of concern he found in the bill for the rights of society at large. This self-styled "Social Christian" claimed that Jefferson's statute would exalt individual freedom at the expense of the collective rights of the majority. Viewed from the perspective of the social contract, the preeminent value which must be maintained was not the separate rights of each person but the common interest of the group. The individual must yield to the will of the majority for the sake of the common good. At the same time each person maintained his personal liberty in his freedom to express his opinion and to cast his vote in determining the will of that majority and fixing the rules by which the society would live. Furthermore, this author insisted that it was well within the power

[27] Boyd, *Papers of Jefferson* 2: 548, 3: 68.

[28] *Va. Gaz.* (Dixon & Nicholson), Aug. 14, 1779.

of the majority to determine that moral precepts and religious teaching would promote the temporal welfare and happiness of society. Consequently the majority had a right to institutionalize these values by establishing places of public worship, providing financial support for Christian teachers of various denominations, and requiring attendance at religious exercises.

The author of this particular article promoted the establishment of Christianity as the religion of the state on the grounds that the vast majority of Virginians were Christians. As for the others— "Jews, Mohamedans, Atheists or Deists"—they might be tolerated, but on the basis of public utility they had no right to hold public office or promote their own "singular opinions." Nor should they be exempted from contributions to the support of those churches whose function was to serve the common good of society. He defended the concept of an assessment on the grounds that it was crucial to have regular churches and preachers rather than depend upon the services of an itinerant clergy. It would also guarantee a supply of competent ministers. In addition, it would prove of major benefit to the poor of the community, those who were not capable of self-education in values, by providing them with services for which the wealthy bore the major burden of the cost. Finally, he urged that attendance at religious gatherings be compulsory since they were the cement of society and a force for the cultivation of public virtue and the common good of the state. At the same time, he cautioned that it was not necessary for government to make any other regulations for Christian churches beyond those required to ensure peace and concord; in all other areas, each religious society should be free "as to their modes of worship and the internal government of their church."[29]

When the Assembly convened in October, public sentiment was clearly weighted against Jefferson's bill. A long petition from Lancaster County feared that its passage would beget a "Licentious Freedom subversive of true piety and civil Society" and wanted it amended to require licenses for both meetinghouses and preachers. Some petitioners from Culpeper County went even further, asking that the bill for religious freedom be rejected and a

[29]Ibid., Sept. 11, Sept. 18, 1779. This was a two-part article.

form of religious establishment instituted. Three more petitions, from widely separated areas, explicitly requested a general assessment for the support of religion. "The great confusion and disorder ... since the Old Establishment has been interrupted" had convinced the petitioners from Essex County that the Assembly must take a firm hand in religious matters. Alarmed at Jefferson's bill, which they considered harmful to Christianity, they found the prospect of a general assessment "most agreeable" and asked that it be coupled with a limitation of public officeholding to those who professed the Christian religion. They also wanted itinerant preaching limited, order maintained in church services, and a ban on any doctrine which tended "to subvert Government or Distress Civil Society." The claims of civil society were also cited in a petition from Lunenburg County as the justification for the Assembly to establish Protestant Christianity together with an assessment to support its ministers.[30]

The final petition presented to the legislature that fall came from Amherst County. It briefly requested the delegates to pass a law requiring an assessment and asked that any toleration granted to Roman Catholics be "guarded & limited," and in particular that no member of that church or any "Jew, Turk or Infidel" be allowed to hold a civil or military position in Virginia. Coming from an area in the western Piedmont where dissenters were supposed to be strongly entrenched, this was a significant petition. It was signed by over one hundred persons, including Joseph and John Cabell, two members of the most prominent family in Amherst. Their two other brothers, Nicholas and William, were both members of the Assembly that fall.[31] Amherst County had sent two other petitions to the legislature earlier in the session

[30] *JHD*, Oct. 21, 1779, p. 19; RP, Oct. 20, Oct. 22, Nov. 3. 1779. The Essex County petition was signed by 165 persons including William Gatewood and Spencer Roane, both of whom as members of the House in 1784 would vote against the assessment proposal. It was also signed by Robert P. Waring, one of the wealthiest men in Virginia; see Jackson Turner Main, "The One Hundred," *William and Mary Quarterly*, 3d ser., 11 (1954): 383.

[31] RP, Nov. 10, 1779. The Cabells belonged to the liberal wing of the established church, and they also had ties with the Presbyterian clergy. In 1774 the Hanover Presbytery had met at Col. William Cabell's home to plan its remonstrance to the

requesting the passage of Jefferson's bill. Claiming the support of
Anglicans, Presbyterians, Baptists, and Methodists, these petitioners had warned that at the thought of binding men to pay
taxes for a form of worship not of their own choice "Religion
looses her Angels Face, and looks pale & Sickly."[32] But the
petition signed by the Cabell brothers effectively canceled the
others out. The only other support in petition form for Jefferson's
bill that session came from Augusta County across the Blue
Ridge.[33]

Most notable for its absence was any public statement from the
Presbyterian ministers and elders commending the bill establishing
religious freedom. Jefferson had privately sent the Reverend John
Todd, a leading figure in the Hanover Presbytery, a copy of the bill
during the summer. He must have hoped that its publication would
evoke public support from the Presbyterian leadership. If so, he
was doomed to disappointment. In August, Todd replied with a
gracious letter, thanking Jefferson and indicating his personal
approval of the bill: "The Sentiments are the Sentiments of my
heart, and therefore [I] cordially approve them. It is my wish the
author of the bill may find men of like Sentiments and abilities
enough to pass it safely thro' the Assembly." But Jefferson would
have to look elsewhere for support, for neither Todd nor the other
members of the Presbytery made their views on the bill a matter
of public record that year.[34]

Assembly (Alexander Brown, *The Cabells and Their Kin* [Boston, 1895], pp. 65-66, 95).
In 1779 William, Joseph, and John Cabell all had sons attending Hampden-Sydney, the
Presbyterian academy in Prince Edward County (Alfred J. Morrison, *The College of
Hampden Sidney: Calendar of Board Minutes, 1776-1786* [Richmond, 1912], pp. 32-34).
That same year Nicholas Cabell was a delegate and William Cabell a senator [Earl G. Swem
and John W. Williams, *A Register of the General Assembly of Virginia, 1776-1918, and
of the Constitutional Conventions* [Richmond, 1918], pp. 8, 10).

[32] RP, Nov. 1, 1779.

[33] Ibid., Oct. 27, 1779.

[34] Boyd, *Papers of Jefferson* 3: 68. Todd was a strong defender of the Revolution
later invited by the Assembly to preach to it in November 1782 at a day of public
thanksgiving. This was an honor usually reserved to the established clergy (Lohrenz, "The
Virginia Clergy," p. 229). The Presbytery apparently did not discuss the church-state
question at its October meeting in 1779 (Minutes of Hanover Presbytery, 1755-86,
microfilm, Union Theological Seminary, Richmond). Nor is there any reference to a
Presbyterian petition in either *JHD* or RP for 1779.

The most plausible explanation for the official silence of the Presbytery might be that a division of opinion existed among its members. Some of the presbyters must have shared Todd's opinion of Jefferson's bill, and perhaps they hoped that their statement of April 1777 would serve as a sufficient indication of their stance. At the same time, Todd was aware, as he indicated in his letter to Jefferson, that "the old detested establishment had warm advocates in the house" and that sentiment for an assessment was growing. It may well have been growing within the ranks of his Presbyterian confreres. Sufficient reasons existed for a change of heart. Over the past three years the established church had steadily declined in power and influence and no longer presented a formidable threat, the economic dislocations of the war undoubtedly sliced into all clerical incomes, and the shortage of ministers was acute. At the fall meeting in 1778 the Presbytery summarized its problems: "the growing extent of our Churches; the critical state of religious Affairs, the great variety of Denominations multiplying in the State, the Danger of the Extinction of our own Churches, unless some speedy and effectual Means be adopted to present the Evil." The ministers and elders agreed to consider "altering the usual course of Education" in order to get more men into the pulpits.[35]

Rapprochement with the Anglicans was another possibility. The Reverend Samuel Stanhope Smith, the president of Hampden-Sydney Academy, had written to Jefferson in the spring of 1779 about the latter's proposal for a statewide system of education. Although enthusiastically endorsing the plan, Smith thought it would founder because of the mutual jealousies of the various religious groups in Virginia. In particular, he pointed out that both the Presbyterians and the Anglicans would want to dominate the College of William and Mary, which was to be the apex of the proposed system. Whichever church controlled that institution could in turn impose its religious views on the educational network throughout the commonwealth. The solution to this impasse,

[35]Minutes of Hanover Presbytery, Oct. 30, 1778. The number of ministers belonging to the Presbytery grew throughout the war years; for example: 1776, 9 ministers; 1778, 11; 1781, 17; 1783, 21; 1785, 25. Yet there was never sufficient clergy to satisfy the demands for their services (ibid., 1776-85, passim).

Smith believed, lay in a reunion of the Christians in Virginia. "Good God," he exclaimed, "What suspicions, what animosities divide the disciples of a religion whose ruling maxim is charity and love!" Now was the chosen moment, Smith insisted, "to heal these divisions"; and he placed his immediate hopes in "a union, at least of the two capital sects of christians [in] this state." United in faith they would be able to reach common agreement and cooperation in this vital matter of education. Not only was union necessary; it was also attainable if only the Anglicans would descend from their "pride and insolence," while the Presbyterians eased their "rigour and austerity."[36]

The amount of support for this project which Smith aroused among his Presbyterian colleagues is unknown, but apparently he was not working alone. The Reverend David Griffith, a leader of Virginia Anglicans after the Revolution, also expressed a desire to one of his fellow clergymen for a "coalition" with the other religious groups; but by 1783 he would become convinced that this was impossible because of their implacable hatred for his church. All of them, with the exception of the Quakers and Methodists, were its "avowed enemies" bent on its "destruction."[37] Griffith had good reason for this judgment. The level of antagonism and bitterness which is so apparent in the press and petitions of the period makes it clear that while some ministers might have proposed a scheme of union, they would have been hard pressed to convince the rank and file of their congregations. Not only were the churches separated in polity and certain aspects of doctrine and worship, but they distrusted one another's motives and sincerity. This was not an ecumenical age.

However, in 1779 Smith remained optimistic. Though he would soon leave Virginia to assume a professorship at the College of New Jersey, his thoughts were directed toward doing all in his power to effect such a reunion. Religion and education were the most important concerns of his life; and, in marked contrast to Jefferson, he saw the two as necessarily joined. Also in contradiction to the position of Jefferson's bill on religious freedom, Smith believed that civil government should support religion. Shortly

[36]Boyd, *Papers of Jefferson* 2: 248.   [37]Meade, *Old Churches* 2: 264-65.

after the Revolution, he commented to a foreign correspondent on the problems facing the churches in America, the general religious indifference, and the laissez-faire attitude of the states, and concluded: "The civil power is too inattentive to the influence which religion would have on the good government of the state." Smith noted the tendency of Americans to think "that heaven will take care of the church, if they take care of the state." The net result of this policy was to leave "the care of religion solely to providence, and its ministers"; and he considered this "one of the fruits of our extreme idea of liberty and one of its most injurious effects."[38] Smith's influence in the Hanover Presbytery was great; and his opinions were shared by others, including his brother, John Blair Smith.[39] But they did not sway Todd. Lacking a consensus, the Presbyterian clergy and elders issued no recommendations to the Assembly in 1779.

Unlike their more conservative Presbyterian brethren, the Separate Baptists went on record in their General Association meeting of October, declaring their complete approval of the bill for religious freedom. They further ordered that this approbation be published in the press, but the only petition they submitted to the legislature that fall dealt exclusively with their continued concern for a measure which would legalize marriages performed by dissenting ministers.[40]

[38]Michael Kraus, "Charles Nisbet and Samuel Stanhope Smith—Two Eighteenth Century Educators," *Princeton University Library Chronicle* 6 (1944): 26, 33.

[39]Another example might be provided by Caleb Wallace, who was the deputy of the Presbytery to the Assembly of 1776 to present its memorial. At that time he strongly opposed any kind of establishment. During the latter years of the Revolution he gave up the ministry and moved to Kentucky, where he became a prominent political figure. The influence of Smith showed in a series of questions Wallace posed in early 1785. In seeking advice on a form of government he raised the issues: "Is the belief of a God indispensable to civil Society?" and "As Christianity is generally confessed to be highly conducive to the interests of Civil Society; may it be established by Laws, or unbelievers be subjected to Civil Incapacities?" (Rutland, *Papers of Madison* 8: 219; see also William H. Whitsitt, *The Life and Times of Judge Caleb Wallace, Some Time a Justice of the Court of Appeals of Kentucky,* Filson Club Publications, 4 [Louisville, 1888], pp. 40-41, 50-51).

[40]*JHD,* Oct. 25, 1779, p. 23: William Henry Foote, *Sketches of Virginia, Historical and Biographical, First Series* (Richmond, 1850), pp. 330-31. A copy of the *Va. Gaz.* in which the Baptist memorial was printed has not been located.

The reaction in the press and the religious petitions clearly showed that the weight of public opinion favored some form of governmental intervention in religious matters, and this sentiment found support in the House of Delegates. Jefferson's bill was not even considered that fall. Instead, shortly after the Assembly had settled down to business, a select committee was ordered to prepare and bring in a bill "concerning religion." James Henry, a delegate from Accomack County on the Eastern Shore, was appointed chairman of a group which included Carter Braxton, George Mason, and John Tyler. Ten days later, on October 25, the bill was presented on the floor of the House and passed its first reading.[41]

The bill would have fixed the boundaries of toleration in Virginia, established certain varieties of Christianity as the religion of the state, provided for the incorporation of these religious bodies, and instituted an assessment to support their ministers and churches. In effect, therefore, the delegates compressed four different measures within the bonds of one act: toleration, establishment, incorporation, and assessment. With the sole exception of the assessment proviso, all of these measures had been included as part of the South Carolina Constitution adopted in 1778. The drafting committee obviously utilized this document, as the proposed bill repeated practically verbatim its provisions on toleration, establishment, and incorporation. However, where the South Carolina Constitution explicitly instituted the voluntary system of support, the Virginia bill provided for an assessment.[42]

The opening clause effectively repudiated the sixteenth article of the Declaration of Rights. Only those individuals and groups who subscribed to a belief in one God, a future life, and the necessity of public worship were to be "freely tolerated." Although this was ostensibly done in the name of encouraging "Religion and

[41]*JHD*, Oct. 15, Oct. 25, 1779, pp. 10, 24.

[42]A "bill concerning religion," Oct. 25, 1779, in House of Delegates Bills, Resolutions, etc., Box 3, Rough Bills, Oct. 1779, VSL. Both the initial draft proposed by the committee and the final working copy are available, so it is clear what amendments were made in the course of the debates. All the quotations in the text are taken from the final copy, which is reproduced in Appendix I. For the South Carolina Constitution, on which the first half of the bill was based, see Thorpe, *Constitutions* 6: 3255-57.

virtue, and for removing all restraints on the mind in its inquiries after truth," the bill was actually closing off certain areas of debate. Down the street at the Governor's Palace, Jefferson must have shuddered at these restrictions.

The bill then proceeded to establish Christianity as the religion of the commonwealth with equal civil and religious privileges, including the right of incorporation, for all those denominations which would submit to a set of five articles. These were:

First, That there is one Eternal God and a future State of Rewards and punishments.

Secondly, That God is publickly to be Worshiped.

Thirdly, That the Christian Religion is the true Religion.

Fourthly, That the Holy Scriptures of the old and new Testament are of divine inspiration, and are the only rule of Faith.

Fifthly, That it is the duty of every Man, when thereunto called by those who Govern, to bear Witness to truth.

The first two articles were identical to the test for toleration. But the third article eliminated establishment for the Jewish community in Richmond, and a strict interpretation of the fourth article might have precluded Catholics who accepted church tradition as part of the "rule of faith" and Quakers who held to the doctrine of the "Inward Light."[43]

Having sufficiently narrowed the scope of toleration, as more than one of the petitions that session had requested, the bill then moved into the area of church polity and ministerial services. Each clergyman must be selected either by a majority of his congregation or by persons chosen by that majority to select him. Before assuming his pastoral duties, he must declare before "some Court of Record" in the state that he would "teach nothing (as required

[43]For the Jewish community in Richmond, see Leon Hukner, "The Jews in Virginia from the Earliest Times to the Close of the Eighteenth Century," *Publications of the American Jewish Historical Society,* no. 20 (1911): 100-105. For Quaker belief, see Jones, *Quakers in the American Colonies,* pp. 32-36.

The delegates may not have intended to exclude either Catholics or Quakers. The South Carolina Constitution and the initial draft presented by the committee provided for the establishment of Protestant Christianity, and the word "Protestant" was dropped during the debates. But at the same time, "only" was added before "rule of faith" in the fourth article.

of necessity to eternal Salvation) but that which he shall be persuaded may be concluded and proved from the Scriptures."[44] In addition, he had to promise to be careful about his work, study, and prayer and to attempt to lead an exemplary life, maintaining peace and charity within the community. The rationale for requiring this oath was to ensure that "the State may have Security for the due discharge of the Pastoral Office." In other words, the government was assuming complete responsibility for the clergy. The bill also provided that the churches would maintain the proper posture of devotion toward their earthly as well as their heavenly creator: "No person whatsoever shall speak anything in their Religious Assemblies disrespectfully or Seditiously of the Government of this State."[45] There would be no repetition of those days before the Revolution when ministers in Sunday sermons denounced the Stamp Act and urged resistance to the authority of the royal governors.

The second half of the bill was concerned with the assessment. It briefly justified the measure on the grounds that "permanent encouragement may be given for providing a sufficient number of ministers and teachers." The tax was to be paid either in tobacco or money on the basis of the number of tithables; and each person could determine which religious society, among those belonging to the establishment, would receive his allotment. The sheriff of each county charged with the actual collection and distribution of the taxes, and the trustees appointed by each denomination would determine how their share of the funds was to be spent.[46]

Careful provisions were made for all contingencies. Should anyone fail to pay the tax, the sheriff could use force if necessary to collect it on behalf of the religious society in which the unwilling contributor was enrolled. In cases where no religious affiliation was designated, the county court was to divide the nonmember's

---

[44]The requirement for attestation before the court was added during the debate in the House.

[45]The initial draft of the committee had added "or Treason" after "Seditiously," but this addition was dropped during the House debate.

[46]In the section on the assessment, a number of minor changes were made by the House. However, the only major alteration was the substitution of county court, sheriff, and clerk in the place of the vestry for the administration of the act.

taxes among the various established churches of his local parish in proportion to the amount of assessed taxes they had already received. Much the same procedure was to be followed if a religious group failed to appoint someone to receive its portion of the assessment. The desired purpose of these extensive provisions was to close tightly all loopholes and require everyone to provide financial support for those religious groups which would form the Christian establishment of Virginia. Finally, in addition to technical matters of sheriffs' bonds and clerks' fees, the bill would repeal that act of 1748 which provided for clerical salaries and which the Assembly had been suspending from session to session since 1776. It also would revoke that portion of another colonial law which required established clergy to be ordained by a bishop in England.

The day after the bill was presented from committee, it barely squeaked through a second reading; but the small majority who favored it managed to defeat an attempt to postpone the measure until the following spring, and it was referred to a Committee of the Whole for further discussion.[47] The amount of opposition it generated is not surprising, for the delegates must have been aware that this measure, if passed, would mean a major retreat from the philosophy of the sixteenth article of the Declaration of Rights and a reversal of the direction in which the legislature had been slowly moving since the Revolution began. Governor Jefferson must have itched to join the debates on the floor of the House. On the other side of the political question, though equally removed from the immediate decision, Edmund Pendleton unburdened himself to an old friend:

I consider it still more Ominous for our virtue that a Bill . . . for regulating Religion has produced warm debates, and . . . [I] fear for it's fate, and I cannot keep out of my mind two lines of a song lately made on the declining state of Britain
        Must Religion expire on the ground?
        And must Virtue Sink down by her side?[48]

[47]*JHD*, Oct. 26, 1779, p. 24.
[48]Mays, *Letters of Pendleton* 1: 303.

While the Assembly debated the bill, the press came out with several articles defending the measure. The *Virginia Gazette* carried an ironical column which pretended aversion for the projected establishment and assessment. A self-styled "Friend to Liberty" argued that although everyone acknowledged the value of religion to the welfare of society, yet government had no right to infringe on human freedom. His reductio ad absurdum insisted that all forms of instruction should only be tolerated since they impinged upon the ideas which men form unaided for themselves. In the final analysis, though the state should be toppled as a result of granting total freedom of opinion, Virginians could be comforted by the realization that it had been done only out of "a zealous enthusiastick regard for the rights of human nature." The assessment must be rejected, for it would render the clergy independent of the people, whereas if kept in financial bondage, they "will flatter our passions and teach us how we may go on to sin, and yet live."[49]

In a more direct if somewhat hysterical fashion, another press writer attacked Jefferson's bill for proposing a freedom of opinion and expression which would effectively undermine the coercive powers of the state by making each man's opinion a law unto itself. He staunchly defended the need for Christian leaders in government, equating atheists in administration with allowing "a fox to guard the hen houses." If the assessment was not passed, he warned his readers that God would soon be little known in Virginia.[50]

But press campaigns, clerical problems, and religious petitions notwithstanding, the House in the end shelved the bill "concerning religion." On November 15, exactly a month after it had been ordered, the delegates buried the proposal until the next session. It was never resurrected. Pendleton correctly noted that the legislature had "rejected the proposition . . . and left every man to do what is right in his own eyes." One small section of the bill was reclaimed, however, for George Mason and two other delegates were ordered to bring in a measure repealing the act of 1748

[49] *Va. Gaz.* (Clarkson & Davis), Oct. 30, 1779.

[50] Ibid., Nov. 6, 1779.

which provided salaries for the established clergy. The game of suspending enforcement from session to session was at an end, and the bill passed into law shortly before Christmas.[51]

At the same time, the House showed its reluctance to make the rejection of the assessment definitive. In an effort to preclude further hopes and false optimism for the possible reestablishment of state support, Mason and his cohorts had affixed a preamble to this repeal bill, stating that the measure was being passed so that the people would never have to fear "being compelled to contribute to the Support or Maintenance of the former established Church" and that the church members should neither expect its reestablishment nor avoid "proper Measures, among themselves, for the Support and Maintenance of their own Religion and Ministers." However, this attempt at realism was struck out by the House.[52]

Mason's other attempt that session to place the Church of England in Virginia on a practical basis was equally unsuccessful. He had been appointed chairman of a committee to bring in a bill "for saving and securing the property of the church heretofore by law established," a measure presented as part of the revisal of the laws in the last session but postponed at that time. Mason now revised the bill, so that in lieu of the missing ecclesiastical administration, the church members and vestries would be able to remove incompetent or disloyal clergy. Final action on this measure was also postponed.[53] The House considered one other proposal pertaining to religion, the change in the marriage laws requested by the Baptists. That also was rejected by the delegates on its first reading.[54]

[51]*JHD*, Nov. 15, Dec. 13, Dec. 18, 1779, pp. 56-57, 87, 97; Mays, *Letters of Pendleton* 1: 306.

[52]Rutland, *Papers of Mason* 2: 553.

[53]*JHD*, Nov. 15, 1779, p. 57; Rutland, *Papers of Mason* 2: 590-92. As originally drafted, its purpose was to provide the established church with a secure title to the property it had owned at the time of the Revolution. Boyd, *Papers of Jefferson* 2: 553-55, contains the text of the bill as it was presented in the revisal. But Boyd's note which states that after its postponement in the spring session of 1779 nothing was done until 1785 is incorrect.

[54]*JHD*, Nov. 8, Nov. 29, 1779, pp. 46, 73.

In matters of religion and the relationship of church and state, the Assembly during these years of Revolution generally appeared as a master of indecision, ordering bills to be drafted, debating them at length, and then postponing or rejecting them. The expenditure of great quantities of energy produced only meager results. The single major legislative change was the ending of taxation for the support of the Church of England in Virginia. Even the passage of this bill only made definitive a practice begun in the session of 1776. While this absence of decisive action may be partially understood in terms of the overwhelming concern for the prosecution of the Revolution and the economic hardships which war had imposed upon the commonwealth, the major explanation lies in the composition of the House of Delegates. There the opposing forces were very evenly divided, and the crucial decision on the future status of the churches and religion would have to wait until one side or the other gained a preponderance. Eventually this would be achieved, but only by the force of public opinion among the people themselves.

The failure to pass an assessment was not the only defeat suffered in the fall of 1779 by the supporters of the established church. Perhaps even more crucial in terms of its long-range effect upon the church and its ministry was the revision of the educational system at the College of William and Mary and the consequent elimination of the chair of theology.[55] Here too the hand of Jefferson was at work. Describing the college as it existed before his "reforms," Jefferson wrote: "The College of William and Mary was an establishment purely of the Church of England; and Visitors were required to be all of that Church; the Professors to subscribe its thirty-nine Articles; its Students to learn its Catechism; and one of its fundamental objects was declared to be, to raise up Ministers for that Church."[56] Up until the Revolution, the college had performed that function with fair success, and most of the Virginia candidates for the ministry received their theological training there. The events of 1776, however, decimated the student body as those who were of age entered military service. In

[55] Brydon, *Virginia's Mother Church* 2: 590-92.

[56] Ford, *Works of Jefferson* 1: 75-76.

addition, the tory sentiments of President John Camm and most of the faculty made their replacement necessary. In 1777 the Reverend James Madison, second cousin to the young politician from Orange and a good friend to both his cousin and Jefferson, was appointed president of the college by the Visitors. He was assisted in the classes by two other clergymen, John Bracken and Robert Andrews.[57] They might have resumed the work of training ministers but for the changes in the curriculum initiated in 1779 under the direction of Jefferson.

As part of his revision of the laws, Jefferson had proposed sweeping educational innovations and reforms on every level in the state. One of his principal proposals concerned the transformation of the College of William and Mary from a private institution operated on the basis of a colonial charter into a secular university dependent upon the government. The bill did not pass, however, and Jefferson later blamed its defeat on the identification of the college with "the Anglican sect."[58] Samuel Stanhope Smith had rested his objections to the bill on the close link which the college maintained with the Church of England. Jefferson was prepared to put those fears to rest. Although the fullness of his vision would have to wait until the foundation of the University of Virginia several decades later, shortly after assuming the position of governor, Jefferson was appointed to the Board of Visitors of the college. In this capacity he proceeded to initiate many of the changes proposed in his bill. Among these were the elimination of the grammar school (in which the students learned their catechism) together with the chairs of theology and oriental languages, the latter involving the study of Scripture.[59]

---

[57]"Journal of the President and Masters or Professors of William and Mary College," *William and Mary Quarterly,* 1st ser., 15 (1907): 164-65.

[58]Boyd, *Papers of Jefferson* 2: 535-43; Ford, *Works of Jefferson* 1: 76.

[59]Ford, *Works of Jefferson* 1: 78. The "Journal of the President of William and Mary," p. 169, dates this visitation in December 1779. Madison and Andrews were retained on the faculty, while three laymen were added: George Wythe, James McClurg, and Charles Bellini. Another, more subtle indication of the transformation of the school was the elimination of the title "Rev." before the names of Madison and Andrews in the journal. A very useful study of Jefferson's position on church, state, and education is Robert M. Healey, *Jefferson on Religion in Public Education* (New Haven, 1962).

The removal of the theological education from the curriculum did not appear to bother the Anglican minister who presided over the changes. In the summer of 1780, President Madison wrote to Ezra Stiles, the president of Yale, and enthusiastically recounted the reforms recently made at William and Mary. He also explained the reason for dropping the study of theology: "It was formerly instituted for the Purpose of the Church of England, which was here established, but it is now thought that Establishments in Favor of any particular Sect are incompatible with the Freedom of a Republic, and therefore, the Professorship is entirely dropped."[60] Madison was a young man, a dedicated republican, and perhaps heavily under the influence of Jefferson. At least he shared with the governor a commitment to education as the principal means by which knowledge and virtue would advance.[61] His commitment to the ministry was less firm, and in 1781 he wrote his cousin, the other Madison, that he was "gradually undergoing a Conversion" and expected to leave both the ministry and the college to take up the profession of law. The latter career did not particularly appeal to him, but he thought it would be more financially beneficial, as well as "more fashionable."[62] The future first bishop of Virginia

[60]F. B. Dexter, ed., *The Literary Diary of Ezra Stiles* (New York, 1901), 2: 447. Not all the faculty were happy with the changes. Rev. John Bracken had been dropped from the faculty along with the elimination of the grammar school ("Journal of the President of William and Mary," p. 267; Rutherfoord Goodwin, "The Rev. John Bracken, 1745-1818: Rector of Bruton Parish and President of William and Mary College in Virginia," *Historical Magazine of the Protestant Episcopal Church* 10 (1941): 378-84).

[61]Charles Crowe, "Bishop James Madison and the Republic of Virtue," *Journal of Southern History* 30 (1964): 58-70; Dexter, *Literary Diary of Stiles* 2: 446-47.

[62]Hutchinson, *Papers of Madison* 2: 294. In a letter to his brother later that same year, Madison wrote: "my prospects are very gloomy. . . . These are miserable Times to most of us down here. We know not that any Thing we have is safe for a week, tho I have suffered nothing material as yet" (James Madison to William Madison, July 21, 1781, Xerox of typescript, Bishop James Madison Papers, Virginia Historical Society, Richmond [hereafter VHS], original in Pierpont Morgan Library, New York City). He was, of course, referring to the invasion of Virginia by the British. The college revived after Yorktown and granted its reformer Jefferson a Doctor of Laws degree ("Journal of the President of William and Mary," p. 73). With the restoration of peace, Madison also began to make a decent living. Jefferson reported to Stiles in 1784 that there were 80 undergraduate students at the college and that Madison was receiving a salary of approximately £400 a year (Dexter, *Literary Diary of Stiles* 3: 125).

was not interested in a pastoral ministry, nor does he appear to have reflected upon the effect which the reforms at William and Mary would work on his church.

A harbinger of an equally serious problem to plague the church after the Revolution came from the evangelical wing. Despite the embarrassment created by John Wesley's denunciation of the colonial revolt, the Methodist movement in Virginia continued to gain strength during the early years of the war. However, its development was increasingly hampered by the diminishing numbers of established clergy available to administer the sacraments. Consequently, in May 1779, at a meeting attended primarily by younger Methodist preachers from Virginia and North Carolina circuits, the young exhorters determined to take matters into their own hands and confer ordination among themselves. This radical departure from Anglican usage, denounced by Devereux Jarratt as "a most unwarrantable usurpation and a flagrant violation of all order," split the Methodists in the South into two opposing factions with much resultant bitterness. The following year a conference of preachers from states north of Virginia met under the direction of Francis Asbury, Wesley's surrogate in America, and condemned the action taken by their hotheaded brethren. Asbury subsequently attended a Virginia conference to pour oil on the troubled waters and persuaded the young preachers to refrain from administering the sacraments until Wesley could be consulted. Harmony was restored between Jarratt and the preachers, and the Methodists reunited. But it was a fragile peace. The needs of a growing cure could not be met by a church suffering acutely from lack of clergy and without means to provide them.[63]

Asbury, returning from the Virginia meeting, stopped off to visit Jarratt and heard him preach an "excellent sermon." They spent the evening together, and afterwards in his journal Asbury spelled out much of the predicament of the Anglican ministry in

[63]Sweet, *Methodism in American History,* pp. 79-97; Brydon, *Virginia's Mother Church* 2: 204-8; Jarratt, *Life,* 112, 114. Edward Dromgoole, a Methodist preacher, attended the 1779 conference and later wrote of his disapproval. He noted that the division lasted about two years (Edward Dromgoole Papers, microfilm, Southern Historical Collection, University of North Carolina Library, Chapel Hill [hereafter So. Hist. Coll., UNC]).

Virginia: "He labours, but the people give him little or nothing." The regular clergy of the Church of England had been sadly depleted since the beginning of the Revolution. In addition to the tories who had left either the state or the ministry, eighteen Anglican clergymen died during the early years of the war; and there were no replacements. Others had entered military service as chaplains or in positions of command. Some of those left behind to tend the religious flocks proved to be subjects of controversy or went into semiretirement when their salaries were ended. Many of the churches and chapels stood vacant. If services were held, they often had to be conducted by lay readers.[64]

At the other end of the ecclesiastical spectrum, the Baptists did not suffer from a shortage of preachers—they had approximately one hundred in Virginia—nor did they lack the energy or the initiative to challenge the prerogatives of the establishment. When the prominent Baptist minister John Leland applied in 1781 to the vestry of St. Thomas Parish in Orange County for the use of one of the parish chapels, he claimed the right to preach there on the grounds that the buildings were the community property of the state. Replying for the vestrymen, the father of James Madison informed Leland that the vestry found his request "new and . . . unprecedented" and that the rights which he had asserted were without validity for the property was "reserved to the use of the Church by law established."[65]

On other fronts, the Baptists were somewhat successful. In a series of petitions through the early years of the 1780s, they continued to pressure the Assembly to alter the vestry and marriage laws. Although the legislature had generally acceded to requests from individual parishes to dissolve and reconstitute the membership of the vestries, thus ending the self-perpetuation of those bodies, vestrymen were still expected to swear conformity to the doctrine and discipline of the Church of England and the right to

[64]Clark, *Journal of Asbury* 1: 351; Lohrenz, "Virginia Clergy," pp. 112-20, Brydon, *Virginia's Mother Church* 2: 422-23. For examples of the controversies surrounding various Episcopal clergy, see RP, Nov. 3, 1779, Nov. 10, Nov. 23, Dec. 13, 1780, Nov. 13, 1783.

[65]Meade, *Old Churches* 2: 87. Lohrenz, "Virginia Clergy," p. 251, estimated the number of ministers.

elect vestries was supposed to be limited to members of that church. Neither requirement was absolutely enforced. It was not unusual, especially in frontier areas, for vestrymen to be political Anglicans and religious dissenters. Nevertheless, the legal limitation on membership and the civil functions involved in their duties were constant thorns in the sides of those who wanted the church disestablished.[66]

The reservation of the right to perform marriages to established clergy was another major irritant to the dissenters, for it served as an explicit reminder of the superior position held by the Church of England in Virginia. As in the case of the vestry laws, however, compliance with this law was practically impossible due to the lack of Anglican ministers, especially beyond the Blue Ridge. Those who were available to perform the service sometimes demanded exorbitant fees, especially after the legislature ended their accustomed salaries. Repeatedly in the years after 1778 Baptist petitions asked for a change in this law and the right of their own clergy to perform marriages.[67]

The Assembly responded to both vestry and marriage complaints, but stopped short of meeting the full demands of the dissenters. In the spring session of 1780 bills were prepared to dissolve the vestries and change the marriage laws so that the service might be performed by any minister "regularly ordained according to the rules of his society." However, the actual bill which eliminated the vestries and transferred their civil functions to a new group called overseers of the poor applied only to certain counties in areas beyond the Blue Ridge, while the marriage bill passed the House only to languish in the Senate. In the fall session the latter measure was reintroduced and finally passed only after the Senate added certain amendments. The new marriage law provided that each county court would license four dissenting ministers from each religious society who were to perform marriages in that county only. Of course all clergymen of the Church

[66]See, for example, the petition from Amelia County in *JHD*, May 12, 1780, p. 8, and the Baptist petition in RP, Nov. 8, 1780.

[67]*JHD*, Oct. 25, 1779, p. 23, June 5, 1780, p. 35, Nov. 8, 1780, p. 11; RP, Nov. 8, 1780.

of England remained free to do so anywhere in the state. Neither the vestry nor the marriage acts satisfied the Baptists, and during the succeeding years they continued to petition the legislature for that religious equality which they considered to be not "a Privilege either to grant or withhold at Pleasure, but as what we have a just Claim to as Freemen of the Commonwealth."[68]

What is remarkable, however, is that in those years when the British carried the war into Virginia, the Assembly found time to address itself to any purely domestic matters. By the spring session of 1780 the government had moved from Williamsburg, exchanging, in one participant's opinion, the salt-sea breezes of the Tidewater for the "thin putrid" air of Richmond.[69] If the trading center on the fall line was more central for the purposes of administration and more convenient for the legislators from the West, it was also further removed from the menace of invasion from the Chesapeake. Unfortunately it was not distant enough. That spring the collapse of Charleston before the British fleet opened the southern campaign; and the following January, as Governor Jefferson watched from across the James River, Benedict Arnold briefly occupied Richmond with His Majesty's regulars. In May these forces joined at Petersburg with troops under Cornwallis, and Virginia became the final battleground of the Revolution. Meanwhile the exiled Assembly met first in Charlottesville and then, its dignity as well as its effectiveness in shreds, fled across the Blue Ridge to escape from Banastre Tarleton's dragoons. Since Jefferson declined to stand for reelection when his term expired during its flight, the rump legislature which convened at Staunton elected General Thomas Nelson, ranking officer of the militia, to succeed him. Further battles were expected throughout Virginia, but Cornwallis had turned back to the sea and a rendezvous at Yorktown.

Retirement from the anxieties of a wartime executive provided

---

[68]*JHD*, June 8, July 7, 1780, pp. 39-40, 79, Dec. 2, Dec. 18, 1780, pp. 35, 55. Vestry legislation is found in Hening, *Statutes at Large* 10: 288-90, 11: 62-63. Marriage legislation in ibid., 10: 85-89. For the Baptist petition, see RP, May 31, 1783; other petitions from the Baptists are in RP, June 3, 1782, and May 30, 1783.

[69]Hutchinson, *Papers of Madison* 2: 30.

Jefferson with the opportunity to complete his *Notes on Virginia.* Perhaps more clearly and succinctly than in any of his other writings, the brief passage on liberty of conscience illustrates his mature belief in the totally private nature of religion and his confidence in the ultimate power of the reasoning person to arrive at truth:

> The rights of conscience we never submitted, we could not submit. We are answerable for them to our God. The legitimate powers of government extend to such acts only as are injurious to others. But it does me no injury for my neighbour to say there are twenty gods, or no god. It neither picks my pocket nor breaks my leg. If it be said, his testimony in a court of justice cannot be relied on, reject it then, and be the stigma on him. Constraint may make him worse by making him a hypocrite, but it will never make him a truer man. It may fix him obstinately in his errors, but will not cure them. Reason and free enquiry are the only effectual agents against error. Give a loose to them. They will support the true religion, by bringing every false one to their tribunal, to the test of their investigation.[70]

Two years later, in his second attempt at writing a state constitution for Virginia, Jefferson fleshed out his views on religion in a paragraph defining the limits of the power to be exercised by the legislature: "The General assembly shall not have power ... to abridge the civil rights of any person on account of his religious belief; to restrain him from professing and supporting that belief, or to compel him to contributions, other than those he shall himself have stipulated, for the support of that or any other."[71] Gone from this new constitutional draft was any mention of court jurisdiction over ecclesiastical laws or oaths of office for clergymen. The only residue of Jefferson's wariness of organized religion

[70]Jefferson, *Notes on Virginia,* p. 159; Malone, *Jefferson* 1: 373-75.

[71]Boyd, *Papers of Jefferson* 6: 298. Jefferson was convinced that the Virginia Constitution then in effect was invalid, since it had been enacted by the convention of 1776 without ratification by the people. Even though it had come to be regarded as a fundamental law, its status was in fact that of a piece of legislation. Jefferson also thought it had serious flaws, particularly in the extensive powers granted to the lower house. For these reasons, he drafted a constitution in 1783, hoping that the end of the war would turn the politicians toward a revision of their own institutions. In this expectation he was to be disappointed. The constitution of 1776 was not revised until 1830 (ibid., 6: 278-80).

was the provision excluding all "Ministers of the Gospel" from holding office in the legislature.[72] Madison, reviewing Jefferson's draft in 1788, criticized this exclusion of the clergy, pointing out that to deprive them of the right to hold office on the basis of their religious profession was a violation of "another article of the plan itself which exempts religion from the cognizance of Civil power."[73] Jefferson would eventually come around to Madison's viewpoint, but in the 1780s he remained concerned with the potential power of the clergy in political life.[74]

The Richmond press announced the formal end of the war in December 1783, printing the full text of the Treaty of Paris. "The *time* is now arrived," the *Virginia Gazette* proclaimed, "when every thing is to give way to *peace*."[75] With the Revolution successfully concluded, the government could now turn its full attention to domestic concerns. In the fall Assembly that year, two fresh petitions urging a general assessment set the stage for the political-religious conflict which would rage for the next three years.[76] The decisive battle that would settle the relationship of the state to the churches in Virginia was about to begin.

[72]Ibid., 6: 297. This was not an innovation on Jefferson's part, however, since clergy had been forbidden seats in the Assembly in the colonial period and the constitution of 1776 continued this practice (Rutland, *Papers of Mason* 1: 307). It was also commonly accepted in most of the state constitutions written at that time (Gordon Wood, *The Creation of the American Republic, 1776-1787* [Chapel Hill, N.C., 1969], p. 148).

[73]Boyd, *Papers of Jefferson* 6: 311. Madison had settled his own problems with the clergy before he wrote this critique.

[74]In 1785 Jefferson explained the reason for clerical exclusion from the Assembly to a French correspondent: "if admitted into the legislature at all, the probability is that they would form its majority. For they are all dispersed through every county in the state, they have influence with the people, and great opportunity of persuading them to elect them" (ibid., 8: 470). Only one clergyman on active duty appears to have been elected during the Confederation period. He was John Corbley of Monongalia, and although he claimed that he did not receive any "stipend or gratuity" for his clerical services, he was not allowed to take his seat in the legislature (*JHD*, Nov. 1, 1777, p. 9).

[75]*Virginia Gazette, and Independent Chronicle*, Dec. 13, 1783.

[76]RP, Nov. 8, Nov. 27, 1783.

Chapter Three
The Legislation of Virtue
1783–1784

HIS reputation enhanced by his early outspoken opposition to Great Britain and a highly successful three years as governor of Virginia, Patrick Henry emerged from the Revolution as the most popular politician in the state and the outstanding leader of the Assembly. Although more striking than handsome in appearance, with his flashing blue eyes and forceful voice Henry had a commanding presence on the floor of the House of Delegates. More important than his physical attributes, however, were his practical mind and shrewd knowledge of politics.[1] Thomas Jefferson, who detested Henry, might privately impugn his personal courage and characterize him as "all tongue without either head or heart," but as governor as well as legislator Henry had proved far more successful than Jefferson.[2]

During the concluding years of the war, two major factions contended for power in the Assembly; one was controlled by Henry and the other by Richard Henry Lee and his younger brother Arthur. Like Jefferson, the Lees disliked Henry personally and resented his political power. Edmund Randolph informed Madison of their consuming ambition and the tactics of private calumny and public bitterness they used against Henry.[3] But to no avail. In the legislative session of 1783 Henry had flexed his political muscles, supported John Tyler against Richard Henry Lee

[1] William Wirt Henry, *Patrick Henry: Life, Correspondence, and Speeches* (New York, 1891), 2: 242-45, contains the recollections of Spencer Roane.

[2] Boyd, *Papers of Jefferson* 6: 205. Jefferson apparently considered Henry responsible for George Nicholas's motion in the Assembly for an investigation into Jefferson's conduct as governor during the British invasion of 1781 (ibid., 6: 85, 144). Nicholas later became a close associate of Jefferson.

[3] Hutchinson, *Papers of Madison* 4: 354-55; Henry, *Patrick Henry* 2: 241; Boyd, *Papers of Jefferson* 6: 266.

in a contest for the position of Speaker of the House, and had the satisfaction of seeing his friend chosen by the lopsided margin of 61 to 40.[4] John Marshall, a young lawyer serving his first term as a legislator that year, was particularly impressed by Henry's abilities in debate and remarked, as did other observers, on the immensity of his influence over the Assembly.[5] No one could match him. The opposition might question Henry's motives and offer crude comments about his rustic background and political machinations; but he, not they, emerged triumphant.

It was natural, therefore, that men should turn to him for leadership in the postwar years. Writing from his retirement in 1783, George Mason congratulated Henry on the achievement of independence and noted some of his own rather typical anxieties concerning Virginia's future: "whether our Independence shall prove a Blessing or a Curse, must depend upon our own Wisdom or Folly, Virtue or Wickedness; judging of the future from the Past, the Prospect is not promising. Justice & Virtue are the vital Principles of republican Government; but among us, a Depravity of Manners and Morals prevails, to the Destruction of all Confidence between Man & Man."[6] Mason appealed to Henry as the one man capable of doing more good "than any Man in this State" to exert his powers in the days ahead. Mason's concern for virtue was not unusual in Virginia or throughout the independent confederation. A central theme of both civil and religious leadership in the new republic was the need for public virtue to sustain the relationships within society which made self-government possible. This public virtue, the willingness to subordinate one's private good for the sake of the whole community, rested upon the sum total of each man's private virtues and his cooperation in culti-

[4]*JHD*, May 12, 1783, p. 4. For Tyler's admiration for Henry, see Lyon Gardiner Tyler, *The Letters and Times of the Tylers* (Richmond, 1884-85), 1:83.

[5]John Marshall to unknown correspondent, Dec. 12, 1783, John Marshall Papers, Library of Congress (hereafter LC); Henry, *Patrick Henry* 2: 241-42; Johann David Schoepf, *Travels in the Confederation, 1783-1784,* trans. and ed. Alfred J. Morrison (Philadelphia, 1911), 2: 56. Schoepf reported that Henry "appears to have the greatest influence over the House. He has a high-flown and bold delivery, deals more in words than in reasons, and not so long ago was a country schoolteacher."

[6]Rutland, *Papers of Mason* 2: 770.

vating and practicing them.[7] Mason's concern was primarily within
the area of legislative activity; and he wanted the Assembly to
revise certain laws, secure justice in contractual obligations (especially in the payment of British debts), and in general provide the
legal basis for fair relationships among men.[8] Operating within the
same conceptual framework, however, it was also quite logical to
link both the maintenance of public virtue and the success of the
republican experiment with the survival of religion. It was this line
of thought that Henry chose to follow. Deeply concerned over the
growing influence of continental rationalism and perhaps developing more religious sensibilities in his older years, he put behind
him those pre-Revolutionary struggles when he had championed
the Virginia taxpayers against what appeared as the unjust demands
of a rapacious clergy.[9]

Henry found ample support for his new position in the pages of
the public press. In September 1783 the *Virginia Gazette* published
an article which emphasized the need for public virtue to ensure
the success of republicanism and called upon the legislature to
concern itself with *"public virtue, being the public care."* Appealing to the paternal instincts of the delegates, the writer urged them
to assume the role of "nursing fathers to the church," so that
truth and honesty might be maintained and the liberty of unborn
generations secured. In very general terms, he proposed that the
Assembly "form a genuine system and mode of worship, on the
true basis of Christian freedom," with the hope that such comprehensive legislative support for religion might eventually result
in a union of all groups of Protestants.[10] A more concrete proposal
was submitted in the same newspaper that November. "Philan-
thropos" reiterated the concern for morality and the suppression

[7] Wood, *Creation of the American Republic,* pp. 65-70, 117-18, 427-28.

[8] Rutland, *Papers of Mason* 2: 768, 770-72, 774-76.

[9] Henry, *Patrick Henry* 2: 200, asserted that Henry's concern for the "undermining
influence of French infidelity" was responsible for "much of his subsequent political
course." Francis L. Hawks, *Contributions to the Ecclesiastical History of the United
States of America* (New York, 1836), 1: 100-101, stated, on the basis of a letter from
Henry's widow and children, that Henry had been an Episcopalian and received communion regularly during and after his terms as governor.

[10] *Virginia Gazette, or the American Advertizer,* Sept. 13, 1783.

of vice and suggested a system whereby each parish would maintain a clergyman approved either by the church or the state and
chosen on a yearly basis by the people through a regularly elected
vestry.[11]

When the legislature convened that fall, the House received two
petitions advocating a general assessment, the first such memorials
offered for its consideration since 1779. From Lunenburg County
came "a humble Petition and remonstrance" purporting to represent the views of all Christian groups within the state. This petition
attributed the decline of religion in Virginia since the suspension
of clerical salaries to a lack of zeal on the part of Christians and
pointed out the additional burden which had been placed on the
shoulders of those who recognized their responsibility to support
religion "even with their last mite." While professing a desire for a
liberal policy of toleration, the petitioners also called for the
maintenance of "the reformed Christian religion" by an equitable
system of assessment.[12] Amherst County residents submitted a
longer and more flowery memorial in November 1783, stating
their satisfaction at the conclusion of the Revolution together
with their anxiety about the decline of religion. The worship of
God had been replaced by "Vice and Immorality, Lewdness &
Prophanity," and they urged the Assembly to find a solution in
the passage of laws which would both punish vice and promote
Christianity. A comprehensive system should be established "On
the Broad Basis of Gospel Liberty & Christian Charity—Divested of
Past Prejudices and Bigotry." They coupled this call for a religion
of love with an insistence that it be drawn up at once while "No
Proud or lordly Prelate, No bigoted Presbytery can Awe your
Deliberations" and suggested that the assessment should be moderate, "especially at first," and leave each taxpayer free to determine which church or minister would receive his allotment.[13]

The presentation of these three petitions together with the
articles in the press indicate a revival of interest in some definitive
settlement of the status of religion in Virginia. However, the

[11]Ibid., Nov. 15, Nov. 22, 1783. This article was published in two parts.

[12]RP, Nov. 8, 1783.

[13]Ibid., Nov. 27, 1783.

sentiment for an assessment was not unanimous. Another writer in the *Gazette,* an opponent of that proposal, noted the statewide concern over the ambiguous religious situation and claimed that many people, although opposed to an establishment, were unwittingly supporting an assessment without realizing its implications. He argued that assessment and establishment were necessarily connected, for to levy taxes for clerical salaries would effectually establish the clergy. Once more the by now familiar arguments were trotted forward: "The Church and the State are two societies, and in their natures and designs, as different as Heaven and earth. And to unite them in one, is greatly to injure, if not utterly to ruin both together."[14] The author further warned that when government intruded itself into matters of religion, the legislators would find themselves fixing creedal formulas and forms of worship. Then, inevitably, persecution would once again rear its ugly head.

The delegates must have blanched at the thought of drawing up creeds, for they had difficulties enough attempting to compose a prayer for their own use. Reviving a practice which had lapsed at the time of the British invasion, the House appointed a personal chaplain at the May session of 1783.[15] Simultaneously, the delegates had accepted a motion offered by Patrick Henry that a prayer should be written which would be suitable for "all persuasions."[16] This nondenominational effort was to be composed by the chaplain and approved by the committee for religion, but several different attempts were made without ready agreement. The bill "concerning religion" of 1779 had contained a set of five creedal articles, but it had been rejected. That was one experiment the legislature would not attempt again.

In other religious matters, the House thus far had shown no inclination toward a swift solution. In both the spring and fall sessions the Baptists had again submitted their regular memorials for a change in the marriage and vestry laws; their petitions had

---

[14] *Va. Gaz., or the American Advertizer,* Nov. 8, 1783.

[15] *JHD,* May 15, 1783, p. 7. The chaplain was Benjamin Blagrove, an Episcopalian clergyman at nearby Manchester Parish in Chesterfield County.

[16] Hutchinson, ed., *Papers of Madison* 7: 46.

been found reasonable; bills had been drafted, passed at the initial stages, and then postponed. However, a new note had been injected into the deliberations of the Assembly by the presentation of the assessment proposals. When the committee for religion recommended that the assessment issue be postponed, Patrick Henry persuaded the House to reject the committee's resolution; and at the end of November, the delegates voted to take up the question in the Committee of the Whole.[17] The debates and discussions in this forum settled nothing, and no bill was drafted, but assessment was certain to be on the agenda for the opening session of 1784.

The April elections in that first springtime of full-fledged independence produced a fresh crop of delegates for the May Assembly. Fully half of those chosen were not incumbents, while one third had never served in the legislature before. Governor Benjamin Harrison saw in the turnover a possibility for genuine reform in the Assembly and commented in a letter to Jefferson on the increased participation by the people in the elections. Many of the new delegates were veterans, having served in the Virginia line of the militia during the Revolution; and, on the whole, they were a younger group. One observer, noting the unfamiliar faces, added hopefully: "We may expect new Measures."[18]

The capital in which they assembled had less than a thousand inhabitants; but when the legislature met, the population swelled with a variety of people come to trade, lobby with the delegates, or merely enjoy the social season that always accompanied the

[17] For the Baptist petitions and legislative measures concerning them, see *JHD*, May 30, 31, June 2, 19, 23, 1783, pp. 26-27, 29, 30, 67, 78; and Nov. 6, 15, Dec. 16-19, 1783, pp. 10, 19, 66, 68, 73. In the spring session of 1783 the legislature passed another marriage bill liberalizing the laws for the counties beyond the mountains. Most probably this was in response to a petition from Lincoln County in Kentucky which had requested a bill "to authorize the solemnization of the rites of matrimony, by some civil power" (*JHD*, May 21, June 24-27, 1783, pp. 15, 81, 85, 90; text is in Hening, *Statutes at Large*, 11: 281-82). For the assessment issue, see *JHD*, Nov. 15, 27, pp. 19, 37. Henry's role in this session was described by John Buchanan in a letter to David Griffith (Meade, *Old Churches* 2: 266).

[18] Boyd, *Papers of Jefferson* 7: 103, 257. Of the 152 delegates from 72 counties and 2 cities, 74 were not incumbents and 53 were totally new to the legislature (Swem, *Register*, pp. 17-20).

sessions. Richmond was a nondescript town, built almost entirely of wood and stinking from the smoke of the coal mined a few miles beyond its boundaries. A small frame building served as the capitol and doubled for balls, banquets, and occasional church services. After a day spent in legislative or committee meetings, the assemblymen and others crowded into Formicola's tavern in the evenings to talk politics, barter votes, and exchange news, gossip, and bawdy jokes.[19] The town quickly lapsed into somnolence when the sessions ended, but for two months in the spring and again in the fall, Richmond was the most interesting place to be in Virginia.

Although the Assembly was scheduled to begin meeting on May 5, a quorum was not present until almost a week later. Difficulties with the dirt roads, many of which were little more than cow paths in the western part of the state, as well as washed-out bridges and rain-swollen creeks, usually delayed the travels of most people. Moreover, it was traditional for the members to dribble into the session rather than arrive promptly. Lee and Henry were not present on the first full day of the session, though John Tyler was there to be reelected Speaker without opposition. In his family hagiography, Tyler's grandson wrote of the House during this period as a "model of decorum" which "revived the memory of the golden days of John Robinson." However, the observations of a contemporary foreign traveler were probably more accurate. He found the lack of dignity incredible and was shocked by the casual manner of transacting business: "It is said of the Assembly: It sits; but this is not a just expression, for these members show themselves in every possible position rather than that of sitting still, with dignity and attention. . . . independence prevails even here. During the visits I made I saw this estimable assembly quiet not 5 minutes together."[20]

Nevertheless, they met. Perhaps the most important new member in the House was James Madison. After serving four years in the Continental Congress, he had returned to Virginia to stand

[19]Schoepf, *Travels* 2: 49-68 passim.
[20]Tyler, *Life and Times of the Tylers* 1: 91; Schoepf, *Travels* 2: 55.

again for election to the legislature in his home county of Orange.
It was almost a foregone conclusion not only that he would be
elected but that a position of leadership awaited him in the
Assembly. Edmund Randolph, the attorney general of Virginia,
informed Jefferson that Madison was the most likely candidate to
assume command of the newer and younger delegates. With many
of them, Randolph pointed out, Madison was already being considered "as a general, of whom much has been preconceived to
his advantage." William Short confirmed this view of his possibilities. "The Assembly . . . have formed great hopes of Mr. Madison,"
he told Jefferson, "and those who know him best think he will
not disappoint their most sanguine Expectations." The committee
assignments, always an indication of strength, reinforced these
observations. Madison had no sooner arrived than he was appointed
to five of the six standing committees of the House and was made
chairman of the committee on commerce. In that position he
might hope to press home his proposal to make Norfolk the sole
port of entry for foreign shipping.[21]

Madison's bill for establishing a single port was only one of a
number of serious issues confronting the Assembly. Moreover, in a
series of contests, he and Henry clashed—on the collection of
taxes, the payment of British debts, and the advisability of a new
constitution for Virginia. In each case Madison favored the
measure, while Henry was opposed, and in each case Henry's
views prevailed. He was still the guiding star, capable of changing
votes and reversing decisions by the sheer brilliance of his ora-
tory.[22] Another member of the House at this time, Spencer
Roane, later recalled: "As an orator, Mr. Henry demolished
Madison with as much ease as Sampson did the cords that bound

[21] Boyd, *Papers of Jefferson* 7: 257, 260; *JHD*, May 12, 1784, pp. 5-6. For Madison's
interest in the port bill and a general summary of the session's business, see Rutland,
Papers of Madison 8: 35-38, 64-65.

[22] See, for example, Archibald Stuart to William Wirt, Aug. 25, 1816, Archibald
Stuart Papers, Earl Gregg Swem Library, College of William and Mary in Virginia,
Williamsburg (hereafter Swem Lib., College of William and Mary). There were nine
recorded votes in the May session of 1784, and in eight of these votes both Henry and
Madison participated. In four of these votes they disagreed, but in every case Henry's
position was sustained (*JHD*, May session, 1784, passim).

him before he was shorn."[23] In fairness to Madison, it should be noted that his mind rather than his voice was his key attribute.

The two leaders were also divided on another issue. Even before the opening of the session, Madison had learned from Philip Mazzei that Henry favored a general assessment for the support of religion. When the legislature met, Henry was still keeping his opinion on this matter private, perhaps waiting until he could survey the mood of the delegates and see what the religious petitions would hold.[24] He did not have a long wait. The House had barely organized itself for the session when a petition was received from Warwick County requesting a general assessment. In a calm, matter-of-fact tone, this memorial pointed out that since the question of independence had finally been settled, it was now time for the legislature to turn its attention to matters of internal policy and particularly to concern itself with "the too general Neglect of Religion and Morality in this State." The petitioners thought a general assessment would best remedy this situation and help them to become "as good Christians, as they mean to be Citizens."[25] The House referred the petition to the committee for religion.

Within the next two weeks both major dissenting denominations expressed their desires to the legislature. The Baptists in familiar fashion repeated their demands for a change in the marriage and vestry laws and also expressed their pique that past assemblies had paid them so little attention, treating them as "not worthy good Members of civil society."[26] They did not mention the possibility of an assessment, nor did the Presbyterian petition which arrived in the House the same day. Like the Baptists, the Presbyterians were upset over the general inequality of religious groups in the state. The ministers and elders had met earlier that month and instructed John Blair Smith and James Waddel to draft a memorial to the legislature. It was a far different document from their last

[23]Henry, *Patrick Henry* 2: 242.

[24]Boyd, *Papers of Jefferson* 7: 122, 260. In fact, Madison had sent Mazzei to visit Henry and report back on his plans for the coming session.

[25]RP, May 15, 1784.

[26]Ibid., May 26, 1784.

petition in 1777. Then the Presbytery had attacked any intervention of the government in religion; now it objected to the
special privileges extended to one church but withheld from the
others. The petitioners singled out the "unjust preeminence"
granted the former Church of England, citing as examples its
continuing title as the "established Mother Church," its retention
of the church buildings and glebes, and the discriminatory marriage
and vestries laws.

Perhaps the most interesting complaint was that this church was
"incorporated" and could hold property "for ecclesiastical purposes without trouble or risk in securing it, while other Christian
communities were obliged to trust to the precarious fidelity of
Trustees chosen for the purpose." Incorporation was to become a
thorny issue, but the Presbytery misread the actual condition of
the establishment. As the state church of Virginia, the former
Church of England was not civilly incorporated as a separate
entity. Rather it was an arm of the government and therefore
under the control of the legislature. Church property was secure
because it was state property, and every aspect of the church's
internal operation remained subject to laws enacted during the
colonial period and not repealed by the Assembly. Those outside
the establishment fold tended to overlook the severe limitations
this condition imposed on the church's freedom while bridling at
what appeared as a position of honor and influence not shared by
the other churches. It was within this framework that the Presbytery asked the Assembly to remove all inequalities and preserve
"a proper regard to every religious denomination as the common
protectors of piety and virtue."[27] And it was on this basis that the
legislature, when considering an incorporation for the renamed
Episcopal church, would read the Presbyterians' petition as requesting an incorporation for themselves.

Both the Baptist and Presbyterian petitions were referred to the
committee for religion; and on the following day, May 27, chairman Wilson Miles Cary reported to the House that the committee
had found the Warwick petition for a general assessment to be
reasonable. Together with men such as Edmund Pendleton and the

[27]Minutes of Hanover Presbytery, May 19-20, 1784; RP, May 26, 1784.

late Robert Carter Nicholas, Cary represented the best of the old guard established laymen, dedicated to maintaining the church of their forefathers. Since he was a delegate from Warwick County, he may well have had a hand in writing and circulating the assessment petition. Instead of either rejecting or accepting the committee report, the delegates approved a motion to submit the measure to a discussion by the Committee of the Whole. The assessment issue was therefore in the same position in which it had rested at the end of the second session of 1783.[28]

One week later another petition for a general assessment was presented from Powhatan County, indicating the petitioners' willingness to pay taxes for the support of a minister of their own choice.[29] A much more significant memorial, however, arrived that day from the clergy of "the Protestant Episcopal Church in Virginia in Convention." It had been an historic meeting. The clergy of what was still, in some respects, the established church had finally come together without a summons from any bishop, commissary, or legislature and were prepared to act in concert. More important than any other motive was the realization that religion in general and their church in particular were at a critical juncture and that the Assembly would not move to help them unless prodded.

The declining state of religion was obvious to those who had eyes to observe it. The impressions conveyed by petitions requesting an assessment were confirmed by a contemporary visitor who commented on the religious situation and compared Virginia with other states: "If the Virginians themselves did not freely and openly admit that zeal for religion, and religion generally, is now very faint among them, the fact might easily be divined from other circumstances. Considering the extent of the state, one sees not only a smaller number of houses of worship than in the other provinces, but what there are in a ruinous or ruined condition; and the clergy for the most part dead or driven away and their places unfilled."[30] During the Revolution the number of established

[28]*JHD*, May 26, May 27, 1784, pp. 20-21, 23.

[29]RP, June 4, 1784.

[30]Schoepf, *Travels* 2: 62-63.

clergy actively engaged in the ministry had been cut in half, and by the close of the war approximately forty parishes were without resident pastors.[31] A major problem of the ministers who remained at their posts was financial. When clerical salaries had first been suspended in 1776, a voluntary subscription system had been attempted. Jefferson himself had drawn up the list for his local rector, Charles Clay, and even made the most generous offering, six pounds a year.[32] In their advertisements for clergymen during the war years, the vestries or church wardens generally held out the prospect of a generous subscription.[33] But the system did not work.

Alexander Balmain's situation was typical. Of Scottish birth, Balmain came to Virginia before the Revolution as a tutor to the family of Richard Henry Lee. After returning to England for ordination, he became rector of Augusta Parish beyond the Blue Ridge; and at the time of the conflict with Great Britain, he was an outspoken patriot, serving as a member of the Augusta County committee of safety and then as a chaplain to the Virginia line. Balmain was a well-respected and even devout minister. The prayers which he either composed himself or copied into his memorandum book reflect the traditional piety of the middle path of Anglicanism rather than a rationalist viewpoint. At the conclusion of the war, he accepted the rectorship of Frederick Parish in the northern part of the Valley and attempted to raise a subscription to support himself and his wife. Fortunately they had no children, for the voluntary system produced only meager results. In 1783 Balmain was ministering to two congregations and listed subscriptions from a total of sixty-eight men. He also noted the names of those who had called upon his services but failed to contribute to his support in any way. Among them was Charles

---

[31] Brydon, *Virginia's Mother Church* 2: 429. His estimate is that of the pre-Revolutionary clergy, 56 were still in the active ministry. For a list of parishes and incumbent ministers, see ibid., 2: 608-12.

[32] Boyd, *Papers of Jefferson* 2: 6-8.

[33] *Va. Gaz.* (Purdie) Nov. 7, 1777, April 3, Aug. 21, 1778; *Va. Gaz.* (Dixon & Nicholson), Mar. 26, June 19, Oct. 30, 1779.

Mynn Thruston, who had once been an established clergyman himself before giving up the ministry for politics and a career as the "Fighting Parson" during the Revolutionary War. Although Thruston had summoned Balmain to his home on two occasions to baptize his children, he had not joined in the subscription. Writing to his brother in Scotland, Balmain explained his predicament: "The revolution, however important in its effects, has been fatal to the Clergy of Virginia. From a fixed salary they are reduced to depend on a precarious subscription for bread. The Establishment abolished, every sect upon the same level, & every man at liberty to contribute or not to the support of the Minister of his own persuasion as he judges best. In a country too where religion is little regarded, you may easily conceive the subsistence of the Clergy cannot be very liberal."[34]

The problem of salaries, however, was only one aspect of a much more fundamental difficulty—the complete dependence of the church upon the legislature. It was this more central issue to which the Reverend David Griffith addressed himself at the end of the war. Griffith was a New Yorker, and after studying medicine in England he had served as a surgeon with the colonial army during the Indian wars and then engaged in private practice. One kind of healing had led to an interest in another. Griffith had taken orders in 1770 and assumed the rectorship of Shelburne Parish in Loudoun County. Like Balmain, he was a chaplain in the Revolution and afterwards resumed a parochial cure, Fairfax Parish,

---

[34] Alexander Balmain to John Balmain, May 8, 1783, in Alexander Balmain's Memorandum Book, photostat in Swem Lib., College of William and Mary. This book is an invaluable source of information of Balmain's activities and problems after the Revolution. He continued on as rector of Frederick Parish until his death about 1820. During his ministry, he performed a large number of marriages including that of James Madison, his wife's cousin, to Dolley Payne Todd on Sept. 15, 1794, for which the groom made the princely offering of £5.4.10.

For the various ideological parties among American Anglicans, see Clara O. Loveland, *The Critical Years: The Reconstruction of the Anglican Church in the United States of America* (Greenwich, Conn., 1956), pp. 8-9.

For Thruston, see Lyon G. Tyler, ed., *Encyclopedia of Virginia Biography* (New York, 1915), 1: 342. Thruston served in the Assembly of 1785, where he voted in favor of the bill for religious freedom. He was also elected as a vestryman for Frederick Parish that same year.

where George Washington was one of his parishioners as well as his friend.[35]

Griffith had no illusions about the difficulties faced by the church, nor did he lack energy in attempting to meet them. In 1783 he wrote John Buchanan, a Richmond clergyman, proposing that a convention of the clergy be assembled to plan the restructuring of the church. He emphasized the urgency of affairs: "Considering her present situation and circumstances,—without ordination, without government, without support, unprotected by the laws, and yet laboring under injurious restrictions from laws which yet exist,—these things considered, her destruction is sure as fate, unless some mode is adopted for her preservation." While Griffith believed that the dissenters were intent upon the ruin of the former established church, he made it clear to Buchanan that without immediate action no outside force would be necessary to bring about its destruction. Hoping that someone or some group closer to the center of government would lead the movement to reorganize the church, he proposed that the clergy in the Richmond area summon all the Virginia ministers to meet in April 1784 before the Assembly convened. The timing would be crucial, he explained, for "we must necessarily have recourse to it for the repeal of those existing laws which made a part of the old Establishment, and which, while they do exist, must prove ruinous to the Church in spite of any regulations the clergy may adopt." In concluding he pointed out that although he had hoped for some form of reunion with the dissenting churches, this now appeared impossible; and he reiterated his belief that if the church was to survive its present anguish, the clergy would have to assume a position of leadership.[36]

It was a bold suggestion, as Buchanan's reply made clear. The ministers in the area of the capital had done nothing, nor even considered taking the initiative in the reconstruction of the church. Buchanan informed Griffith that "they seemed to despair of any thing being done effectually without its originating in the Assem-

[35]George M. Brydon, "David Griffith, 1742-1789: First Bishop Elect of Virginia," *Historical Magazine of the Protestant Episcopal Church* 9 (1940): 194-230.

[36]Meade, *Old Churches* 2: 264-65.

bly."[37] The older clergy were trained to respond to the leadership of powers beyond themselves; yet they were well aware of the current problems and lack of organization within the church. Buchanan himself had formerly believed that the legislature was the one to take any steps to save the church and had personally hoped that the assessment would pass in the fall session of 1783. Some of the ministers feared that any initiative from the clergy would arouse the fury of the dissenters, and laymen of the caliber of Governor Harrison agreed with this viewpoint. It was the responsibility of the Assembly to act, the delegates ought to act, and their failure to do so was disgraceful. However, Griffith's letter evidently provided a new avenue of thought as well as action. In April 1784 a notice was printed in the *Virginia Gazette* calling the clergy of the "EPISCOPAL church in Virginia" to a convention in Richmond on June 2. It was signed by three clergymen, Miles Selden and John Buchanan from Henrico Parish in Richmond and William Leigh from Dale Parish in adjacent Chesterfield County.[38]

The meeting lasted for three days, but no record of the names or number of the clergy who responded to this invitation exists. Those ministers in attendance chose Samuel Sheild, the rector of St. Alsaph's Parish in Caroline County and a close friend of Edmund Pendleton, as their presiding officer. A graduate of William and Mary, Sheild was one of the youngest clergymen in Virginia. His sermons were noted for their evangelical flavor. One aristocratic lady, returning from a service conducted by Sheild, called for a maid to remove her brocaded dresses "for she had heard so much of hell, damnation and death that it would take her all evening to get cool."[39]

However, the petition to the legislature, which Sheild signed on behalf of the clergy, was quite calm and reasoned. The primary

[37]Ibid., 2: 266. Brydon makes a strong case for the position that the established church was more subject to discrimination at this point than were the dissenters, for while the latter were free to set up their own congregations and regulate their own affairs, the established clergy were still controlled by the legislature (*Virginia's Mother Church* 2: 439-41).

[38]*Va. Gaz., or the American Advertizer*, April 11, 1784.

[39]Lyon G. Tyler, "Sheild Family," *William and Mary Quarterly*, 1st ser., 3 (1895): 271; Mays, *Pendleton* 2: 165, 380-81.

concern of the ministers was the restraint imposed upon them by
the Assembly's legal control. They asked the legislature to transfer
that control to themselves first by repealing the colonial laws
which prescribed creeds, liturgical rites, and qualifications of
ministers and, second, by incorporating them as the "clergy of the
Protestant Episcopal Church in Virginia . . . to regulate all the
spiritual concerns of that Church—alter its form of worship, and
institute such canons, by-laws, and rules for the government and
good order thereof, as are suited to their religious principles."
They considered this as their "immediate duty and a right always
granted to the ministers of every Christian church,"[40] but Griffith
later wrote that the assembled ministers had thought it improper
and even dangerous to proceed without definite authorization
from the legislature. He explained their predicament to the future
bishop William White: "The Episcopal Church in Virginia is so
fettered by Laws; that the Clergy could do no more than petition
for a repeal of those laws—for liberty to introduce Ordination and
Government, and to revise and alter the Liturgy."[41] Incorporation
would give them liberty. With regard to the temporal administration of the church, the clergy asked that the vestry laws be altered
to eliminate the vestries' secular function of caring for the parish
poor as well as any prescribed method of selecting vestrymen or
requiring oaths of office. However, the ministers did request the
Assembly to ensure that future vestries would be composed "from
among and by such persons only as are members of the Episcopal
Church."

   In essence, therefore, the clergy convention wanted the authority to govern the church with an emphasis on their jurisdiction in
all matters normally regulated by canon law, while the vestries
would confine their attention to temporal church matters. In the
context of the colonial period and the traditional subservience of
the Virginia ministry to lay control, this petition was an extraordinary document. The clergy, at least at this stage in the trans-

---

[40] RP, June 4, 1784.

[41] Griffith to White, July 26, 1784, Bishop William White Papers, Archives and
Historical Collections of the Episcopal Church, Historical Society of the Episcopal
Church, Austin, Texas (hereafter Hist. Soc. Episcopal Church, Austin).

formation of their church, lacked neither energy nor boldness. They were also aware that the alteration of the church's name as well as its government and form of worship would provide additional ammunition to those dissenters who had already expressed a desire to have the state divide up the church's property. In an effort to forestall this move, their petition requested the Assembly to reaffirm their title to the glebes, churches, and other property which they had held as the established church. Finally, in a veiled reference to the prospect of an assessment, the ministers noted that it would be desirable for the legislature to assume "the patronage and care of the Christian religion."[42]

Like the Baptist and Presbyterian petitions which had preceded it, the memorial from the Episcopal clergy was referred to the committee for religion. Within a week Wilson Miles Cary reported the committee's decision on these religious petitions. In general the members attempted to satisfy all requests. Their report stated that the petition of the Episcopal ministers with respect to self-government, the changes in vestry laws, and the measure to secure their property was reasonable. The same verdict was given to the Baptist and Presbyterian petitions for a change in the marriage and vestry laws, and the report added that "all legal distinctions in favor of any particular religious society, may be abolished." Approving the request of the clergy of the Episcopal church for the right to incorporate, it gave the Presbyterians the same right and offered to extend that service to any other religious group which might apply for it. All of these resolutions were approved by the House and the committee for religion was ordered to draw up bills pursuant to them.[43]

For the most part, however, the matter languished in committee. Only two measures were ultimately drafted in legislative form and debated on the floor of the House. One of these, a marriage bill, finally passed the House only to be defeated in the Senate.[44] The

---

[42] RP, June 4, 1784.

[43] *JHD*, June 8, 1784, p. 48.

[44] The House ordered the bill to be brought in on June 21, discussed it June 25, and passed it by a vote of 50 to 30 on June 28. However, the bill was not acceptable to the Senate, and the session ended on June 30 before any compromise could be reached

other debated measure, a bill to incorporate the Episcopal church, was reported out of the committee for religion on June 16 by Joseph Jones of King George County. Despite his close friendship with Madison and Jefferson, Jones was a staunch member of the Episcopal church and would later vote in favor of both the assessment and the incorporation bills. However, the incorporation bill at this session was discussed for less than a week and then postponed until the next session. Madison later reported its contents and fate in a revealing letter to Jefferson.

The Episcopal Clergy introduced a notable project for re-establishing their independence of the laity. The foundation of it was that the whole body should be legally incorporated, invested with the present property of the Church, made capable of acquiring indefinitely—empowered to make canons & by laws not contrary to the laws of the land, and incumbents when once chosen by Vestries to be immovable otherwise than by sentence of the Convocation. Extraordinary as such a project was, it was preserved from a dishonorable death by the talents of Mr. Henry. It lies over for another Session.[45]

Meanwhile the assessment issue which had been taken up by the Committee of the Whole progressed no further. "The friends of the measure," Madison noted, "did not chuse to try their strength in the House."[46]

While the Assembly temporized on the religious issues, the press remained relatively quiet. Only one brief article, a series of rhetorical questions posed by a self-styled "Locke," attacked the Episcopal clergy for their privileged position in the commonwealth. A much longer, unsigned piece preferred to denounce Virginians in general for their neglect of religion and prevailing vices. Since Yorktown they had "revelled in the enchanting lap of luxury" and forgotten their Creator and religious duties. Blame for this condition was divided equally between the "coldness and indifference" of the ministry and the failure of the upper classes to set a good

---

(ibid., pp. 71, 79, 82). Neither Henry nor Madison participated in the roll-call vote in the House.

[45] Rutland, *Papers of Madison* 8: 93-94; *JHD*, June 16, June 25, 1784, pp. 58, 79.

[46] Rutland, *Papers of Madison* 8: 93.

example. The author called upon the legislature, magistrates, and ministers to inaugurate a moral reformation in the state.[47]

Perhaps an article published a month after the session ended best captured the mood of the delegates as well as the temper in the countryside. Earlier in the spring a long poem ridiculing the Methodists had been published in the *Gazette*. Decrying this venture in bigotry, "Pacificus" now responded with a plea "to avoid every thing that might give further occasion for strifes, animosities, and party disputes." He pointed out that although the Revolution was now successfully concluded, the new government remained untried and political differences faced the state. It was therefore incumbent upon all citizens to cooperate together for the peace and tranquillity of society. The spring session of the legislature, he noted, had shown great "caution and prudence" in postponing a decision on the religious questions until the sentiments of the population could be gauged. Concluding the article, he summarized the task awaiting the delegates at the fall session: "to reconcile all parties and obviate all future causes of dissention on the subject of religion; by forming such a system as might reasonably be expected to give general satisfaction to all."[48] It was a noble goal, but one impossible to attain in a society so seriously divided on the question of the role of government in the promotion of virtue, morality, and religion. The failure of the legislators, however, did not result from lack of effort.

The fall session of 1784 was scheduled to begin on Monday, October 18; but a quorum was not present to organize the House until almost two weeks later. Since the arrival of the legislators also marked the beginning of the social season in Richmond, many of the delegates who should have attended the Assembly were probably present instead at the races which began on Tuesday, October 27, and concluded on Thursday with a ball in the capitol at which the honored guest was General Nathanael Green. The gentlemen spent the following day recovering from the numerous toasts drunk to the leader of the southern campaign; and finally,

---

[47] *Virginia Gazette, and Weekly Advertizer,* May 8, June 12, 1784.

[48] *Va. Gaz., or the American Advertizer,* July 31, 1784. The poem against the Methodists appeared in the same paper on May 29, 1784.

on Saturday, a sufficient number of delegates were present in the Assembly to call the House to order. On Monday, Speaker Tyler announced the committee appointments for the session. He considerably revised the committee for religion by reducing its membership from the spring total of twenty-nine to only sixteen delegates for the fall and heavily weighting it with older men of considerable legislative experience. Tyler's predilection for the assessment and incorporation bills was obvious, for almost all the committee members were known Episcopalians and only one came from a county west of the Blue Ridge Mountains. For the chairman of the group, Tyler selected William Norvell of James City County, a veteran delegate and devout member of the Episcopal church.[49]

The House had scarcely settled down to business when two petitions supporting the assessment were presented. From Isle of Wight County came a stout plea for the measure on the grounds that since the advancement of religion was of general advantage to the entire community, everyone should be required to contribute to it.[50] The same point was driven home by an even more forceful missive from Amelia County which insisted that the delegates should operate on "the principle of public utility" by doing all in their power to promote religion, since it was the basis and bulwark for the survival of government. These petitioners requested the financial support of "pure reformed Christianity," so that good candidates would be encouraged to enter the ministry. The distinctive features of this memorial, however, were the requests that the Episcopal church be legally secured in all its property and granted the rights of "self-government and particularly to confer orders according to the Episcopal mode," in order to provide sufficient clergy for the empty parishes in Virginia.[51]

---

[49]Ibid., Oct. 30, 1784; *JHD*, Oct. 30, Nov. 1, 1784, pp. 5, 6. One member, Jones of King George County, was added on Nov. 5; two more delegates, Mann Page and Benjamin Harrison (after he retired from the governor's seat), were added on Dec. 4 (ibid., pp. 13, 56). On the resolution in favor of the assessment, the committee split 8 to 6 for the resolution; on the resolution for incorporation of religious societies, the vote would be 11 to 4 in favor of the measure. For Novell, see Tyler, *Encyclopedia* 1: 299.

[50]*JHD*, Nov. 4, 1784, p. 11.

[51]RP, Nov. 8, 1784. This petition was very well subscribed with 158 signatures, including those of John Booker, Jr., a delegate who would not be present to vote on the

Several days later, on November 11, the Baptists presented their memorial to the legislature. Earlier in the fall they had held the first meeting of the recently formed General Committee, which included representatives from the Ketocton Association of Regulars as well as the far more numerous Separate Baptists. Despite the concern expressed by some Baptists that this committee might develop the aspects of a synod or presbytery, its sole function was to act as a clearinghouse for political activity, considering all Baptist grievances and funneling petitions to the Assembly. With this responsibility in mind, the General Committee drew up a statement to submit to the legislature that fall. In essence it was a repetition of the earlier Baptist memorials against the vestry and marriage laws. Although the General Committee meeting reportedly went on record as opposed to either an assessment or an incorporation of religious bodies, neither item was mentioned in its petition that November. However, it did include a request for the elimination of special privileges for any one group very similar to the Presbyterian memorial of the previous spring. In particular, the Baptists petitioned "that all Distinctions in your Laws may be done away, and that no order or Denomination of Christians in this Commonwealth have any separate Privileges allowed them more than their Brethren of other Religious Societies distinguished by other names; lest they tyrannize over them."[52] Conceivably, the legislature could have understood this statement to imply that the Baptists would not object either to an assessment or an incorporation provided that they were included in the project.

After receiving the petition and referring it to the committee for religion, the House acted on the assessment issue. The question had lingered in the Committee of the Whole since the spring session, and so it was from this committee that Thomas Mathews of Norfolk presented the following resolution: "that the people of this Commonwealth, according to their respectful abilities, ought to pay a moderate tax or contribution, annually, for the support

---

day of the assessment resolution, and Peter Jones, one of the wealthiest men in the state (Main, "The One Hundred," p. 377).

[52] Benedict, *History of Baptist Denomination* 2: 58-60; RP, Nov. 11, 1784. For the statement that this meeting had opposed the assessment and incorporation proposals, see Robert B. Semple, *A History of the Rise and Progress of the Baptists in Virginia* (Richmond, 1810), pp. 69-70.

of the christian religion, or of some christian church, denomination or communion of christians, or of some form of christian worship."[53] The resolution passed by a vote of 47 to 32, and a ten-man committee, chaired by Patrick Henry, was immediately appointed to draft the bill.[54] Despite the margin of votes, not all observers were convinced that the measure was secure. Writing to Jefferson the following day, Governor Harrison informed him of the business of the House and commented: "I think it doubtful whether they will be able to carry the bill through the House."[55]

When composing this letter, Harrison may have been unaware of the Presbyterian petition being presented that day to the Assembly. It would provide a severe jolt to the antiassessment forces. The Hanover Presbytery had held its semiannual meeting at Timber Ridge Church during the last week of October. While the members of the legislature were betting on the horse races, the ministers and elders of the church were locked in serious discussion over the problems of the church. At the opening of their meeting, a letter from a congregation in Bedford County complained in words reminiscent of Jonathan Boucher of "the Intrusion of the ignorant tho' designing Sectaries" and asked the Presbytery to send a minister capable of dealing with this "dangerous Situation."[56] The ministers were hard pressed to satisfy all the calls for their services, for though their numbers had doubled since 1779 the demands had substantially increased. Financial concerns were also pressing. Although they had a decided advantage over the Episcopalian clergy in that they could select and discipline their own ministers, they could not ensure them a decent salary. Two years earlier the Presbytery had recommended that each congregation form a

---

[53] *JHD*, Nov. 11, 1784, p. 19. Madison later told Jefferson that Henry had made the motion (Boyd, *Papers of Jefferson* 7: 594), but in the *Journal* Mathews, an opponent of the measure, is listed as offering the resolution. He probably presided over the Committee of the Whole.

[54] *JHD*, Nov. 11, 1784, p. 11. The other members of the committee were Corbin, Jones of King George, Coles, Norvell, Wray, Jones of Dinwiddie, Carter Henry Harrison, Tazewell, and Prentis. All of them had voted for the assessment resolution.

[55] Boyd, *Papers of Jefferson* 7: 519. Harrison may have had in mind the fact that 54 delegates were either not present or else abstained on the vote.

[56] Minutes of Hanover Presbytery, Oct. 26, 1784.

salary committee and appoint a treasurer, but apparently nothing had been done.[57] Without a fixed income, each pastor depended upon his popularity with the people and their free-will offerings. As Samuel Stanhope Smith remarked, there were "few inducements to a man to enter into the church."[58] Well aware of its lack of clergy, their financial insecurity, and the obvious decline in religious sentiments among Virginians, the Presbytery appointed John Blair Smith and William Graham to draft a memorial to the Assembly.

The two ministers were widely divided in their views on the church-state relationship. John Smith had succeeded to the presidency of Hampden-Sydney College when his brother had gone to the College of New Jersey. Like his brother, John believed that civil government should support religion provided that it was done on the basis of equality for all religious groups and without interference in their systems of worship or government. He had recently experienced the assistance of the state in alleviating his own financial difficulties. Only that spring the trustees of Hampden-Sydney had successfully petitioned the Assembly for a grant of some four hundred acres of land near the college which had been confiscated from a British business firm during the Revolution. The legislature had granted their request without requiring any control over the school. Smith was also conversant with the pluralism of Virginia society. Liberal Episcopalians such as the Cabells of Amherst County sent their sons to his institution, and Patrick Henry was a close personal friend. Given the problems of his church, his own experience, and his brother's influence, it is not surprising that John Smith favored an assessment.[59]

Over in the Valley, however, where Presbyterians comprised the dominant religious group, William Graham, president of rival Liberty Hall College, was unalterably opposed to an assessment,

---

[57]Ibid., Oct. 24, 1782. The Presbytery asked these committees to forward an annual report, but there is no evidence in the Minutes that this was ever done.

[58]Kraus, "Nisbet and Smith," p. 24.

[59]*JHD*, June 1, 1783, p. 30; Hening, *Statutes at Large* 11: 392-93; Charles Grier Sellers, Jr., "John Blair Smith," *Journal of the Presbyterian Historical Society* 34 (1956): 208-11.

an incorporation, or any other measure which would intrude the
government into the affairs of the church. The disagreement which
followed between Graham and Smith would rupture their relationship for several years.[60]

That fall of 1784 Smith dominated the Presbytery, and the
ministers and elders authorized a memorial reflecting his viewpoint. After the customary complaints against the continued
privileges of the establishment, the petition attacked certain
features of the incorporation plan presented by the Episcopal
clergy convention the previous spring. In particular, two points
galled the Presbyterians: first, the desire of the clergy to incorporate themselves separately from the laity and, second, their
request to the legislature for authorization to regulate spiritual
concerns for the church. The Presbytery was not adverse to the
idea of civil incorporation, since it was clearly necessary for the
purposes of owning and managing property. What they minded
was any plan which would separate clergy from laity and hand
over the legal title to the former. This highly irregular move would
make the ministers "independent . . . of the churches" and in the
past had created a clergy distinguished for their "ignorance,
immorality, and neglect of the duties of their Station." In a
private letter sent to Madison the previous summer, Smith had
found this portion of the Episcopal request "very insulting to the
members of their communion" for it portended a clerical domina-
tion unsuitable in a free society.[61]

The Presbyterian clergy made it clear that they desired no such
incorporation for themselves. Although not explicitly stated in
their memorial, at stake was the very nature of Presbyterianism,
which defined the church as the corporate body of believers and
vested its government in lay elders as well as ministers. To incorporate the entire body was acceptable, but for civil government to
make a legal distinction within the church violated their religious
sensibilities. This was closely related to a second concern. For the

---

[60]Sellers, "John Blair Smith," p. 212; William Hill, *Autobiographical Sketches of
Dr. William Hill . . . and Biographical Sketches . . . of the Reverend Dr. Moses Hoge of
Virginia* (rept. Richmond, 1968), p. 113.

[61]Rutland, *Papers of Madison* 7: 81.

House to assume any jurisdiction whatsoever over any church's polity, doctrine, or worship was anathema. The request of the Episcopal clergy presumed that the legislature had authority in this area; but its concerns were wholly "human affairs," not spiritual matters. The church's authority and the direction of ministers came from God, not men.

But the most significant section of the memorial dealt with the justification for an assessment and, in effect, requested one. The petition proclaimed that although religion would never depend upon civil authority for its survival, the converse was not true. Government required the service and support of religion to maintain the social fabric and preserve the bonds of trust and justice in the state. Therefore it ought to encourage religious worship and nourish those institutions which fostered it. An assessment would in reality be a measure to assist the state, not the church. In this respect, the memorial was echoing the arguments used by pro-assessment petitions for the past decade.

The presbyters then proceeded to state the terms on which an assessment bill would be acceptable. If the Assembly thought such a measure necessary, it must be conceived on "the most liberal plan." That is, it must contain nothing inimical to the Declaration of Rights nor interfere in "religion as a spiritual system." This latter condition meant that the bill must not include "Articles of Faith, that are not essential to the preservation of Society," prescribe norms for worship or church government, or render the clergy independent of the laity. Above all, it must not meddle in the sacred matter of individual conscience.[62]

After approving their memorial, the Presbyterian leaders listed in their minutes the precise terms for an acceptable assessment plan.

1. Religion as a Spiritual System is not to be considered as an object of human Legislation; but may in a civil view, as preserving the existence & promoting the happiness of Society.

2. That public Worship, and public periodical Instructions to the people, be maintained in this view by a general Assessment for this purpose.

[62]RP, Nov. 12, 1784.

3. That every man as a good Citizen, be obliged to declare himself attached to some religious Community, publicly known to profess the belief of one God, his righteous providence, our accountableness to him, and a future State of rewards and punishments.

4. That every Citizen should have a liberty annually to direct his assessed proportion to such Community as he chuses.

5. That twelve Tithables or more, to the amount of one hundred & fifty Families, as near as local Circumstances will admit, shall be incorporated, & exclusively direct the application of the money contributed for their support.

The Presbytery then appointed four members, Smith, Graham, Todd, and Montgomery, to attend the session and present both the memorial and the assessment plan.[63]

The Presbyterian petition was a blow to the antiassessment forces. Madison, summarizing their position on the issue, grimly informed James Monroe: "The Presbyterian Clergy have remonstrated against any narrow principles, but indirectly favor a more comprehensive establishment." Later he would become even more bitter toward those he had counted on as his allies. The following April he blasted the ministers for being "as ready to set up an establishment which is to take them in as they were to pull down that which shut them out." There had been, he thought, a "shameful contrast" in the memorials which they had submitted to the legislature.[64]

Having now heard from the major religious bodies in the state, the House sifted and discussed their petitions in the Committee of the Whole for almost a week.[65] Perhaps believing they could main-

---

[63]Minutes of Hanover Presbytery, Oct. 28, 1784. But it is likely that only Smith and Todd remained at the session as they were the only ones who signed the letter to the Assembly on Nov. 18, 1784, clarifying the position of the Presbytery on incorporation (RP, Nov. 18, 1784).

This recital of events and motivations conflicts with the generally accepted account of the reasons for the memorial of the Hanover Presbytery and what that memorial implied. For a discussion of the historiographical problem, see Fred J. Hood, "Revolution and Religious Liberty: The Conservation of the Theocratic Concept in Virginia," *Church History* 40 (1971): 179-80.

[64]Rutland, *Papers of Madison* 8: 137, 261.

[65]The Presbyterian petition was submitted to the Committee of the Whole on Nov. 12, 1784. The next day the Baptist petition was assigned to that committee, and

tain harmony among the various denominations by appeasing all of them at once, the legislators approved two major proposals on November 17. The first resolution, after citing the Presbyterian and Baptist petitions, stated that the acts pertaining to marriage and vestry laws should be changed, while the second resolution approved of the passage of bills "for the incorporation of all societies of the christian religion, which may apply for the same." This latter measure passed by the lopsided majority of 62 to 23, with eleven delegates who had voted against assessment switching sides. Since the Episcopalian ministers were the only group which had formally requested incorporation, a committee to be chaired by Carter Henry Harrison was immediately ordered to draft a bill "to incorporate the clergy of the Protestant Episcopal Church."[66]

The delegates were mistaken, however, if they believed that the incorporation resolution would quiet the Presbyterians. Obviously disturbed by the prospect of a bill incorporating the Episcopalian clergy, John Blair Smith and John Todd submitted a tense petition the following day which repeated their objections against the incorporation of ministers independently of their congregations and warned the Assembly not to assume the right to grant "any Powers of Church Government" or pass any other than a strictly civil incorporation bill.[67] The Presbyterian leaders had quick reflexes. They were also aware of the division within their own ranks. Indeed, the split among the Presbyterians soon became apparent to the legislature as well. William Graham and his allies had not been idle since the presbyters' meeting, and from heavily Presbyterian counties in the Valley came strong denunciations of the proposed assessment and incorporation. One petition from Rockbridge condemned the Episcopalian clergy for even requesting "distinctions incompatible with . . . political EQUALITY" and threatened that an assessment would render the clergy independent of the people and fill up the ministerial ranks with "Fools,

---

on Nov. 16 the spring petition of the Presbytery was also ordered to the same group (*JHD*, pp. 21, 22, 25).

[66] *JHD*, Nov. 17, 1784, p. 27.

[67] RP, Nov. 18, 1784. The petition is dated as having been composed that same day in Richmond. John Smith may have wanted to clarify his position in view of the fact that a number of the "Aye" votes for incorporation had come from Presbyterian areas.

Sots, and Gamblers." A memorial from Rockingham County warned that the legislature which this year could take "five Dollars" might next year take "Fifty" and give it to whomever it pleased. The petitioners insisted that if Christianity had not been founded or propagated by a tax, it should not need one now to keep itself in existence.[68]

However, from Prince Edward County, home of John Smith, came a letter published in the *Virginia Gazette* and signed by "80 of the most respectable inhabitants," which instructed their delegates to support the assessment. The contents of this letter carefully mirrored the distinction made by the Presbyterian petition between civil support for religion and the intrusion of government into purely spiritual affairs. In fact, it repeated almost verbatim the terms laid down by the Hanover Presbytery in October on which an assessment would be acceptable.[69]

While the Presbyterians publicly aired their disagreement over the assessment, other petitions favoring the measure flowed into the Assembly. Although the rest of the state remained quiet on the issue, support for the bill was well organized in the Southside. During the remainder of the session, six more counties below the James submitted one or more proassessment petitions. The most comprehensive memorial came from Surry. Contrasting the thanksgiving due the "god of Battles" with the feeble means provided for his worship, this petition insisted on the value of religion as a prop to civil government. A well-ordered religious system inculcated respect and obedience to the laws and authority of the state, guaranteeing the fidelity of the governors as well as the docility of the governed. The memorial also pointed out that while religion was necessary in any society, it was even more vital to a republic because that form of government was so dependent upon the virtue of its citizens. When men were given such complete freedom, religion kept liberty from becoming license. Repeating what

[68]Ibid., Dec. 1, Nov. 18, 1784. The *Va. Gaz. and Weekly Advertiser,* Nov. 13, 1784, also published a letter from Botetourt County to its delegates, instructing them to vote against the assessment. In fact, none of the Valley delegates had voted for the assessment resolution, while only the two delegates from Botetourt, Archibald Stuart and George Hancock, voted in favor of the incorporation resolution.
[69]*Va. Gaz. and Weekly Advertiser,* Nov. 20, 1784.

by now had become a fundamental principle of the proassessment argument, the petition insisted that *"whatever is to conduce equally to the Advantage of all, should be borne Equally by all."* Consequently the voluntary subscription system, which had proved incapable of maintaining the ministry, was also unjust for thrusting upon the conscientious few a burden which should be borne by all the members of society.[70]

Against what appeared from the petitions to be growing support for the assessment bill, Madison fought back in debate. Sometime during this period he delivered one of his rare speeches, and it was entirely devoted to the subject of assessment. Religion, he informed his fellow delegates, was not within the legitimate area of governmental activity. The tendency, once the state intervened, was to establish Christianity, then to require uniformity and pass penal laws to secure it. The real question before the Assembly was not whether religion was necessary for the state, but whether religious establishments were necessary for religion. Man had a natural tendency toward religious belief, but both history and experience showed that establishments had hindered rather than helped the development of that faith. Patrick Henry had warned the House of the destruction of states, but this had taken place where establishments existed.

Focusing his attack more precisely on the assessment, Madison pointed out the lack of experience with such a measure. He then enumerated the states in America where complete freedom of belief prevailed and the background for this practice in primitive and Reformation Christianity. If Virginia defied this growing pattern of religious liberty by instituting a policy of establishment, it would be closing the door to immigration and encouraging dissenters to forsake the state for other, freer climes. The whole question of an assessment, Madison pointed out, had arisen because people believed that problems in the commonwealth were directly related to the condition of religion; but this simply was not the case. Virginia had become depressed by the dislocations of war, bad laws, the poor administration of justice, and the

[70]RP, Dec. 1, 1784. Other proassessment petitions came from Halifax, Mecklenburg, Lunenburg, Amelia, and Dinwiddie Counties (*JHD*, Nov. 20, 1784, p. 32; RP, Dec. 1, 1784).

general difficulties of transition and change necessitated by the Revolution. Now it was also suffering because of the policies and hopes of those who favored assessment rather than measures which would truly benefit the people. The solution to the evils in the state would not be solved by a new kind of establishment of religion but by attention to the areas of public and personal life which needed correction. A new code of laws and justice were urgently required for external order; in the interior sphere, men must learn to promote virtue by personal example rather than legislation. If there was any place for government intervention, it was in the encouragement and support of education. Finally, Madison addressed himself to the implicit limitations of the bill. How could a legislature begin to determine what constituted the Christian religion? Was it necessary for them to investigate trans- lations of the Bible, to study the doctrines of the Trinity and the nature of Christ, in order to judge whether or not this or that group met the test of genuine Christianity? The end product of this course of action would be to rely upon the government to fix the measure of orthodoxy and heresy, which would be to dishonor Christianity and violate the Declaration of Rights.[71]

It was a long speech and covered all of the sensitive areas; but as an orator Madison was no match for Henry. He had other weapons, however, to use against the bill. If reason could not win the day, perhaps removal of the opposition would help the case. Since Benjamin Harrison had served three consecutive terms as governor, he was not eligible for reelection. The House of Dele- gates, the real locus of power in the governmental structure, was responsible for choosing the chief magistrate of the state; and the post was again within Henry's grasp if he so wished. With obvious relief, Madison informed Monroe late in November of Henry's election, "a circumstance very inauspicious to his offspring" in the House.[72]

Henry thus abandoned his program in the legislature in mid- stream. During the Revolution he had found the executive position

---

[71]Rutland, *Papers of Madison* 8: 195-99, contains an outline of the speech which he delivered.

[72]Ibid., 8: 158.

one of honor and prestige and even managed to control the council, without whose approval the governor could not act. Although another prominent Virginian described the role as "a vox et praeterea nihil," Henry had found it to his liking. In addition, he had personal reasons for accepting the governorship. Richmond was a far more interesting place for his aristocratic wife and gave access to more potential husbands for his marriageable daughters than his Piedmont plantation did.[73] He had carried the assessment resolution, taken comfort in the support of the Hanover Presbytery, and been elected governor just before the overwhelming vote in favor of incorporation of religious societies. He may well have believed that the coalition now formed between the Presbyterians and Episcopalians ensured the passage of the assessment bill. But, as Edmund Randolph pointed out, "Omnipotent as Henry was while present and asserting himself in the Assembly, he had one defect in his politics; he was apt to be contented with some *general* vote of success, but his genius did not lead him into detail. For a debate on great *general* principles, he was never surpassed here; but more laborious men, who seized occasions of modifying propositions which they had lost on a vote or of renewing them at more fortunate seasons, often accomplished their purpose after he had retired from the session." His election was unopposed and very probably took place with the calculated support of Madison.[74]

With Henry removed from the legislative arena, Madison's course was appreciably eased. It was also to his good fortune that Richard Henry Lee, elected as a delegate from Westmoreland County, was now serving as president of the Confederation Congress. The radical Lee, a warm friend of the Episcopal church

[73]Ralph Wormeley, Jr., to Arthur Lee, Dec. 25, 1786, Arthur Lee Papers, Houghton Library, Harvard University, Cambridge, Mass. For other reasons why Henry accepted the governorship, see Robert Douthat Meade, *Patrick Henry* (Philadelphia, 1957-69), 2: 282-83. Meade, however, is not a reliable source for the religious controversies of the period. For example, he stated that the bill for the incorporation of the Protestant Episcopal church did not pass at the session of 1784 (ibid., 2: 281).

[74]Randolph, *History of Virginia*, p. 278. That Madison urged the election of Henry has been accepted by the biographers of both men; see Brant, *Madison* 2: 345-46, and Meade, *Patrick Henry* 2: 281-82.

and a firm believer in the need for public virtue to maintain the republican experiment, would have assumed his usual position of leadership in the Assembly. From a distance, however, he could only lobby by mail for the causes in which he took a personal interest. The fate of the assessment bill concerned him. Writing to Madison in November, Lee urged the necessity of the measure on the grounds of securing "our morals." For him the condition of things was clear: "Refiners may weave as fine a web of reason as they please, but the experience of all times shews Religion to be the guardian of morals—And he must be a very inattentive observer in our Country, who does not see that avarice is accomplishing the destruction of religion, for want of a legal obligation to contribute something to its support." Lee added a pertinent observation on the interpretation of the Declaration of Rights. That document, he pointed out, "rather contends against forcing modes of faith or forms of worship, than against compelling contribution for the support of religion in general." In concluding his remarks, he praised the "liberal ground" of the Presbyterian petition. Any assessment, he observed, should extend itself to the support of all religions, not just Christianity.[75] Lee was apparently unaware of the specifics of the Presbyterian proposal; nevertheless, it was indeed to Madison's advantage that he was absent from the House that fall.

With Henry out of the legislature, the supporters of the religious bills had lost the man whom Samuel Sheild called "the great pillar of our Cause."[76] But the battle for the measures was not over; it merely passed to less competent generals. The division in the House over the questions of church and state did not follow any standard alignment of party blocs or factions in Virginia during the mid-1780s. Thus men who thought very differently about the payment of British debts, the collection of taxes, and the manumission of slaves often found themselves on the same side in the matters of assessment and incorporation.[77]

[75]James Curtis Ballagh, ed., *The Letters of Richard Henry Lee* (rept., New York, 1970), 2: 304-5.

[76]Samuel Sheild to David Griffith, Dec. 20, 1784, David Griffith Papers, VHS.

[77]For an analysis of the voting patterns in the House during this period, see Jackson Turner Main, *Political Parties before the Constitution* (Chapel Hill, N.C., 1973),

The Harrison clan was one group firmly backing both issues. After Henry's election, Benjamin Harrison resumed his seat in the Assembly, joining his son, Carter Bassett Harrison, and his brother, Carter Henry Harrison. Carter Henry Harrison had emerged during the session as a power in the House and a member of all the major committees, including those specifically appointed to draft the bills of assessment and incorporation. Well-entrenched, wealthy Virginia aristocrats, the Harrisons had a bloodline unsurpassed among the first families of the commonwealth and sufficiently fertile to connect them with virtually every important person in the state. Leadership had been their prerogative throughout the colonial period, and at the time of the Revolution they had strongly supported the break with England. Hot-tempered in the cause of freedom, they were equally warm in their attachment to the Episcopal church. During an argument with John Blair Smith, most probably over the terms of the incorporation act, Carter Henry Harrison exclaimed that the "greatest curse which heaven sent at any time into this Country, was sending Dissenters into it."[78] Harrison was not interested in coming to terms with the opposition, nor was he capable of ingratiating himself with potential allies. No less devoted to the church, though perhaps more tactful in its cause, were other prominent delegates including Henry Tazewell, Francis Corbin, and Joseph Jones of King George County. Jones in particular was a close friend and con-

---

pp. 244-67 passim, and Norman K. Risjord and Gordon DenBoer, "The Evolution of Political Parties in Virginia, 1782-1800," *Journal of American History* 60 (1974), 961-70. Neither Main nor Risjord and DenBoer have much to say concerning the religious questions other than to point out that they failed to follow the division on other questions. However, they do note the sectional cleavage in the voting. Main also states that "a very sharp division occurred between the delegates of small property, who opposed any state support for religious purposes, and wealthy delegates, who favored this"; and he notes that educated delegates "were more inclined to approve close state-church relations than those without education" (ibid., p. 260). I think this statement is misleading. There were men of wealth and education on both sides of the question; for an evaluation of the major figures in the House, see Appendix II.

[78]Rutland, *Papers of Madison* 8: 282. Smith wrote Madison in May 1785 to ask his verification of the remarks, but Madison refused to become involved "in any case where the characters of Gentlemen are concerned" (ibid., 8: 283).

For the Harrisons, see W. G. Stanard, "Harrison of James River," *Virginia Magazine of History and Biography* 30-33 (1922-25): passim, and 36 (1934): 183-87.

fidant of Madison, but in the area of religion the two men were poles apart.

Madison also had his allies, and they comprised liberal Episcopalians such as French Strother and Wilson Cary Nicholas, Valley Presbyterians of the caliber of Zachariah Johnston, and some men like John Breckinridge who apparently belonged to no religious group. Strother was a long-standing, though iconoclastic, member of the established church and served as both vestryman and churchwarden during the latter years of the Revolution. He was also extremely popular with the dissenters. While a justice of the peace, Strother had released a Baptist preacher from the Culpeper jail during the dead of night and substituted a slave in his place.[79] Nicholas was much younger and represented not only one of the best families in the state but also a complete reversal of the older generation's views on the relationship of religion to the state.

On the Presbyterian side of the question, Zachariah Johnston was perhaps the best known. The son of Scotch-Irish immigrants, he had served in the war and then come into the legislature from Augusta County in 1778. Johnston had not attended the spring session of 1784, since he had planned at that time to inspect his western lands. From the falls of the Ohio in May he wrote a letter to his wife which reveals the personal nature of his faith. He urged her to maintain "secret and family Devotion," to "Call on the God of heaven in Sincerity," and to "Acknowledge him in all your ways."[80] Johnston was a thoroughly pious man, but during the debates in the House he had announced that although he considered himself a "rigid Presbyterian" born and bred, "the very day that the Presbyterians shall be established by law and become a body politic, the same day Zachariah Johnston will become a dissenter. Dissent from that religion I cannot in honesty, but from that establishment I will."[81]

[79]Philip Slaughter, *A History of St. Mark's Parish, Culpeper County, Virginia,* rept. in *Notes on Culpeper County, Virginia,* comp. Raleigh Travers Green (Baltimore, 1958), pp. 83-84.

[80]Zachariah to Ann Johnston, May 11, 1784, Zachariah Johnston Papers, VSL.

[81]Quoted in M. W. Paxton, "Zachariah Johnston of Augusta and Rockbridge and His Times," Ms, VHS. Paxton dated this speech as having been given in the session of

Breckinridge had also spoken out against the bills. Madison had befriended the young man during the previous year while he was a student at William and Mary. The budding politician responded to Madison's kindness with respect bordering on adulation. Despite his Scotch-Irish background, Breckinridge apparently discarded his Presbyterianism while in college, for his speech against the assessment proclaimed that he was "not attached particularly to any fixed mode of worship," and he denied that organized religion had any effect on the morals of society. Elsewhere he argued that education was the crucial thing: "'Tis Education alone that makes the Man, and is the parent of every Virtue; it is the most sacred, the most useful, and at the same time, the most neglected thing in every Country."[82]

Perhaps with the hope that an emphasis on education might win additional support for the assessment, the drafting committee revised the title of the bill. When presented as a resolution, the measure had been designed to support Christian ministers, churches, and worship. However, when the committee had completed its work, the measure was designated as a bill "establishing a provision for teachers of the christian religion."[83]

The assessment bill had in fact remained in the drafting committee so long that at one point Madison questioned whether it would ever be presented.[84] The month of November dragged by with very little business accomplished. Speaker Tyler was disgusted. He wrote to Monroe on November 26: "We are doing nothing yet, a great waste of time much to our disgrace."[85] How-

---

1785; however, it seems more appropriately located in the session of 1784. See also Howard McKnight Wilson, *The Tinkling Spring, Headwater of Freedom: A Study of the Church and Her People, 1732-1952* (Fishersville, Va., 1954), pp. 222-36.

[82] Breckinridge Family Papers, 1784, LC. The two speeches were entitled "What is the best form of government" and "On a General Assessment for the Support of Religion." They were composed before the beginning of the first session and written out in longhand for delivery in the House. For Breckinridge's close relationship with Madison, see John Breckinridge to Lettice Breckinridge, Aug. 17, 1783, ibid.

[83] *JHD*, Dec. 2, 1784, p. 51.

[84] Rutland, *Papers of Madison* 8: 155.

[85] Letter in *William and Mary Quarterly*, 1st ser., 1 (1892): 100-101.

ever, on that same day, Francis Corbin presented the draft of the assessment bill to the House, and it passed its first two readings on that day and the one following.[86] These votes were more perfunctory than a genuine test of the issue, and Madison remained optimistic that the bill would be defeated. "Its friends," he informed Monroe later that week, "are much disheartened at the loss of Mr. Henry. Its fate is I think very uncertain."[87]

For the time being, the assessment question was left in abeyance while the Assembly turned its attention to the bill, presented by Carter Henry Harrison, "for incorporating the Protestant Episcopal Church." After quickly sailing through the preliminary readings, the bill was debated in the Committee of the Whole, engrossed in its final form, and passed by the House by a vote of 47 to 38 on December 22.[88]

In essence the bill organized the Protestant Episcopal Church and put it on an operating basis independent of the state. Each parish vestry and clergyman was to be constituted as "a body corporate and politic" and given possession and control over all parish property together with the ordinary duties and rights of corporations. Vestry meetings, elections, voting procedures, and other routine matters were all specified by the bill; and it also stated that no one could participate in vestry elections "who does not profess himself a member of the Protestant Episcopal Church, and actually contribute toward its support." All past laws dealing with any of these matters or pertaining in any way to church affairs were declared repealed. As the legislative and governing body of the church, the bill established a convention composed of the clergyman and one layman from each parish, the latter to be chosen by the vestry. The Convention was also given authority to remove incompetent or scandalous ministers, although it could

[86]*JHD*, Dec. 2, Dec. 3, 1784, pp. 51, 52.

[87]Rutland, *Papers of Madison* 8: 175.

[88]The incorporation bill was presented on Dec. 11, passed the first two readings that same day, debated in the Committee of the Whole on Dec. 18 and 20, engrossed on Dec. 21, and passed on Dec. 22 (*JHD*, pp. 65-66, 75, 77-79). The Senate originally wanted some amendments to the bill, but it did not press for them and the bill went into law as approved by the House (ibid., Dec. 24, Dec. 28, 1784, pp. 83, 91).

neither remove nor appoint a clergyman to a parish without the approval of a majority of the elected vestry.[89]

The Assembly had rejected the request of the Episcopal clergy of the previous June which had asked for their own incorporation. Instead, the delegates instituted a form of church government which would be representative of the membership as a whole. Nevertheless, Madison later reported that even broader lay representation had been envisioned. He stated that the House had determined that two lay deputies from each parish should attend the Convention, but that this particular amendment had somehow been omitted from the final form of the bill.[90] Madison himself had voted for the measure. As he told Jefferson: "the necessity of some sort of incorporation for the purpose of holding & managing the property of the Church could not well be denied." But more important, the passage of the incorporation act was part of Madison's strategy to defeat the assessment. Had the incorporation failed, he believed that "would have doubled the eagerness and the pretexts for a much greater evil, a General Assessment, which there is good ground to believe was parried by this partial gratification of its warmest votaries."[91] The advocates of the religious bills had gotten the smaller half of the loaf. Even then it was a close vote. Of the delegates who had voted against the incorporation resolution on November 17, Madison was the only one to support the finished bill, while a number of those who had supported the resolution were either absent or voted against the bill on December 22.

The House then began to move on the assessment bill. During the following day it was discussed and amended in the Committee

---

[89]Hening, *Statutes at Large* 11: 532-37.

[90]Rutland, *Papers of Madison* 8: 217, 228. Madison also stated "that the act is so constructed as to deprive the Vestries of the uncontrolled right of electing clergymen, unless it be referred to them by the canons of the Convention" (ibid., 8: 228). However, Madison's judgment does not appear to agree with the text of the bill, which clearly gave the vestries this power (Hening, *Statutes at Large* 11: 537).

[91]Rutland, *Papers of Madison* 8: 229. Madison was philosophical about the passage of the incorporation act. As he told his father, "If it be unpopular among the laity it will be soon repealed and will be a standing lesson to them of the danger of referring religious matters to the legislature" (ibid., 8: 217).

of the Whole and then presented to the floor of the House. At this critical juncture, Benjamin Harrison made a motion which played into the hands of the bill's opponents. During the course of debate, the decision had been reached to liberalize the bill by dropping the word "christian" and opening up the measure to any group which might consider itself a religion. But Harrison, with what Madison termed *"pathetic zeal,"* was instrumental in having this decision reversed and the limitation reinstated in the text.[92]

The bill had now achieved its definitive form and was ordered to be engrossed by the tenuous margin of 44 to 42. Its formal title was "A Bill establishing a provision for Teachers of the Christian Religion." It was a very different measure from the assessment bill "concerning religion" of 1779. This new proposal was a much shorter document, and it did not mention the establishment of Christianity or set any doctrinal articles or forms of church worship or polity. While the 1779 bill had been directly oriented toward the public worship of God, the 1784 proposal was concerned with the religious instruction of man. As stated in the brief preamble, its basic justification was that "a general diffusion of Christian knowledge hath a natural tendency to correct the morals of men, restrain their vices, and preserve the peace of society." Instructors were needed to diffuse this knowledge, and it was appropriate for the government to assist them in their work. All of those liable for taxation were therefore to pay a to-be-determined percentage based upon their property. The money would be collected by the sheriff and given to the Christian church designated by the taxpayer. These revenues were restricted to the support of the minister and church buildings. However, in a clause which later provoked much controversy, the bill made an exception for Quakers and Mennonites. Realizing that these communities had no formal clergy, the legislature permitted them to place their tax money in a "general fund" and spend it "in a manner . . . best calculated to promote their particular mode of worship." If an individual was not a member of any church or refused to declare his preference, his share of the revenues would be alloted

---

[92]Ibid., 8: 229; *JHD*, Dec. 22-23, 1784, pp. 80-81.

for schools in the county where he resided. The bill also declared that this measure did not violate either the Declaration of Rights or the basic equality of all Christian groups. In essence, it was designed to keep the Christian ministry, and particularly the clergy of the Episcopal church, active and solvent.[93]

The day after its engrossment, Christmas Eve, the bill was postponed in its final reading until the Assembly would meet again the following fall. The motion to delay the decision on the assessment was carried by a vote of 45 to 38. Madison's strategy proved successful, as eight delegates who had supported the incorporation act voted with him to postpone assessment. They provided the margin of victory. (Map 1 shows the geographical distribution of the vote.) A further motion was passed to print up the engrossed bill together with the roll-call vote on postponement. Twelve copies of this handbill were to be given to each member of the Assembly for distribution in his county in order to ascertain the opinion of the people on the measure.[94]

With but two weeks remaining in the session, the delegates now turned their attention to other pressing business, including the highly controversial questions of taxes and the payment of British debts. Nevertheless, two other religious issues still eluded settlement. At the same time as it had passed the incorporation resolution in November, the House had also approved a resolution to alter the marriage and vestry laws in accordance with the petitions presented by the Baptists and Presbyterians. An eight-man committee, chaired by Thomas Mathews, had been appointed to draw up the necessary legislation. However, this committee, perhaps because it was dominated by men who favored the Episcopal church, apparently accomplished very little.[95] The session was well into December before a bill "to amend the several acts, concerning marriages" was presented to the House. In less than a week the delegates approved the measure and sent it on to the Senate,

---

[93]For the complete text of the proposed assessment bill, see Appendix I; for the vote on engrossment, see Rutland, *Papers of Madison* 8: 200.

[94]*JHD*, Dec. 24, 1784, p. 82.

[95]Ibid., Nov. 17, 1784, p. 27. The committee was composed of Mathews, Jones of King George, Corbin, Briggs, Brent, Carter H. Harrison, Henry, and Madison. Only Madison was strongly in favor of total disestablishment.

110

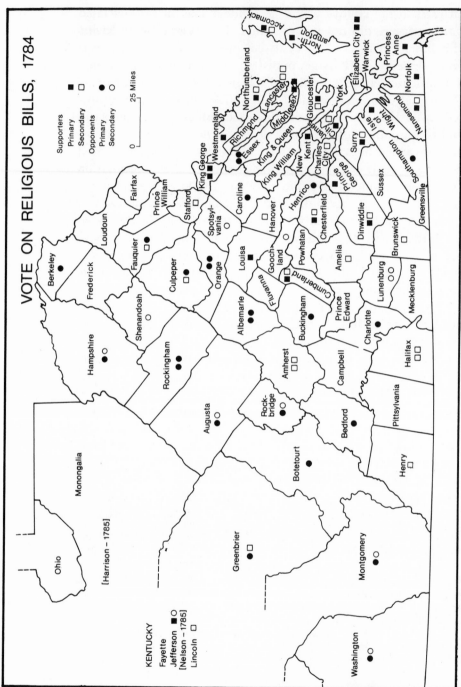

VOTE ON RELIGIOUS BILLS, 1784

Supporters
Primary ■ Secondary □
Opponents
Primary ● Secondary ○

0   25 Miles

KENTUCKY
Fayette
Jefferson ■ ○
[Nelson – 1785]
Lincoln □

[Harrison – 1785]

Map. 1 Vote on Religious Bills (Assessment and Incorporation) in the House of Delegates, Fall 1784 (*JHD*, Fall Session, 1784)

but it must have been rejected there for it was not signed into law.[96] The House had then taken up the incorporation and assessment bills. After disposing of these major issues, the delegates had ordered a new bill "to regulate the solemnization of marriages," with Mann Page as a committee of one to draft and present it. When the delegates returned to work after Christmas, Page submitted the bill, and it swiftly passed the House. This time the Senate concurred, and the bill became law.[97]

The new marriage act authorized "any ordained minister of the gospel in regular communion with any society of christians" to perform the marriage ceremony provided that he served a regular parish or congregation within the state. In an oblique slap at the "enthusiasts," itinerants were specifically excluded. On the other hand, Quakers and Mennonites were permitted their own marriage service of open declaration before their respective communities. The bill also regularized all previous marriages performed by civil officials or "others" due to lack of sufficient authorized clergy.[98] With the passage of this act, the discrimination in favor of the former established clergy which had so irritated the Baptists and Presbyterians was finally brought to an end.

The section of the November resolution pertaining to the vestries met with a less happy fate. Several bills passed in earlier years had transferred the secular functions of the vestries in certain western counties to overseers of the poor. In some cases, however, county sheriffs had neglected to comply with the law and call elections at the proper time. The Assembly now passed a bill to

---

[96]Ibid., Dec. 10, 1784, p. 65. The bill was presented "according to order" by William Ronald. Since he was not an original member of the drafting committee, the bill may be a different one than that drawn up by the group appointed on Nov. 17, or possibly he was later added in place of Henry. The bill was passed and sent to the Senate on Dec. 16, but nothing further was heard of it (ibid., p. 71).

In the *Va. Gaz. and Weekly Advertizer*, Nov. 27, 1784, there was an article on a marriage bill then in the process of discussion. The text of the bill as printed in the *Gazette* was very brief and did not contain the specific restrictions noted in the bill that was finally approved that session.

[97]*JHD*, Dec. 22-30, 1784, pp. 83, 84, 92, 95.

[98]Hening, *Statutes at Large* 11: 503-5.

provide new elections in these counties.[99] The heart of the question was the extension of these laws to the vast majority of the counties where vestries were still performing civil duties. The measure was obviously linked to the incorporation of the Protestant Episcopal Church, and on the same day as that bill cleared the House, a new committee was ordered to draft a bill "for appointing overseers of the poor, within the several parishes of this Commonwealth." Although it was late in the session, this measure should not have aroused much opposition. Nevertheless, a bill was not reported and nothing further was done at that time. Evidently the new vestries to be chosen in April and composed and elected solely by Episcopalians would continue to act in a civil capacity throughout most of the state.[100]

The session finally petered out at the end of the first week of January, and the faithful remnant who had stayed until its conclusion were free to return home. In their baggage they carried the broadsides of the assessment bill for the edification or scorn of their constituents. All things considered, the fall session of 1784 had witnessed the most extensive and open discussion of the religious questions since the beginning of the Revolution. The delegates had heard all sides of the issue. Now the struggle over the relationship of church and state and the best means to ensure virtue in a republican society would pass to the countryside.

[99] *JHD*, Dec. 21, Dec. 23, 1784, pp. 77, 81; Hening, *Statutes at Large* 11: 432-33.

[100] *JHD*, Dec. 22, 1784, p. 80. This committee was composed of Alexander Henderson, Johnston, Tazewell, and Ronald.

Chapter Four

Voluntarism Defended
Spring–Summer 1785

THE delegates had scarcely concluded their business when Madison penned a lengthy epistle to Jefferson, summarizing the politics and legislation of the session. After explaining the assessment proposal, he concluded: "Should the bill ever pass into a law in its present form it may and will be easily eluded. It is chiefly obnoxious on account of its dishonourable principle and dangerous tendency."[1] Not all Virginians would concur with that evaluation. Edmund Pendleton, reporting to Richard Henry Lee on the results of the Assembly's work, remarked with regard to the bills for incorporation and assessment that "some very sagacious gentlemen, can spy designs to revive the former establishment, which I believe, do not exist in the minds of any member of that church, the clergy and a few monarchy men excepted."[2] Pendleton's comment on the ministers is indicative of the division in the church which would surface that year and further hinder the passage of the assessment bill.

Regardless of how the leaders of the state might disagree on the issue, the people now had an opportunity to express their opinions. The reaction was not slow in coming. By March the distribution of the broadside of the assessment proposal had begun to provoke a response, and the opposition quickly took to the press. Early in the spring, the newly founded *Virginia Journal and Alexandria Advertizer* carried both the text of the bill and a series of articles objecting to the plan.[3] In a long essay spread over two issues and liberally spiced with scriptural quotations, "Vigilarius" attacked

---

[1] Boyd, *Papers of Jefferson* 7: 595.

[2] Mays, *Letters of Pendleton* 2: 474.

[3] The newspaper published the text of the assessment bill together with the roll call on the postponement vote on Mar. 17, 1785.

the bill root and branch. Introducing himself as a firm believer in the value of Christianity and a "sincere friend of the Clergy," he rejected the premise that religion needed state assistance. The churches did indeed contribute to the well-being of society, but they would not be assisted in this task by having their ministers transformed into "officers of civil government." Utilizing what by now had become a standard appeal to the experience of primitive Christianity, he pointed out that the voluntary method of support had been the initial practice and had successfully provided a truly "pure and disinterested" ministry. Even amid persecution by the state, the church had flourished. However, when Constantine and his successors had interjected themselves as patrons of religion, corruption and decline had set in. These evils and a host of others had continued wherever church and state had joined forces.

"Vigilarius" argued that rather than promoting the peace and security of the community, the assessment bill would actually injure societal relationships. In elaborating this assertion, he developed two arguments which would be repeated in the months ahead. First, many would consider the assessment a violation of their rights, resist payment of the tax, and have the money taken from them by force. It was a distasteful prospect. Equally objectionable was the discrimination written into the bill itself. Churches with a traditional polity such as the Episcopalians, Presbyterians, and Baptists would have their vestries, elders, or associations distribute their share of the collected funds; but the bill limited the expenditure of this revenue to clerical salaries and church buildings. However, Quakers and Mennonites would pay their taxes into a general fund, and this could be alloted in "a manner which they shall think best calculated to promote their own particular mode of worship."[4] "Vigilarius" insisted that this "invidious distinction" would inevitably increase the mutual hostility already prevalent among Christian groups.

Finally, he pointed out that the bill would not achieve its desired objective of providing a secure living for the clergy, since the ministers would be subjected not only to the whims of individuals who might redirect their taxes from year to year but

[4]Ibid.

also to the annual fluctuations in state tax rates. The consequent insecurity would promote unhealthy competition and envy within ministerial ranks. Moreover, the bill as presently framed would not ensure the religious instruction of the people, for it did not require them to attend services. The same principles which justified salaries for the clergy might also be used to coerce the people to church on Sunday. Indeed, "without this addition, it will be capitally deficient in the means of effecting one of the principal designs which it is expected to promote." He concluded with an appeal to his readers to inform the Assembly by "decent, but spirited" petitions. Even more crucial, men must be chosen for the legislature who favored religious liberty and would go to Richmond with clear instructions to vote against the assessment or any other proposal "which interferes in matters beyond the sphere of their appointment."[5]

Another newspaper opponent of the assessment argued against the proposed bill without ever expressly mentioning it. After a glowing tribute to the "complete triumph" of reason achieved by the Revolution, he noted his sorrow that a solicitation on the question of religion should even be necessary. The sixteenth article of the Declaration of Rights spoke clearly enough; and since it had been framed by a convention, no mere Assembly could alter or annul it. In what had become a general pattern for critics of the assessment proposal, this writer ignored the fact that the same men who had passed the sixteenth article had also raised the possibility of an assessment in 1776. He suggested further that the delegates to the session be ordered by their constituents to enact the bill for religious freedom (which he reprinted) and closed with an appeal to stand firm in the principles of Jefferson, Wythe, and Pendleton.[6]

If this particular issue of the Alexandria newspaper found its way into the hands of Edmund Pendleton, it must have irritated that firm advocate of assessment to see his name used by the opposition, especially when he was doing all in his power to drum up support for the bill. Writing to Richard Henry Lee in April, Pendleton did not venture to predict the outcome of the struggle

[5]Ibid., Mar. 31, April 7, 1785. The article was published in two parts.

[6]Ibid., April 14, 1785.

but noted that "considerable clamours" had been raised against the proposal. Lee had corresponded earlier with Pendleton, stating his reasons for supporting the assessment. The judge now replied that he had taken the liberty of publishing Lee's comments for the benefit of the coming Assembly, "who I fear will need it, as I can truly say, that I have heard of but one elected, who is acquainted with business, and he not a very industrious one."[7]

Pendleton had good reason to be disturbed over the elections. An unusually large number of candidates had resulted in "Great and general efforts" at the polls.[8] The campaign had begun almost immediately after the last session had ended, and the style of electioneering had changed little since the days of the Burgesses. As one observer commented in January, "we live a very Idle life about here—Eating, Drinking and Canvassing for the Next Election takes up a great deal of our time."[9] Throughout Virginia that spring there were many spirited contests. Pendleton noted the rush to get elected and was disgusted with the "frequent and expensive treats" and the "sacrifice of much wine, bottles and glasses to the fortunate Deities." Madison informed Monroe at the end of April that the assessment had influenced the outcome in some cases. In Culpeper County, for example, James Pendleton, a competent legislator well respected by his constituents, was defeated because of his support for the bill.[10]

He was not the only casualty of the April balloting. However, although seventy of the delegates in the 1784 Assembly were not returned to office, it seems unlikely that the assessment played a

---

[7] Mays, *Letters of Pendleton* 2: 478.

[8] Boyd, *Papers of Jefferson* 8: 154.

[9] Joseph Herndon to Rev. James Stevenson, Jan. 18, 1785, Herndon Family Papers, typescript, University of Virginia Library, Charlottesville (hereafter U.Va. Lib.).

For an excellent treatment of election practices in Virginia during this period, see Charles S. Sydnor, *Gentlemen Freeholders: Political Practices in Washington's Virginia* (Chapel Hill, N.C., 1952). The best contemporary document is a play written by Col. Robert Munford entitled *The Candidates; or, the Humours of a Virginia Election.* Written about 1770, it was first published in 1798. It has been reprinted with an introduction by Jay B. Hubbell and Douglass Adair in *William and Mary Quarterly,* 3d ser., 5 (1948): 217-57.

[10] Mays, *Letters of Pendleton* 2: 477; Rutland, *Papers of Madison* 8: 272. See also Madison's comments in May (ibid., 8: 286).

major role in their defeat. Twenty-one of these seventy delegates had been supporters of the assessment and incorporation issues. All but five were replaced by men who, in the next session, would either follow the same voting pattern or abstain on the religious questions. Moreover, there were other issues that spring which could and did defeat candidates. Despite the rumpus stirred up by the assessment proposal and the widespread feelings manifested by the avalanche of petitions the following fall, it did not determine the outcome of the elections as a whole or retire a large number of delegates from office. Nevertheless, it must have played a part in the campaigns and undoubtedly the candidates were expected to take a position on the issue.[11]

While the elections proceeded throughout April, the Episcopalians across Virginia were choosing new vestries in accordance with the terms of the incorporation act. Plans for the church Convention had already been laid. The meeting had been announced on January 1, and a broadside of the act was published together with a postscript informing church members that the Convention would be held in Richmond on May 18. The notice was signed by three clergymen: Miles Selden, the rector of Henrico Parish in the capital, Benjamin Blagrove, the legislature's chaplain, and David Griffith.[12]

Griffith had been extremely active in church affairs ever since the clergy meeting of June 1784. In addition to his organizational work in Virginia, he had maintained close contact with Episcopalian leaders in the other states. While on a business trip to New

---

[11] Swem, *Register*, pp. 19-22. Besides James Pendleton, the four other men who may have been defeated on account of their support for the assessment were John Marshall (Fauquier), John Coleman (Halifax), Philip Barbour (Jefferson), and George Slaughter (Lincoln). Although Alexander Henderson of Fairfax County had supported the assessment, he was probably defeated (if he attempted reelection) by the charge that he had acted in his own self-interest in voting against the opening of the courts of justice for the immediate recovery of debts (*Va. Journal and Alexandria Advertizer*, Mar. 24, 1785). Other important issues included the circuit court bill and the question of compliance with the terms of the treaty with Great Britain. For example, see George Nicholas's comments on the defeat of Edward Carter in Albemarle County in Rutland, *Papers of Madison* 8: 265.

[12] *Va. Gaz., or the American Advertizer*, Feb. 26, 1785; *Va. Journal and Alexandria Advertizer*, Mar. 3, 1785.

York in October, he attended a church meeting. Eight other states had sent representatives to draw up a preliminary set of principles by which the Episcopalians of America might unite and organize their ecclesiastical government. Griffith's presence at the meeting was strictly unofficial, because, as he explained to William White, the Virginia clergy "could not, with propriety and indeed without great danger to the Church," authorize a representative "to agree to the least alteration whatever."[13] His judgment was supported by a Richmond newspaper which reported the meeting and noted that Griffith was there "by permission. The Clergy of [Virginia] being restricted by laws, yet in force there, were not at liberty to send delegates, or conse[n] t to any alteration in the order, government, doctrine, or worship of the Church."[14]

The New York meeting promulgated a list of articles which called for a church unified and governed by a general convention of lay and clerical deputies from every state. Each state should also have a bishop who, by virtue of his office, would be a member of the General Convention. Although the clerical and lay deputies would form one deliberating body, voting would be in separate groups and the concurrence of both would be necessary to pass any legislation. One of the most significant articles pertained to the theology and worship of the church; it stated: "That the said Church shall maintain the Doctrines of the Gospel as now held by the Church of England and shall adhere to the Liturgy of the said Church, as far as shall be consistent with the American Revolution and the Constitutions of the respective States."[15] This conservative proposition together with the provisions for voting in the General Convention would meet with strong resistance at the Richmond meeting the following May.

By the time Griffith returned from New York, the 1784 session was in full swing, and he had an opportunity to observe the fruition of his labors as the Assembly passed what Samuel Sheild

---

[13]Griffith to White, July 26, 1784, Bishop William White Papers, Hist. Soc. Episcopal Church, Austin.

[14]*Va. Gaz. and Weekly Advertizer,* Nov. 6, 1784.

[15]Loveland, *Critical Years,* p. 91.

referred to as "our Bill."[16] However, there was bad news also. The Methodists, those unruly enthusiasts on the left wing of the church, had met and formed a separate denomination, the Methodist Episcopal Church. This division not only reduced the membership of the Episcopal church; it also removed a group which conceivably would have supported the assessment. At the beginning of the Revolution, the active support of the establishment by the Methodists had filled a gap left by more passive members of the church; but in 1785 they would join ranks with the opposition.

Even to a casual observer of religious affairs, this could not have been an entirely unexpected development. The conditions which had provoked the Virginia preachers to their brief flirtation with self-imposed ordination during the war were still very much in evidence. The Methodist movement had emerged from the Revolution with a goodly number of fervent members, especially in Maryland and Virginia. Nevertheless, the lack of clergy was a constant problem and the consequent absence of a vibrant sacramental life became even more acute with the passing years. Francis Asbury made a tour of Virginia in 1784. He was entertained by Devereux Jarratt and found the people in his area "very attentive," but in the central Piedmont there was "poor encouragement for religion" while the inhabitants of the Eastern Shore were "blind in spiritual matters."[17] In addition to the obvious religious decline, there was constant competition from other proselytes. One Methodist preacher noted with horror that some of his flock were attending the meetings of dissenters, while another blamed the "dead weight" of the Baptists and their subtle efforts "to steal away the members."[18]

From the other end of the religious spectrum, the Methodist preachers were exposed to ridicule and criticism. They had never been accepted with any grace by most of the Anglican clergy, and

[16]Sheild to Griffith, Dec. 20, 1784, David Griffith Papers, VHS.

[17]Clark, *Journal of Asbury* 1: 458-59, 470; Emory Stevens Bucke, ed., *The History of American Methodism* (New York, 1964), 1: 196.

[18]Dromgoole Journal, July 10, 1784 and Charles Pettigrew to Edward Dromgoole, Sept. 22, 1784, Edward Dromgoole Papers, microfilm, So. Hist. Coll., UNC.

the rationalist element in the church tended to lump them with the Baptists. One paper carried an article in the summer of 1784 which labeled them as "illiterate zealots" who had abandoned their proper work to engage in a career for which they possessed neither aptitude nor training. This critic offered his reflections in the form of verse:

> Every *mechanic* will commence
> Orator, without *mood* or *tense*;
> *Pudding* is *pudding* still, they know,
> Whether it has a plum or no;
> So, tho' the preacher has no skill,
> A *sermon* is a *sermon* still.[19]

Beset by attacks from the right and erosion on the left, the Methodist preachers met in conference at Baltimore during Christmas 1784. There the appeal to John Wesley which Asbury had promised four years before was returned in the person of Dr. Thomas Coke. An Englishman and a minister of the Church of England, Coke had also been ordained by Wesley the previous September to serve as superintendent for the American Methodists. He now presented himself to the preachers with letters from their British leader, explaining his decision to ordain Coke together with instructions for setting up the liturgy and polity of the new religious body. During the ten days of the meeting, the preachers elected Asbury to serve as joint superintendent with Coke.[20] Although the decision to establish the Methodists as a separate denomination was approved by a majority of the almost sixty preachers present at the meeting, not all the participants concurred. Some thought the action precipitous and questioned Wesley's judgment. After all, he had erred in opposing the American Revolution. One preacher, Thomas Haskins, suggested that the decision be deferred until June and that during the intervening months the Methodist leaders, "as generous & Dutiful Sons of the Episcopal Church to Whom We have from time to time

---

[19] *Va. Gaz., or the American Advertizer,* May 29, 1784.

[20] For a study of this meeting, see N. C. Hughes, Jr., "The Methodist Christmas Conference: Baltimore, Dec. 24, 1784–Jan. 2, 1785," *Maryland Historical Magazine* 54 (1959): 272-92.

publicly professed ourselves to be United," confer with that church's clergy to see if some sort of accommodation could be reached. Haskins's proposal was rejected, and he left the conference fearing for the future of Methodism.[21] His concern was to prove misplaced. The Methodist church would grow to become one of the dominant religious bodies in the new nation. But the effect of the schism on the Episcopal church in Virginia was profound. In one fell swoop its brightest promise of renewal had been lost.

Several months later, in the course of a sermon delivered in Baltimore, Coke offered his apologia for the rupture. The Church of England, he informed his hearers, had become corrupted during the colonial period by an unholy alliance with the state as well as by the link with an English hierarchy manipulated by political interests. As a result of the Revolution, the bonds of spiritual slavery had been struck off and the "hirelings" among the clergy driven from their pulpits. Considering the lack of ministers, God had raised up "sufficient resources in ourselves"; and the time had come to evoke them. To the declaration that the Methodists had placed themselves in schism, he retorted that the majority of Episcopalians were in heresy. They had denied basic doctrines including *"Justification by Faith, the Knowledge of Salvation by the Remission of Sins, and the Witness of the Spirit of God."* In the moral sphere, they justified "as innocent, many of the criminal pleasures of the world,—Card-playing, dancing, theatrical amusements &c.—pleasure utterly inconsistent with union & communion with *God*. And though we admire their *Liturgy* and are determined to *retain* it with a few alterations,—we can not, *we will not* hold connection with them till the *Holy Spirit of God* has made them *see* & *feel*, the evil of their practices, and the importance of doctrines mentioned before."[22]

The Episcopalian most affected by the decision of the Methodists to establish a separate religious body was Devereux Jarratt. Late in the spring of 1785 he wrote one of their preachers a letter

---

[21]Thomas Haskins's Journal, Dec. 22, Dec. 24, 1784, Jan. 1, 1785, LC.

[22]Thomas Coke's Sermon, Mar. 1, 1785, Methodist Church Papers, Duke University Library, Durham, N.C.

filled with bitterness and resentment over the treatment he had received from his erstwhile friends. Jarratt had not been asked to attend the Christmas conference, nor had his invitations to Asbury and Coke to visit him during their trips through Virginia been acknowledged. Although Asbury had been a close associate, he traveled into the Tidewater region that March and even administered the sacraments at one of the churches in James Madison's parish without calling on Jarratt. For one whose "peculiar Attachment" had been the Methodists, the rejection was a cruel and undeserved blow.[23] It must have been all the more difficult to accept since he had met a similar reception from his own brethren in the Episcopal church when he attended the May Convention in Richmond. There he encountered "such a shyness and coldness" from the other clergy that he left the meeting only two hours after it had begun.[24]

In accordance with the notice calling the Convention, the clerical and lay delegates had assembled in the capital on May 18. The interest generated by the proposed meeting was evidenced by the presence of representatives from sixty-nine parishes in forty-eight counties and the town of Williamsburg. Although each parish was entitled to send its minister together with one layman appointed by the vestry, the lay delegates outnumbered the clerics almost two to one. Moreover, despite the presence of ministerial leadership in the persons of Griffith, Madison, and Sheild, the laymen far exceeded the clerical representatives in public stature. Men such as John Tyler, Edmund Randolph, Carter Braxton, and John Page dominated the assemblage. At least fifteen of the members had been in the House of Delegates during the preceding session, while others were state senators, judges, and wealthy plantation owners. The clergy were hopelessly outclassed.[25]

Nevertheless, perhaps in deference to the nature of the convocation, the Convention elected one of the ministers, James Madison,

[23]Jarratt to Dromgoole, May 31, 1785, Dromgoole Papers, microfilm, So. Hist. Coll., UNC. For Asbury's activities, see Clark, *Journal of Asbury* 1: 488.

[24]Jarratt, *Life*, p. 132.

[25]*Journal of a Convention of the Clergy and Laity of the Protestant Episcopal Church of Virginia, Begun and Holden in the City of Richmond, Wednesday, May 18, 1785*, pp. 3-4, rept. in Hawks, *Contributions*, I, app. A total of 71 laymen and 36

as its presiding officer. At the same time it adopted the standing rules of the House of Delegates as its mode of procedure. The opening days of the meeting were relatively peaceful as the delegates determined to publish an address to the church membership and to send representatives to the General Convention which would meet in Philadelphia in September. However, these Virginians were extremely wary of what might be determined by their northern brethren and, at the outset, resolved that their representatives would operate under instructions which would leave the Virginia Convention free "to approve or disapprove of the proceedings" of the gathering in Pennsylvania. While accepting the obvious need for unity among American Episcopalians, they were apprehensive lest control over the Virginia church slip from their grasp. In addition, the Convention took exception to two of the principles proposed at the New York meeting the previous October.

The issue of changes in the doctrine and liturgy of the church produced the major divisions in the Richmond gathering. The clerical delegation generally supported the fourth article of the New York meeting, which stated that the church should retain the doctrine and worship of the Church of England except in those particular instances which clearly violated the new political situation in the United States. Sheild had written earlier to Griffith warmly endorsing this article. "Innovations," he noted, "whether in Politics or Religion have an Aspect peculiarly terrifying to me." He feared that an "innovating Spirit" lured on by the "Charm of Novelty" would wreak havoc on the church. While it was perfectly acceptable to revise those aspects of theology and liturgy which might be "erroneous or unscriptural," all too often a vain display of "critical Talents" led men to carp "at Trifles & make a grammatical Inaccuracy or some such small Matter a Pretence for altering a Form of Prayer which had been established for Ages." Should the church engage in wholesale changes and repudiate the principle laid down by the New York meeting, Sheild believed that the result would be "an irregular, disjointed mungrel kind of Body,

clergy attended the meeting. Of the 15 laymen who had served in the House during the 1784 sessions, almost all had been strong supporters of the assessment and incorporation bills.

not easy to be defined, nor understood,—a Sect divided & subdivided into a Number of Sects, & consequently the Subject of Reproach & Contempt to her Enemies, & of probably Neglect & Disesteem with those of the like Profession, who shall emigrate from other Countries."[26]

There were others at the Convention like Edmund Randolph and John Page, however, who had come to reform the church in precisely those areas where Sheild and the conservatives wished to retain the traditions of the past. Their preoccupation with internal changes dominated the business of the Convention and left little time for the consideration of broader measures, such as the assessment proposal, which would have affected the church as a whole. Randolph was the more liberal of the two lay leaders, having inherited some of the deistical tendencies of his father. Later, under the influence of his wife, Elizabeth Nicholas Randolph, he became a communicant of the church. But in 1784 he had opposed the assessment and sided with Madison, though as attorney general of the state he was not a member of the legislature.[27] Page had also missed the last session while serving on the Maryland-Virginia boundary commission, but he warmly supported the assessment bill. Although a boon companion of Jefferson since their college days together, he had maintained a staunch affinity for the church throughout the vicissitudes of the Revolution. He was so well read in theology that at one time it was suggested he take orders as a preparation for assuming the position of bishop. Page had come to the Convention filled with enthusiasm and fully conscious of his position as *"an Elder of the Church."* Writing to St. George Tucker shortly before the meeting, Page urged him to

[26]Sheild to Griffith, Dec. 20, 1784, David Griffith Papers, VHS. While the majority of the clergy agreed with the position of Sheild, there were exceptions. In this same letter, Sheild noted that "at our last Meeting" (i.e., most probably the clergy meeting in June 1784) some had opted for more sweeping changes. Rev. James Madison may have been in this camp, as his speech to the 1786 Convention indicated an eagerness for the liberal position (Madison, *A Sermon Preached before the Convention of the Protestant Episcopal Church in the State of Virginia, on the Twenty Sixth of May, 1786* [Richmond, 1786]).

[27]Moncure D. Conway, *Omitted Chapters of History Disclosed in the Life and Papers of Edmund Randolph* (New York, 1888), pp. 156-57, 164.

join the "great work" of restoring religion to its "primitive Purity." He looked upon the Convention to inaugurate a "Golden Age" of religion in the world, and for him the work began by cleaning out the dross collected over the centuries.[28]

With the liberal reform segment dominating the discussions, the Convention voted down the conservative clergy and resolved on certain changes in the liturgy and doctrine of the church, some of them rather antitrinitarian in tone. In addition to minor deletions in the services for worship, the Nicene and Athanasian creeds were to be omitted in the future, together with the words "descended into hell" from the Apostles' Creed. The majority also decided to eliminate the rubric which authorized the minister to refuse communion to persons he judged unworthy of receiving the sacrament. Page informed his less theologically conversant hearers that this peculiar practice "derived from popish Artifice" and that it belonged only to the "Searcher of Hearts" to sit in judgment upon men.[29] With such erudition sweeping all before it, the liberals brushed aside the caveats of the clergy and drafted instructions to the delegates who would attend the Philadelphia General Convention to support these changes. Page and Griffith were among those elected to attend the meeting.

The other principle of the New York meeting to which the Virginia Convention took exception pertained to the manner of voting in the General Convention. It stated that although clerical and lay deputies would deliberate together, they would vote as separate bodies, and the two would have to concur in order to pass a measure. But the lay leadership in the commonwealth had dominated the church for too many years to permit the clergy this potential veto over their decisions, and they went on record as opposed to a separation into two houses. Accustomed to command in civil life, it was only too natural that the laity would judge themselves equally competent in matters of religion. William Paca, governor of Maryland, had succinctly expressed their sentiments a few years before: "The Clergy may *assemble* and *propose,*

[28]Page to Tucker, May 7, 1785, Tucker-Coleman Papers, Swem Lib., College of William and Mary. See also Meade, *Old Churches* 1: 148.

[29]Notebook of John Page, Swem Lib., College of William and Mary.

but the Laity must *adopt* or *consent*."[30] This determination to
have effective lay control was reflected in the canons for church
government adopted on the last day of the Convention. Drawing
on the secular model of the House of Delegates, the Convention
like a council was to hold supreme power in the church. On the
parish level, the vestries were given authority to hire and fire the
minister. The bishop, when there was one, would serve as the
regular minister of a parish, and his episcopal functions were
specifically limited to the administration of confirmation and
ordination and a triennial visitation of each parish. Moreover, he
was to be "amenable to the Convention." In concluding their
meeting, the delegates appointed a standing committee to provide
general administration and communication during the interval
before the next Convention. Also, they were to investigate the
possibility of "obtaining consecration for a bishop."[31]

As a testimonial of its work, the Convention approved an
address to the members of the church. In essence, it reviewed the
difficulties under which the church had labored since the beginning of the Revolution and asked their support. At the same time,
it also pointed to the desirability of some form of union with
other Christian churches. "It is our duty," the address stated, "to
be ready to unite upon principles consistent with the gospel, and
bring the Christian Church to unity." This ecumenical thrust was
present in other resolutions and instructions approved by the
Convention. Page had written earlier of his hope that the meeting
would eliminate "everything not essential to the support of
genuine Christianity," so that "all Sects of Christians may be
heartily reconciled to one another."[32] The representatives at the
Convention had obviously attempted to respond to this goal. How-

[30]Paca to General Joseph Reed, Sept. 12, 1783, typescript in Miscellaneous Letters,
Protestant Episcopal Church in U.S.A., Virginia (Diocese) Papers, 1760-1972, VHS.

[31]*Journal of a Convention, 1785*, pp. 8-11. For a review and critique of these
canons, see Brydon, *Virginia's Mother Church* 2: 457-61. He stated: "in the final
analysis, it was these canons which wrecked the Church in Virginia and brought it to
destruction within twenty-five years" (ibid., 2: 460).

[32]*Journal of a Convention, 1785*, p. 8; Page to Tucker, May 7, 1785, Tucker-
Coleman Papers, Swem Lib., College of William and Mary. For adverse comments on the
Convention, see RP, 1786-87, passim.

ever, to the non-Episcopalian observer, the subtle style of the Convention itself spoke more eloquently than the words of its address. The capitol had served as its meeting place, and the governor, his council, and the court justices had been invited to participate in the deliberations. No clearer signs needed to be given that this group of men considered themselves to represent not merely one Christian church within a pluralistic society but the dominant religious body in Virginia.

The reaction to the Convention was not slow in coming. One angry Presbyterian bystander, Archibald Stuart, wrote that "such a set of Bungling thick skulled fat Bellied Disciples of Christ" had never before come together in one place.[33] In August, Jefferson was informed by a Richmond correspondent that the other religious groups, outraged by the "preference" shown the Episcopalians, were busily engaged in publishing articles against them and circulating petitions to repeal the incorporation act.[34] As another commentator cynically remarked, though the members of the old establishment might invite other churches to join in Christian unity, there was little possibility of that occurring. The proclivity for religious warfare dominated their relationships, and "the nearer they approach, the more inveterate is their animosity."[35] Apparently oblivious to the hostility which their meeting had aroused, the members left Richmond pleased with their work. Pendleton wrote Richard Henry Lee that he had learned that "the members were truly respectable, and their proceedings wise and temperate." Page boasted to Jefferson: "we were liberal, and I think we shall reform this episcopal Church so as to make it truly respectable."[36]

Indeed, the delegates to the Convention had shown much more interest in making the church "respectable" than in rendering it solvent. Among the list of woes in their formal address to the membership, they had included the lack of monetary resources. Moreover, they had begged their fellow Episcopalians "to co-

[33]Stuart to John Breckinridge, May 25, 1785, Breckinridge Family Papers, LC.

[34]Boyd, *Papers of Jefferson* 8: 343.

[35]William Nelson, Jr., to William Short, July 17, 1785, William Short Papers, LC.

[36]Mays, *Papers of Pendleton* 2: 480; Boyd, *Papers of Jefferson* 8: 428.

operate fervently in the cause of our church." What that cooperation involved, however, was never explicitly stated. There was no
mention of voluntary subscriptions and no direct financial appeal.
Most significant of all, the address contained not one word about
the assessment.[37] Although a number of delegates were known
supporters of the bill, there were significant exceptions, such as
Spencer Roane and Edmund Randolph. Other laymen at the
Convention, being shrewd politicians, were doubtless aware of the
shifting weight of public opinion. Even before the meeting,
Madison remarked on the waning enthusiasm for the measure on
the part of some Episcopalians. Finally, the tremendous opposition to the bill being mustered by the Presbyterians and Baptists
was becoming apparent, and some delegates may have feared that
an endorsement of the assessment would rouse even more antagonism toward their church. The internal divisions over the advisability of the assessment as well as a reluctance to make themselves
the target of the dissenters' collective wrath may well have been
the dominant factors which kept the members of the Convention
from issuing any statement on the proposed bill.[38]

If the fight for the assessment was to be carried on, it would
have to be done on the local level through parish or county petitions. In addition, individuals would have to attempt to persuade
members of the political "establishment" of the need for the bill.
With this mission in mind, John Page wrote to Thomas Jefferson.
Despite the fact that the Convention had made no mention of the
bill, Page's letter is ample witness that the proposed tax was pre-
eminently a measure to support the Episcopal church. Pointing to
the suffering endured by that religious body during the Revolution
and its loyalty to the cause despite the destruction of the establishment it had enjoyed, Page concluded: "Such disinterestedness

---

[37]*Journal of a Convention,* 1785, p. 8. William Nelson, Jr., in his letter to William
Short of July 17, 1785, stated that the Convention's address included a declaration on
the "propriety of aid from government, for the support of religion" (William Short
Papers, LC). But this was not in the address itself, and Nelson's remarks may have been
based on other (unlocated) data or his own instinctive distrust of the church's activities.

[38]Rutland, *Papers of Madison* 8: 261. Of the 12 members of the Convention who
served in the 1785 session of the House, 3 would vote in favor, 4 against, and 5 abstain
on Jefferson's bill for religious freedom (*JHD,* Dec. 19, 1785, p. 96).

entitles them to Respect, and the Liberality of their religious Sentiments is such, as is sufficient to make any one of a Liberal way of thinking lament that this sect is declining daily; whilst some others the most bigotted and illiberal are gaining ground."[39] He explained to Jefferson that some clergymen were giving up the ministry to feed their families while others who remained at their posts were close to starvation. The choice was clear: if the assessment bill did not pass, then religion would collapse and the commonwealth would be "divided between immorality, and Enthusiastic Bigottry."

Although Page did not mention it in his letter, he and the other members of the Episcopal Convention had witnessed one such "enthusiastic" spectacle. In the course of their meetings, a fanatic "with a stern Countenance & the Boldness of a Saint" marched into the assemblage and declared to the startled members: "In the name of God hear ye the Voice of the Lord, Cease from Oppressing the hand of the Lord . . . he will strip you even as I strip off my Coat." Whereupon the man ripped off his coat, cut off the buttons, and threw the pile down "as a testimony" against them. He then rode off undisturbed on a horse. "I am told he's a man of Property," Archibald Stuart concluded at the end of his recital of the event.[40] For men like Page this kind of affair undoubtedly indicated a dangerous future for religion in Virginia. He pointed out that a trial of voluntary support had been made for the past eight years but had proved unsuccessful and forced the preacher to coddle his congregation if he wished to eat. Outraged by the campaign against the assessment by the press and the use of Jefferson's name and opinions by its foes, Page clung to the rumor that his friend had changed his mind. His hopes were not realized.

Another member of the Convention, Edmund Randolph, was far less sanguine about its work than Page. In the middle of July he sent Madison a copy of the proceedings of the meeting, dedicating it to him, sarcastically, "as a patron of the protestant Episcopal church." Randolph had been disappointed by the Convention, and he doubted that he would attend another. Most probably referring

---

[39] Boyd, *Papers of Jefferson* 8: 428.

[40] Stuart to John Breckinridge, May 25, 1785, Breckinridge Family Papers, LC.

to the clergy, he added: "We have squeezed out a little liberality from them; but at a future day they will be harder than adament, and perhaps credulous, that they possess authority." In reply, Madison pointed out that the Convention's proceedings offered "fresh and forcible arguments against the General Assessment" and enclosed a draft of his memorial against the bill. He had composed it, he noted, at the instigation of "Col. Nicholas of Albemarle."[41]

In the early months of 1785 Madison had thought it better to confine his opposition to the assessment to private correspondence, but he had been eventually dissuaded from this course through the efforts of the Nicholas brothers. Wilson Cary Nicholas had been a leader of the antiassessment forces during the previous session, despite the fact that it was only his first term in the legislature. His election in the spring of 1784 had been attributed to the fact that he had visited the home of every freeholder in Albemarle County. Upon hearing of his victory at the polls, his mother, Anne Cary Nicholas, the sister of Wilson Miles Cary, wrote her congratulations and added a piece of motherly advice. She expressed her hope that he had won freely without binding himself by political promises and "especially that You have not engaged to lend a last hand to pulling down the Church." An "impertinent" newspaper article had informed her that something of that sort was intended, and she implored him: "Never my dear Wilson, let me hear that, by that sacreligious act, You have furnished Yourself with materials to erect a scaffold by which you may climb to the summit of popularity."[42] Nicholas would indeed climb to the upper reaches of political office, and his unwavering support of the bill for religious freedom would give him a major boost. Politically and religiously, he was much more the son of Thomas Jefferson than Robert Carter Nicholas.

His older brother, George Nicholas, shared his views. Wilson Cary had attempted to persuade Madison to enter the contest against the assessment; when his efforts were unsuccessful, he

---

[41] Rutland, *Papers of Madison* 8: 324, 327-28.

[42] Anne Nicholas to Wilson Cary Nicholas, (?) 12, 1784, photocopy in Wilson Cary Nicholas Papers, VHS; see also George Nicholas, "Memoir of Wilson Cary Nicholas," VHS.

turned to his brother to intercede. Writing to Madison in April 1785, the older Nicholas urged him to become involved in a solicitation of the counties. He feared that the silence of the opposition to the assessment would assure its passage. He also pointed to the political realities involved: "A majority of the counties are in favor of the measure but . . . a great majority of the people are against it; but if this majority should not appear by petition the fact will be denied. . . . If you think with me that it will be proper to say something to the Assembly, will you commit it to paper?"[43] Madison agreed and during the next few months composed his "Memorial and Remonstrance," a long statement which in fifteen points reviewed the major arguments against the assessment.[44]

The memorial opened with the statement that if the proposed bill should pass into law, it would be a "dangerous abuse of power." This was the underlying theme, but it picked up various nuances as Madison shifted back and forth, utilizing the different rationalist and pietist objections to the assessment. The philosophical line of attack was his mainstay, and he introduced and concluded the memorial on the note of natural rights and the effect which the assessment bill would have on them. To a great extent, his reasoning in this section was closely related to and probably dependent upon the thought of John Locke as formulated in his *Two Treatises of Government* and the classic *Letter on Toleration*. Introducing his argumentation with an appeal to the sixteenth article of the Declaration of Rights, Madison pointed out that religion had an essentially private note. It depended for its direction on the conscience of the individual. Moreover, man's right to judge in this matter, to direct his own conscience upon the path he deemed proper, was a natural right.

Locke had set up the hypothesis of a natural state in which men existed before entering into civil society. In that condition all were free and equal, each man possessing certain rights: life, liberty (including conscience), and property. All of this was directed by reason, a law of nature; and reason taught men "that being all

[43]Rutland, *Papers of Madison* 8: 264.

[44]Ibid., 8: 295-306.

equal and independent, no one ought to harm another in his Life, Health, Liberty, or Possessions."[45] But, since the state of nature was insufficient to ensure adequately the preservation of these rights, men entered into political society by their own free consent. They did not give up their natural rights; rather, by means of a social contract, each man entered into a society with civil government, handing over his legislative and executive functions in order to preserve his rights in the best possible way. Nevertheless, these rights remained his own possession, nor could they be given up without enslavement. So Locke argued and Madison concurred.

One of the most fundamental of these natural rights was that of conscience, which included religious belief. Madison reasoned that one's religion depended entirely on personal opinion; as such, it was totally the result of personal viewpoint, which should not be coerced or directed by any other man. Nor could it be handed over to another human being, because on an even more basic level its direction belonged to God. There was a correlation operative here: what was a right for man was a duty toward God. This responsibility to God was prior both in time and importance to any obligation which man might have toward civil society or the creature of that society, the civil government. Therefore, religion did not come within the jurisdiction or scope of either society or the legislature. This remained true even though the will of the majority might dictate a religious establishment. In this case the majority would be wrong; it would have become oppressive of a minority and be acting in violation of that group's rights. Furthermore, if the civil government enacted laws for matters of conscience, it might justly be considered a tyrant. Those who were forced to obey such laws became slaves. Madison pointed out that such intrusions into the rights of men must be guarded against at the outset. If the legislature could act in this case, the precedent would be set. It now proposed an establishment of Christianity to the exclusion of all other religions. Would the next step, perhaps, be an attempt to establish this or that particular variety of Christianity, "in exclusion of all other Sects?"

[45]John Locke, *Two Treatises on Government*, ed. Peter Laslett (London, 1967), p. 289.

Man's original state, as Madison again followed Locke, was one of equality with other men. When he entered into a civil society, he gave up only the same powers as his fellows. All men therefore remained on a fundamental level of equality. Consequently, Madison argued that just as the man who chose to believe in God and belong to a religious body exercised his right, so also the same kind of choice belonged to a man who did not believe in God, who was an atheist. The decisions of both men were beyond the power of government; and reprobation, if there was to be any, belonged to God, not men. In this important respect, Madison parted company with Locke. The English theorist had reasoned that freedom of belief could not be extended to nonbelievers. He based this judgment on the idea that the integrity of a society depended upon the trustworthiness of oaths and promises made in the sight of God. The atheist, by removing God from the scene of human endeavor, "dissolves all."[46] The advocates of the assessment had used precisely this argument in pointing out that without the bill, religion in Virginia would collapse. With its downfall, the bonds of trust which made society possible would also dissolve.[47] Madison did not refute this argument. His memorial simply affirmed the right of the man who had no religion to remain in civil society with his rights intact.

However, in pursuit of his argument, Madison ignored the actual text of the proposed bill by implying that nonbelievers would be forced to contribute to religion. He also chose to overlook the polity of the Quaker and Mennonite churches by stating that the bill would violate the equality of all denominations by giving these societies a freedom it denied to the others. The assessment had been carefully drafted to permit those who preferred to support education rather than religion to do so. It also provided for the special situation of the Quakers and Mennonites, who had no formal clergy or body of elders. While asserting that the rights of atheists were ignored by the bill, Madison charged that these religious groups were being granted "extraordinary privileges"

[46]John Locke, *Epistolia de Tolerantia: A Letter on Toleration*, ed. Raymond Klibansky and J. W. Gough (Oxford, 1968), pp. 131-35.

[47]For example, see RP, Nov. 12, 1784 (Presbyterian petition).

which would enable them to proselytize among the other denominations. Here the raw political nature of the memorial becomes most evident, for the author misinterpreted both the terms of the bill and the reality of the religious polity of these groups to press home his argument. What Madison did not misjudge was the opportunity to capitalize on the competition among the churches.

Although the argument from natural rights was most persuasive to the rationalist mind, Madison was careful not to limit his memorial to those grounds alone. Many who might not be able to comprehend or identify with that line of reasoning would be capable of viewing the assessment as an inherent attack upon their own concept of Christianity and the voluntary nature of the church. Consequently, he pointed out that the measure would be a positive harm to the religion instituted by Christ. To employ it in the service of the state was "an unhallowed perversion of the means of salvation." Moreover, Christianity did not need the support of civil government. Reiterating a position consistently maintained by the Baptists for over a decade, he insisted that compulsion was not needed in the cause of Christ. To imply otherwise was to cast doubt on the divine origin and efficacy of the Gospel which Jesus had proclaimed. It was also to miss the lesson of history which proved that ecclesiastical establishments had never assisted the development of pure religion. In addition, the assessment would harm Christianity by hindering the spirit of cooperation and friendship among the churches and would reverse the spirit of toleration so promising in the present age. Finally, it would obstruct the missionary work among nonbelievers by encouraging them to remain out of a state where religion had been established.

Just as the churches did not need state aid in order to survive or achieve their goals, so also civil government did not require the support of an establishment. As Madison reviewed the course of world events, those institutions had in fact injured governments in ages past, either by subjecting civil authority to church control or by assisting the government to tyrannize the people. Moreover, at this point in the development of the state, it would seriously hinder the work of civil authority. First of all, it would make Virginia a less attractive place in which to settle. Instead of increasing the population, the assessment would discourage many from coming into a state where religion was supported by public taxation; and those who dissented from the bill would be motivated to leave the commonwealth for other, freer climes. Most important of all, the proposed bill would serve to discredit the government it was designed to support. This kind of a law required the overwhelming approval of the population, but such was not the case with the assessment. Consequently, the passage of a measure repugnant to the consciences of so many people would have the effect of weakening respect for law in general and thus make the task of government that much more difficult.

Throughout the memorial there is the basic presupposition that the church was a purely voluntary organization outside the sphere or concern of civil government. Only once did Madison imply that there might be some possible relationship between the churches and the state. The state, he noted, had the obligation to protect every citizen in the exercise of his religion, allowing all religious groups to operate freely and preventing any group from injuring or invading the rights of another. That was the limit of the church-state relationship for Madison then and for the rest of his life.[48]

In concluding his memorial, Madison returned once again to the theory of natural rights. In the final analysis, all of the liberties of the people rested upon the same ground. If one was attacked, Madison pointed out, then all of the others were placed in jeopardy. Invoking the solidarity of the rights of man, he ended with an appeal to the "Supreme Lawgiver of the Universe" to illumine the legislature and guide its decisions.

Madison's "Memorial and Remonstrance" was a virtuoso performance, a brilliant display of his command over both the religious and rationalist arguments against a church-state connection as well as his skill in the art of political persuasion. Although he did not wish his authorship to be generally known, Madison was justifiably pleased with his composition. By the end of June it

---

[48] For Madison's later views on the actual situation of the church-state relationship in the United States after his presidency, see Elizabeth Fleet, ed., "Madison's 'Detached Memoranda,'" *William and Mary Quarterly*, 3d ser., 3 (1946): 554-68. For a summary article, see Irving Brant, "Madison: On the Separation of Church and State," ibid., 3d ser., 8 (1951): 3-24.

was already in circulation, and two months later he informed Jefferson that "the opposition to the assessment gains ground. . . . [The remonstrance] will be pretty extensively signed."[49]

George Nicholas was equally satisfied with the finished product and assumed the responsibility for having the memorial distributed in the counties of the central Piedmont and across the Blue Ridge.[50] Meanwhile in the Northern Neck, George Mason had copies printed and then circulated them to his neighbors in Fairfax County, including George Washington. Washington replied to Mason's request that he subscribe with a statement displaying not only his sentiments about the assessment but also his political acuity:

> Altho' no mans Sentiments are more opposed to *any kind* of restraint upon religious principles than mine are; yet I must confess, that I am not amongst the number of those who are so much alarmed at the thoughts of making People pay toward the support of that which they profess, if of the denominations of Christians; or declare themselves Jews, Mahomitans, or otherwise, and thereby obtain proper relief.—As the matter now stands, I wish an assessment had never been agitated—and as it has gone so far, that the bill could die an easy death; because I think it will be productive of more quiet to the State, than by enacting it into a Law; which, in my opinion, would be impolitic, admitting there is a decided majority for it, to the disgust of a respectable minority.— In the first case the matter will soon subside;—in the latter it will rankle, and perhaps convulse the State.[51]

For Washington the feelings of the population spoke more eloquently than the arguments of the rationalists.

Madison and his friends were not working alone that summer. As he had reported to Jefferson in late April, the assessment issue produced "some fermentation below the Mountains and a violent

[49] Boyd, *Papers of Jefferson* 8: 415. Madison was careful to keep his authorship a secret (see Rutland, *Papers of Madison* 8: 328; Rutland, *Papers of Mason* 2: 830-32).

[50] Rutland, *Papers of Madison* 8: 264-65, 316.

[51] Rutland, *Papers of Mason* 2: 832. However, neither Mason nor Washington signed the Fairfax County petition against the assessment. For Washington's views on religious freedom, see Paul F. Buller, Jr., "George Washington and Religious Liberty," *William and Mary Quarterly*, 3d ser., 17 (1960): 486-506.

one beyond them." Over on the west side of the Blue Ridge the Hanover Presbytery had assembled and felt the impact of the reaction there. While the Episcopalians deliberated in Richmond in May, the Presbyterian leaders gathered at Bethel Church in the Valley. After John Smith reported on his activities at the fall session of the Assembly, the ministers and elders received a petition from the Augusta congregation, demanding an explanation of their last memorial. Specifically, the Presbytery was asked to clarify the meaning of the term "*Liberal*" as well as their "Motives and end" in sending the petition to the legislature. In the vote which followed, the Presbyterian leaders went on record as "unanimously" opposed to an assessment.[52]

Why this sudden reversal? Madison claimed that "*fear of their laity or a jealousy of the episcopalians*" motivated their response. Certainly the average Presbyterian layman did not want an assessment. The bulk of the laity came from Scotch-Irish settlers who had emigrated to the New World at least partly because of a desire for religious freedom. After settling the western counties of Virginia, they had practiced their faith in relative freedom and watched their prospects for complete equality grow with the Revolution. From the beginning they had supported their church by voluntary subscriptions. In a church structure dominated by the ministers in presbytery, financial supervision was the principal vehicle ensuring a measure of lay control. Now the assessment bill threatened to reverse the progress toward absolute religious freedom and, in the words of one religious petition, "render the ministry independent of the people."[53]

An equally crucial consideration for the Presbytery may well have been the prospective rejuvenation of the church which had dominated the religious life of Virginia before the Revolution. The act of incorporation confirming the Protestant Episcopal Church in its real property and authorizing it to manage its own affairs stung Presbyterian sensibilities. While the former establishment

[52]Boyd, *Papers of Jefferson* 8: 113; Minutes of Hanover Presbytery, May 19, 1785.

[53]Boyd, *Papers of Jefferson* 8: 415 (italics indicate cipher): *RP*, Dec. 1, 1785. Examples of Presbyterian subscription lists may be found in Tinkling Springs Church, Augusta County, Records, 1741-93, passim, photostat, VSL, and Foote, *Sketches of Virginia*, pp. 97-98.

had languished during the war years, animosity toward it had also softened; but when signs of life returned, the latent hostilities of its opponents once again surfaced. Jefferson had shrewdly forecast this development. After learning of the Episcopal clergy's petition for incorporation in 1784, he wrote Madison that he was "glad the *Episcopalians* have again shown their teeth and fangs. The *dissenters* have almost forgotten them." Privately, Madison also rejoiced over the *"jealousy"* and "mutual hatred" between Episcopalians and Presbyterians evoked by the incorporation act. *"I am far from being sorry for it,"* he informed Jefferson, "as *a coalition between them* could *alone endanger our religious rights* and a tendency to *such an event had been suspected."* Now even John Blair Smith deserted the assessment cause and, "with a temper well-roused," prepared to battle the legislature over the incorporation act."[54]

But the Presbytery's simple resolution against the proposed bill was insufficient. Evidently observers were present to make sure that proper action was taken, for another motion was made and this time "several Members of different Congregations" were included in the vote. All those attending now agreed that "a General Convention of the Presbyterian body was expedient in our present Circumstances." The press later announced that each congregation was requested to send one representative "with full powers in writing to act in the name of the . . . Church."[55]

This extraordinary meeting opened on August 10 at Bethel Church with Jefferson's old friend, John Todd, serving as chairman; and three days later the convention approved a lengthy petition to the Assembly which rejected the assessment as "unnecessary," "impolitic," and "a direct violation of the Declaration of Rights." Gone from this memorial was any mention of the support which religion was supposed to provide the state. Instead it attacked the assessment's preference for Christianity as a prelude to the reestablishment of a state church and pointed out that by certain terms of the incorporation act the Assembly had already begun to favor the Episcopalians "at the expense of the other

[54]Boyd, *Papers of Jefferson* 7: 558, 8: 415 (italics indicate cipher); Rutland, *Papers of Madison* 8: 325.

[55]Minutes of Hanover Presbytery, May 19, 1785; *Va. Gaz., or the American Advertizer,* June 4, 1785.

Denominations." In legislating the polity of that church, the delegates had exercised an unjustifiable "Supremacy in Spirituals," transformed the Episcopal church into the "Church of the State," and granted it a "preeminence over others." Madison's strategy in the last Assembly session again proved successful, for the Presbyterians read the assessment proposal as a veiled attempt on the part of the legislature to further assist the Episcopal church, an intention already manifested by the terms of the incorporation act. Here was the crucial issue: the revival of religious inequities against which the Presbyterians had consistently struggled since the beginning of the Revolution. The convention now asked the Assembly to reject the assessment bill and repeal the "exceptionable parts" of the act of incorporation. Finally, for the first time in the history of their religious memorials, the Presbyterians requested the passage of Jefferson's bill establishing religious freedom.[56]

While the Presbyterians held their convention, the General Committee of the various Baptist associations met in Powhatan County. Like the other religious groups, the Baptists had been affected by the general decline of religious spirit. "God sent them liberty," one early Baptist historian noted, "and with it, leanness of soul."[57] At Broad Run Church in Fauquier County, for example, there had not been a single baptism since 1783. Two years later the church's clerk despondently recorded that "the Lord's Supper has not been celebrated among us, for several years past. Nor has a preached Gospel been attended with any apparent success. . . . It is winter! No wonder the birds are not heard to sing."[58] But waning fervor and declining congregations did not alter Baptist opposition to any form of governmental intervention in religious affairs. Although their memorials to the legislature in 1784 had not mentioned the assessment, their reaction to the proposed bill the following year made it clear that their position on the church-state relationship had not changed since the begin-

[56]RP, Nov. 2, 1785. The text of this petition may have been drafted by William Graham (Sellers, "John Blair Smith," p. 214).

[57]Semple, *Rise of the Baptists in Virginia,* p. 35.

[58]Broad Run Baptist Church, Fauquier County, Records, 1762-83, April 23, 1785, p. 19, photostat, VSL.

ning of the Revolution. During the late spring and early summer of
1785, various petitions were approved by local congregations, and
when the General Committee met in August, the delegates drafted
a tough memorial to the Assembly roundly condemning the
proposed bill.

In forceful evangelical terms, the Baptist leaders denounced the
assessment as an attack on the purity and spiritual nature of the
church. Compulsory contributions would assist neither the church
nor the state. The clergy as the "Voluntary Servants of the
Church" would be best supported by each congregation as the
members should judge appropriate. Moreover, the legislature had
no authority to interject itself in this or any other area of spiritual
ministry. To do so was ultimately to jeopardize the entire fabric
of religious freedom. However, the delegates took note of one
area in which the government might take action. In a pregnant
statement foreshadowing the moral and sabbatarian legislation of
the following century, the Baptist committee pointed out that the
Assembly's contribution to Christianity could best be expressed
by "supporting those Laws of Morality, which are necessary for
Private and Public Happiness." Here, finally, the government
might fulfill its role as the "Guardian" of the people.[59]

The committee's memorial to the legislature did not mention
the incorporation act, and perhaps for this reason the Orange
Baptist Association drafted its own memorial the following month.
In a series of resolutions, it objected to the proposed assessment
as "opening the door to religious Tyranny" and added that the
act incorporating the Protestant Episcopal Church was "inconsistent with american Freedom" and ought to be repealed. Finally, in
what would become the dominant issue in church-state relations
for the next fifteen years, it demanded that the property of the
once established church, since it had been acquired "at the
common expense," should be "devoted to the use of the publick
at large."[60]

---

[59] RP, Nov. 3, 1785. For evidence that religious petitions were already in circulation
before the General Committee met, see Black Creek Church (Baptist), Southampton
County, Records, 1776-1804, May 10, 1785, p. 8, photostat, and Mill Swamp Baptist
Church, Isle of Wight County, Records, 1779-90, June 17, 1785, p. 17, photostat, VSL.

[60] RP, Nov. 17, 1785. This memorial was dated Sept. 17, 1785.

While the opponents of the assessment met in conventions and committees, drafted memorials to the legislature, and circulated petitions against the bill, the advocates of the measure fought back in the public press. One of the Richmond newspapers carried a two-part article in August entitled: "On the IMPORTANCE and NECESSITY of RELIGION to CIVIL SOCIETY." After pointing out that this once commonly held judgment was now in dispute, the anonymous author argued from an analysis of human nature that reason, "benevolence and public spirit," and the offices of civil government were all insufficient by themselves to promote the good order and happiness of society. They required the assistance of religion. Reason alone would never lead a man to yield his own private interests for the common good of society. There was needed belief in God, who made *"self love and social be* finally *the same."* Although reason, if properly followed, would direct men to faith in a supreme being, all too often it stopped short of that conclusion, and then its dictates became "uncertain and precarious." In the same way, "benevolence and public spirit," while they might be of great value, also had opposing tendencies perhaps even more active, and hence were unsatisfactory by themselves. Finally, civil government had always depended for its own success upon religion and in the nature of things must continue to do so. For the bonds of society and trust among men depended upon the veracity of oaths made to God and a belief in divine sanctions. He summarized his position: "In short without *religion* 'tis hard to say what foundation there could be for any such mutual *trust* and *confidence* among men as is necessary for the support of government, the very being of society."[61]

However, religious belief and the public acknowledgment of God had an obviously beneficial effect on the moral order and the relationships among men in society. With these characteristics, "society becomes practicable, and government a blessing." Moreover, Christianity possessed a definite superiority and guided men to nourish and develop their own rational powers, their sense of benevolence, and the offices of the state. Since, therefore, religion was so essential to the well-being of society, the civil magistrates

[61] *Va. Gaz. and Weekly Advertizer,* Aug. 6, 1785.

and all responsible leaders should be expected to encourage and support it. Nor was the personal aspect of religion sufficient; it needed public expression not only for its own maintenance but also to build the common basis of confidence and trust among men. Believing in and worshiping the same God would make men cognizant of the fact that they were all operating under the same general principles. Consequently, the government should be concerned to provide a "competent provision" for those who had devoted their lives to the promotion of religious belief and the inculcation of moral values. The author concluded his essay with a parting shot at those who considered reason sufficient in itself, insisting that instruction and guidance would always be needed from "a standing order of preachers, such as we have hitherto enjoyed."[62]

In a very different style, the same newspaper later that month carried a satirical dialogue between a Presbyterian and a Baptist, thinly disguised as "Mr. Observer Calvinisticus" and "Mr. Timothy Whitfieldensis." Both parties were mocked. "Are you not alarmed at seeing the Episcopal Church once more rearing its head amongst us?" Calvinisticus asked. The Baptist was more concerned about acquiring the church property. "But do you not think," he replied, "we could contrive to take their glebes and churches from them, and enjoy them ourselves." He could hardly manage to get a word in, however, as the Presbyterian monopolized the conversation. In a patronizing fashion, he explained to the ignorant Baptist his foolproof plan to trick the people into opposing the incorporation and assessment bills as well as the legislature which had proposed them. However, avarice finally gained the upper hand, and the two parted as enemies when the Baptist realized that the Presbyterian would not object "to get the glebes and the churches, or to be established either."[63]

This biting satire was perhaps the cleverest piece of writing to emerge from the propaganda war that year, but by the time of its

---

[62]Ibid., Aug. 13, 1785.

[63]Ibid., Aug. 20, 1785. John Calvin was the major influence on John Knox, the founder of Scottish Presbyterianism. George Whitefield, though an Anglican minister, was the leading proponent of the Great Awakening in America, which was identified

publication the battle for the assessment was virtually lost. As spring turned into summer, and summer into early autumn, the opponents of the measure became increasingly confident that the bill would be defeated when the legislature met. In his "Memorial and Remonstrance," Madison had contributed a brilliant statement on behalf of religious liberty. Yet to contemporary observers, the work of the evangelicals and particularly the Presbyterians appeared ever more decisive for the outcome; and these religious groups demanded that the principle of voluntary church support be maintained. "Religion will form a capital figure in the debates of the next assembly," Edmund Randolph informed Arthur Lee in late September. "The Presbyterians will have a sufficient force to prevent the general assessment, & possibly to repeal the act of incorporation."[64] The Episcopalians' efforts to reorganize their church and the cooperation they had received from the legislature had only heightened the antagonism of the former dissenters. On the eve of the session, a Richmond correspondent wrote Jefferson: "The Other Religionists are damned mad at the Establishment and Anathematise the Assembly, and their Elect which they attempt to prove are not those of God."[65] As the legislators arrived in the capital, the assessment bill was apparently a dead issue. What would replace it in the discussions over the relationship of church and state in Virginia remained to be seen.

---

with the rise of the Baptists. At the end of this dialogue, the author stated that the following week there would be an account of a meeting between "Calvinisticus" and an "honest Quaker." However, this issue of the newspaper, Aug. 27, 1785, has not been located.

[64]Randolph to Lee, Sept. 24, 1785, Lee Family Papers, microfilm, U.Va. Lib., Charlottesville.

[65]Boyd, *Papers of Jefferson* 8:641.

Chapter Five

Establishing Religious
Freedom, 1786–1787

"WE SHALL never have monasteries...at least in Virginia,"
William Nelson, Jr., happily informed William Short in April
1786.[1] Though his prediction would one day prove incorrect,
Nelson thus enthusiastically greeted the passage of Jefferson's
bill for religious freedom. In the space of a year, the Assembly
had reversed directions and approved legislation which was the
antithesis of the assessment proposal.

Autumn colors still laced the woods surrounding Richmond as
the delegates drifted into the capital for the single session of 1785.
Although the Assembly was scheduled to convene on Monday,
October 17, another week passed before sufficient members were
present to call the House to order. At the opening meeting,
Benjamin Harrison narrowly defeated his archrival, John Tyler, in
a bitter contest for the Speaker's chair; and the following day the
former governor appointed the committees to manage the session's
business.[2] As chairman of the committee for religion, Harrison
selected Zachariah Johnston. The choice of this rock-ribbed Presbyterian was graphic evidence of the capitulation to the antiassessment forces.[3] The political necessity of such a move became

[1] April 8, 1786, William Short Papers, LC.

[2] *JHD*, Oct. 24, 1785, p. 4. Tyler and Harrison were engaged in a vendetta arising out
of the spring elections in which Harrison held Tyler responsible for his defeat in
Charles City County. He subsequently crossed the James River and was elected from
Surry. During the second week of the session Harrison barely survived a challenge to his
seat on the grounds of residency by a vote of 57 to 49 (ibid., Nov. 3, 1785; Mays, *Letters
of Pendleton* 2: 279; Boyd, *Papers of Jefferson* 8: 641-42, 9: 194). Madison and Carter
Braxton were also considered potential candidates for the position of Speaker, but
neither was nominated (William Nelson, Jr., to William Short, Oct. 16, 1785, William
Short Papers, LC; Boyd, *Papers of Jefferson* 8: 642, 645).

[3] *JHD*, Oct. 25, 1785. Of the other members appointed to the committee, five had
been strong supporters and five strong opponents of the assessment and incorporation

obvious during the next month and a half as an unprecedented tidal wave of religious petitions engulfed the Assembly.

Of the more than one hundred memorials which swamped the legislative table that session, only eleven supported the proposed assessment. These came from ten counties located principally in the lower region of the Northern Neck and the Southside (see Map 2).[4] Most of these petitions were relatively brief and undramatic compositions which commended the legislature for proposing the bill and urged its enactment. With more or less detail, they rehearsed the standard arguments in favor of governmental support for religion. On the basis of history and human experience, they asserted, mankind had learned the importance of religion to the well-being of society. Indeed, as one petition pointed out, a belief in God and the practice of religion had always been considered "the most solid Basis of Private and public Virtue . . . at every Period of Time and in every Corner of the Globe." They had helped to suppress immorality, exterminate vice, and restrain the twin evils of "Enthusiasm and Superstition."[5] Religion, at least the right kind of religion, was therefore necessarily linked to the peace and prosperity of civil governments.

Governments in turn had traditionally recognized the importance of religious observance and acted to preserve and strengthen it. The assessment bill, drawn up by a legislature obviously moved by "Divine Influence," ensured the continuation of this relationship between church and state without infringing upon either the civil or religious liberties of the people. The proposed assessment instituted no establishment. Instead it was both just and impartial, providing a nonpreferential system which would benefit all members of society without coercing them in matters of conscience.

---

bills introduced into the 1784 session. However, in 1785 the overwhelming majority of the committees, including these members, endorsed Jefferson's bill.

[4]A total of 101 petitions were submitted that fall on the assessment issue. All but 3 are available in RP, and these 3 are listed in *JHD*. This count of the petitions lists identical petitions received on the same day from the same county as a single petition. All other petitions are counted separately, including those from the Presbyterian supporters and those in support of the "Memorial and Remonstrance" by James Madison.

[5]RP, Surry County, Nov. 14, 1785. In citing petitions for this chapter, the county from which each came will be given either in the text or in the notes, since so many petitions were received on the same dates.

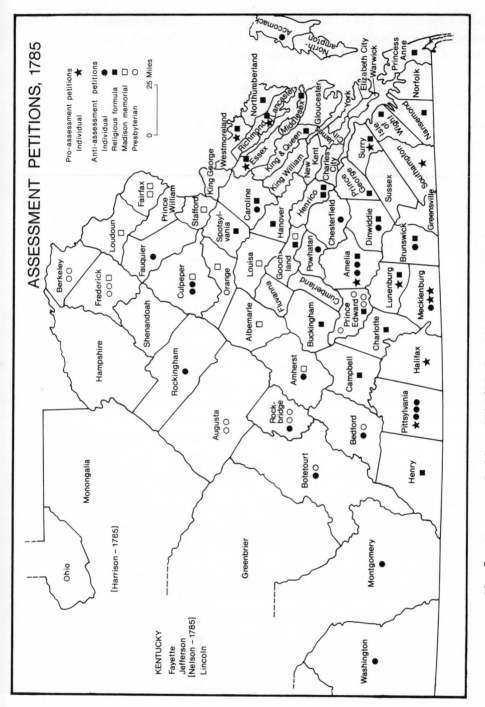

Map 2   Assessment Petitions, 1785 (RP, October-December 1785)

Further, it relieved the hardships and inequities of the voluntary method of support which had been tried and found ineffectual. More specifically, the proposed bill would offer a reasonable encouragement for competent candidates to undertake the academic preparation requisite for a ministerial career. They could proceed with a sure expectation that the time spent in studies would gain for them "a Decent and Respectable Rank in life."[6]

The proassessment petitions were calm, logical, even dispassionate documents. If their wording at times betrays a tinge of elitism, it also reflects the viewpoint of men who wished to live in a society ordered and organized by traditional values. The total list of signatures on these memorials numbered just over a thousand. In ordinary years, this would have been considered an impressive display of strength, but in 1785, for every man who signed a petition in favor of the bill, twelve others subscribed to a memorial against it.

The ninety petitions opposing the assessment came from virtually every county of the state with the exception of the lower Tidewater and the extreme West. These petitions can be divided into four distinct groups. The first of these, comprising thirteen identical memorials with approximately seventeen hundred signatures, followed Madison's remonstrance; and the primary agents for their circulation had been George Nicholas and George Mason. When urging Madison to compose the memorial in April, Nicholas had optimistically promised to give it extensive publicity throughout the central, southern, and western areas of the state. However, the longhand versions which he and his friends most probably copied were eventually submitted from only six counties in the central Piedmont.[7] In the meantime, Mason had the remonstrance printed and distributed through the Northern Neck, and these broadsides were sent to the legislature from four counties in this region.[8]

[6]Ibid., Mecklenburg County, Oct. 26, 1785, Essex County, Nov. 2, 1785.

[7]Rutland, *Papers of Madison* 8: 264-65, 316-17. These counties were Orange, Amherst, Albemarle, Culpeper, Louisa, and Goochland. In addition, one other handwritten memorial was submitted without any indication of the county.

[8]Rutland, *Papers of Mason* 2: 830-33. These counties were Loudoun, Fairfax, Stafford, and Frederick.

A second group of petitions, equally well subscribed, came directly from religious bodies of Baptists, Presbyterians, and Quakers. The Baptist and Presbyterian memorials have been discussed earlier; and the latter, drawn up on August 25 by the convention at Bethel Church, was subsequently endorsed by twenty-one other petitions from local congregations of Presbyterians in Prince Edward County and throughout the Valley.[9] The Quakers also submitted a memorial signed by four hundred of "Your real Friends" protesting against the assessment. They stated that the proposal was based upon principles repugnant to their view of Christianity. Since "Christian knowledge" was not dependent upon human assistance or mediation but came directly from Christ himself, there was no need to make "Provisions for learned Teachers." The Quakers acknowledged the intended "favour" of the legislature in writing special provisions into the proposed bill for the benefit of their particular polity; yet to them the measure was "an Infringement of Religious and Civil Liberty Established by the Bill of Rights."[10]

The most numerous series of petitions submitted that fall, however, came neither from recognized religious groups nor from Madison's supporters. The largest subscription went to a formula petition, drawn up by an unknown author and widely circulated through most of the central and southern sections of Virginia. Briefly summarized, this set of almost identical petitions opposed the assessment on the grounds that it was "contrary to the Spirit of the Gospel, and the Bill of Rights." The former clearly held priority in their consideration. Appealing to the practice of Christ and the early church and reciting the subsequent lurid history of Christianity beginning with the patronage of Constantine, this formula argued that the current decline in religious practice and the simultaneous growth of deism was due to other causes than the removal of religious establishments. Moreover, this could be solved by enacting laws against vice and immorality, their vigorous enforcement by conscientious government officials, and a con-

[9]RP, Nov. 18, 1785. Most of them were submitted on this date. Those which are themselves dated indicate they circulated between Aug. 25 and Sept. 14, 1785.

[10]Ibid., Nov. 14, 1785.

verted ministry living upright lives and teaching sound doctrine based on the scriptures. An assessment, on the other hand, would harm the progress of religion by encouraging a hireling clergy intent only on temporal profit. As the example of Pennsylvania proved, there was no need to link religion and government in order to preserve the state; and to do so in Virginia would furthermore be a violation of the Declaration of Rights.[11]

The chief significance of this petition rests in its commitment to the advancement of Christianity. The maintenance of government and the legal requirements of the Declaration of Rights hold second place in the argument. The men who signed such petitions were neither rationalists nor indifferent to the progress of organized religion. Rather, they were evangelical Christians believing deeply in the principle of voluntary support. A wide gap existed between these advocates of voluntarism and the supporters of the assessment; but an even greater distance, though perhaps unrecognized at the time, separated both of these groups from those who embraced the principles of Madison and Jefferson.[12]

The fourth group of antiassessment petitions were the most varied of the lot. Composed by different individuals or groups in counties from the Eastern Shore to the extreme southwestern corner of the state, they also represented an equally broad spectrum of thought. From Montgomery County, for example, came a petition written by John Breckinridge and signed by some three hundred freeholders. In tones reminiscent of his patron, James Madison, he argued that although good morals were part of the object of government, civil laws were insufficient to ensure them. It was not possible, Breckinridge wrote, for the legislature to "seize the Principle of Religion in Man," and it was "inconsistent with natural right" to attempt to do so. Government should

[11]Ibid., Goochland County, Nov. 2, 1785. This formula petition also came in a shorter version.

[12]This "formula" and those modeled upon it may well have been the work of the Baptists. It reflects their thought, especially with regard to the ministry; and Semple speaks of a formula drawn up by the General Committee which was to circulate among the counties (*Rise of the Baptists in Virginia,* p. 71). Lohrenz, "Virginia Clergy," pp. 349-50, states that the Baptists drew up a number of petitions which were usually written out and signed by one of their preachers.

rather confine itself to those areas of society pertaining to "the Public Welfare" and leave religion and civil regulations "forever distinct."[13]

Other petitions, primarily from the western counties, echoed this insistence on the separate natures of religion and government. The object of the latter, one proclaimed, was the "Proper Regulation of the External conduct of men towards each other," while religion was directed toward "our internal or spiritual welfare and is beyond the reach of human laws."[14] A Rockbridge petition insisted that the powers of the legislators had been delegated to them by the people only to make those laws which would "promote the happiness of Society." This did not extend to the regulation or control of religious matters, which should not be made "the Object of Human Legislation."[15] Still another memorial pointed out that "civil policy . . . can never make us christians, neither can christianity be benefitted by the Laws of the commonwealth, but only by the constitutions of Christ."[16]

Although most of the independent petitions agreed with Breckinridge's views on the separate natures of civil and religious jurisdictions, few subscribed to his further statement that the advancement of religion would be secure when "unbiased and unprejudiced Reason" was given "full Scope." Many of these memorials displayed a more than perfunctory interest in the future of the Christian Gospel. As in the formula petitions, the requirements of a truly zealous and disinterested ministry were repeatedly urged as major arguments against the assessment. Compulsive support would raise up "a lazy, indolent Clergy," independent of the people and unconcerned for their spiritual needs. Although it was true that a shortage of ministers existed now due to the dislocations of the Revolution, this could eventually be remedied. In the meantime,

[13]RP, Nov. 15, 1785. This petition is in Breckinridge's handwriting. He had been defeated in his bid for reelection to the Assembly, a fact lamented by Madison (Archibald Stuart to Breckinridge, Oct. 24, 1785, Breckinridge Family Papers, LC).

[14]RP, Botetourt County, Nov. 29, 1785.

[15]Ibid., Nov. 2, 1785.

[16]Ibid., Washington County, Dec. 10, 1785.

Virginia was well rid of those "Hirelings who got into the Priest's Office Merely out of Temporal Motives."[17]

Another frequently voiced complaint against the proposed bill was directed at the Harrison amendment which limited the provisions to those professing Christianity. Seizing upon this restriction as a violation of the toleration granted by the Declaration of Rights, many of the petitions voiced a deeper fear of the direction this sort of legislation might eventually take. The assessment was but a "Stepping Stone to an Establishment . . . a Snake in the Grass," which would ultimately result in extensive governmental regulation of both churches and ministry, turning the legislators into "judges of Heresy and kindling Smithfield Fires in America."[18] There should be no room for "Compulsion" in matters of religion, another petition insisted.[19] The whole business smacked of a dangerous precedent to our liberties. Should the principle be established now, it might eventually be used to prefer one church over another. The government which today can require a man to pay a certain sum to his own religious society, might tomorrow force all to contribute to the same religious society.[20] For many who protested against the proposed assessment, the implications of the bill were more serious than the text itself.

Others saw it as a ploy to save the tottering Episcopal church or viewed the Assembly as desiring to play the role of "Elders and Governors of the Churches."[21] It would be more appropriate, another writer suggested, if the legislators themselves inaugurated the reform of society by restraining their financial extravagances and doing away with moral evils such as "open Barrels of Liquid fire, at the Elections." Thus he implored the assemblymen to "be no longer Votaries to Bacchus, nor Sing the Song of frantic Mirth,

[17]Ibid., Fauquier County, Nov. 29, 1785.

[18]Ibid., Amelia County, Nov. ?, 1785. An identical petition was submitted from Accomack County, Oct. 28, 1785.

[19]Ibid., Brunswick County, Nov. 28, 1785.

[20]Ibid., Amherst County, Dec. 10, 1785, Bedford County, Oct. 27, 1785.

[21]Ibid., Amelia County, Nov. ?, 1785.

but Te deum." In the same vein, he charged that the assessment would also be totally ineffectual in achieving the goal of restoring religion in the state. After all, it would surely not change the deists: "Will the Deist come to hear preaching? How then are they to be Converted? The Learned Minister is paid to overthrow Deism by preaching to thirty honest professors, and the Deist many miles from church [is] laughing in his Sleeve or toping at a tavern. . . . How many Deists have the Orthodox Clergy converted Lately?"[22]

In fact, the orthodox clergy in the person of their most prominent representative, David Griffith, had been engaged during the fall in precisely that task. As delegates from the Protestant Episcopal Church in Virginia, he and John Page attended the General Convention meeting in Philadelphia. There Page's proposal to eliminate the first section from the litanies and replace them with a vague prayer of his own composition was "warmly opposed" by Griffith, who stated that if this change was approved, "the Convention would be called Deists or Socinians at least." Page eventually withdrew his amendment, but not before he took time to expose Griffith's "hasty & irrational Objections."[23]

That two men so different in outlook on theological questions should have represented the church in Virginia is ample witness to the internal divisions manifested not only over doctrine and liturgy but also in their response to the church-state issues that year. Fundamentally, the Episcopal church had no response. Despite the obvious benefit they would reap from an assessment bill and the fact that the shortage of ministers was growing more critical each year, the Episcopalians both in and out of the Assembly held no common positions. Their May Convention had taken no stand, and only one petition supporting the assessment was received from an Episcopalian congregation that fall. In the following year, when the movement to repeal the incorporation act threatened their structure and property, local congregations would galvanize for political action, but in 1785, alone among the major religious bodies in Virginia, the Episcopal church was mute.[24]

[22]Ibid., Amelia County, Nov. 9, 1785.

[23]Notebook of John Page, Swem Library, College of William and Mary.

[24]That year Robert Andrews, a member of the faculty at William and Mary and rector of York-Hampton Parish (York County) left the ministry, and at least two other

Madison was euphoric. As he noted in his report to Jefferson at the close of the session, "The steps taken throughout the Country to defeat the General Assessment had produced all the effect that could have been wished."[25] Even had the memorials been less overwhelming in their opposition, it is likely that the critical economic and financial conditions would have at least postponed the assessment bill that fall. As it turned out, that situation helped finish it off.

At work were a complicated set of closely related problems. With the conclusion of the Revolution, Virginia had experienced a brief surge of prosperity, brought on primarily by the repeal of trade restrictions with Great Britain. While the price of tobacco, the chief staple commodity, remained at a high level, reasonably good conditions prevailed. During this boomlet, however, the seeds of future disaster were planted as the demands for imports from both foreign countries and northern states created a tremendous drain on the available hard currency. Archibald Stuart told Jefferson that "Extravagance and dissipation had seized all Ranks of People," and that his fellow citizens were foolishly bringing into the state even those goods which might be grown or produced in Virginia.[26] By February 1785 one westerner complained that "all our money as fast as we get it, goes to the eastward";[27] and from the East it flowed out, mainly to British creditors. The pattern of chronic indebtedness, the curse of Virginia planters throughout the period before the Revolution, now reasserted itself as a pattern of

---

parishes, Elizabeth City (Elizabeth City County) and Hanover (King George County) fell vacant (Boyd, *Papers of Jefferson* 8: 428; *Va. Gaz. and Weekly Advertizer,* May 28, 1785 ; *Va. Gaz. and American Advertizer,* Sept. 10, 1785).

The single Episcopal petition was from Southampton County (RP, Dec. 10, 1785).

[25] Rutland, *Papers of Madison* 8: 473.

[26] Boyd, *Papers of Jefferson* 8: 645. The most thorough treatment of the economic and financial problems of Virginia during this period may be found in Louis Maganzin, "Economic Depression in Maryland and Virginia, 1783-1787" (Ph.D. diss., Georgetown University, 1967). Also useful are Alan Schaffer, "Virginia's 'Critical Period,' " in *The Old Dominion: Essays for Thomas Perkins Abernathy,* ed. Darrett B. Rutman (Charlottesville, 1964), and Myra Lakoff Rich, "The Experimental Years: Virginia, 1781-1789" (Ph.D. diss., Yale University, 1966), pp. 205-11. For a summary of these problems as affecting political groups in the legislature, see Main, *Political Parties before the Constitution,* pp. 250-55.

[27] Arthur Campbell to Robert Preston, Feb. 7, 1785, Robert Preston Papers, VHS.

life. When the price of tobacco faltered in the summer of 1785 and then plummeted throughout the fall and winter, the economic situation reached critical proportions.[28]

Simultaneously it became virtually impossible to collect taxes. Even during the short-lived prosperity, complaints about the high taxes had remained prevalent. Richard Henry Lee told Madison in November 1784 that he believed the collective taxes paid by Virginians amounted "in the aggregate to a heavier taxation than prevails in any other part of the world!"[29] With the rate of taxation, the state of indebtedness increased. One Tidewater planter informed his British factor: "Our taxes are high and urgent, and probably I shall draw on you for about £200 before long."[30] Sensitive to the burdens placed on the voters, the legislature in May 1784 delayed the collection of taxes for that year until the following January, and then in the fall session cut the tax for 1785 in half.[31] Nevertheless, one recent arrival wrote an Irish correspondent in the spring of 1785 that the taxes appeared to increase and "lie heavy upon Men of property." He had heard Virginians boast that their state was "the Richest," but from those who had moved about the other areas of the new nation he had learned that it was "esteemed the Poorest," except perhaps in furniture and horseflesh.[32] The former, it should be noted, was imported.

When the price of tobacco collapsed in the fall, even the half tax of 1785 was postponed by the Assembly.[33] In connection with their protest against the assessment, several of the petitions urged the legislature to turn down the proposal on the grounds of

[28]In Richmond the price of tobacco in the spring of 1785 was about 36 shillings; during the summer it dropped to 30, then to 24 shillings by the end of December (Thomas Rutherfoord to Messrs. Hawsley and Rutherfoord, Aug. 16, Nov. 12, Dec. 26, 1785, Thomas Rutherfoord Letterbook, VHS). Rutherfoord also commented on the serious decline of trade and lack of currency.

[29]Rutland, *Papers of Madison* 8: 145. John Francis Mercer, another congressman that year, agreed: "We pay greater Taxes than any people under the Sun" (ibid., 8: 135).

[30]Robert Beverley to Samuel Gest, Nov. 25, 1784, Robert Beverley Letterbook, LC.

[31]Hening, *Statutes at Large* 11: 368-69, 540-41.

[32]John Joyce to Robert Dickson, Mar. 25, 1785, *Virginia Magazine of History and Biography* 23 (1915): 441.

[33]Hening, *Statutes at Large* 12: 93-96.

the excessive taxes already laid on the populace. A memorial from Brunswick County pointed out: "our Taxes already are equal to the Abilities of the People in general." From Amelia County the plea was more hysterical in tone: "The people are borne down with Taxes, Have Mercy!" An assessment for religious teachers would be "very oppressive," yet another memorial complained, "as we are Burdened already equal to our Strength."[34] When the delegates met in October, there was serious discussion of printing paper money, and a bill eliminating the tax entirely for that year was proposed and almost passed during the session.[35] Reflecting upon the economic and financial difficulties besetting Virginia, one historian of the period concluded that an added tax "for any purpose, religious or political," would have been an impossibility.[36]

Within this social, economic, and political framework, the ideal moment had arrived for Madison to introduce Jefferson's bill for establishing religious liberty. He also was presented with a perfect occasion. Not only had Hanover Presbytery expressly petitioned for its passage, but it was also a part of the revision of the laws to be considered by the Assembly that fall. This revisal, the cooperative work of Jefferson, Pendleton, and Wythe, had originally been presented to the House in the May session of 1779. It had been largely ignored then, and little was achieved during the remainder of the war years. From time to time individual bills were singled out and passed, but the main body of the work remained untouched. When the Revolution had been completed and peace achieved, Madison had been instrumental in having the Assembly authorize the printing of five hundred copies of the revisal. Now, in his position as chairman of the committee on the courts of justice, he presented over one hundred bills for the consideration

---

[34] RP, Nov. 28, 1785, Nov. 9, 1785, and Pittsylvania County, Nov. 7, 1785. Another petition against taxes in general was published in the *Va. Gaz. and Weekly Advertizer*, Nov. 5, 1785.

[35] Rutland, *Papers of Madison* 8: 477-78. For the "clamor for paper money," see Edmund Randolph to Arthur Lee, Sept. 24, 1784, Lee Family Papers, microfilm, U.Va. Lib.

[36] Hugh Blair Grigsby, *The History of the Virginia Federal Convention of 1788* (rept. New York, 1970), 2: 127.

of the House. Bill number 82 was the crucial measure on religious freedom.[37]

At the outset the revisal met with far greater acceptance than Madison had expected. Throughout November the work sped along in orderly fashion, and the young legislator was clearly in command of the situation. "He has astonished mankind," Archibald Stuart reported, "and has by means perfectly constitutional become almost a Dictator."[38] Within the space of six weeks, the delegates had moved through almost half of the code, despite the regular motions offered by the opposition to cut off further consideration until another session. Then in early December the scene abruptly changed. More and more objections were raised concerning the amount of time devoted to the revisal, until an irritated Madison told Washington: "We . . . might by this time have been at the end of it had the time wasted in disputing whether it could be finished at this Session been spent in forwarding the work."[39]

All along the major opponents to the revisal had been Speaker Harrison, whose enmity Madison had earned, and Charles Mynn Thruston, the onetime "Fighting Parson" from Frederick County.[40] Late in the session a new force joined them in the person of John Francis Mercer, who had been chosen by a special election to replace the recently deceased William Brent of Stafford County. Though despised by Jefferson, who had served with him in Congress and thought that "Vanity and ambition" were his "ruling passions," Mercer was a talented, well-connected young

[37]*JHD*, Oct. 31, 1785, pp. 12-14. The Hanover Presbytery had asked that "full Equality in all things, & ample Protection & Security to Religious Liberty" be given by adopting Jefferson's bill (RP, Nov. 3, 1785). For background on the revisal, see Boyd, *Papers of Jefferson* 2: 305-24. For the 1784 activity and Madison's resolution for the printing of the code, see Rutland, *Papers of Madison* 8: 47-49, 94.

[38]Stuart to John Breckinridge, Dec. 7, 1785, Breckinridge Family Papers, LC. Madison noted his own surprise at the initial ease of his labors in a letter to Jefferson (Rutland, *Papers of Madison* 8: 473).

[39]Rutland, *Papers of Madison* 8:439.

[40]Ibid., 8: 473. In light of his subsequent problem with Harrison, it was perhaps unwise that Madison had voted to unseat him on the residency issue in early November (*JHD*, Nov. 3, 1785, pp. 21-22).

man with a long and successful political career before him.[41]
When he joined the House he impressed Madison with his "unceas-
ing hostility" toward the revisal and appears to have made a major
contribution toward preventing further consideration of the project.[42]

Faced with this growing opposition, Madison gave up hope for
an orderly completion of the code and determined to jump ahead
to a few bills which he considered of major importance. He picked
out the religious liberty bill and presented it to the House on
December 14. The measure was debated in the Committee of the
Whole on the following day. There was, as Madison soon informed
Monroe, "warm opposition" to the proposal, especially from
Mercer and Francis Corbin.[43] The son of the king's receiver
general before the Revolution, Corbin came from one of the most
prominent families in Virginia. A young man like Mercer—they
were both only twenty-six years old—he was serving his second
term in the House, and as a devout Episcopalian, Corbin had
strongly espoused the assessment in the preceding session.[44]

It may well have been Mercer or Corbin, or even perhaps
Speaker Harrison, who proposed during the debate in the Committee of the Whole that Jefferson's preamble be slightly modified.
Where the text stated that coercion in matters of religion was "a
departure from the plan of the holy author of our religion," the
amendment suggested that the "holy author" be specified by
including the words "Jesus Christ." Madison later claimed that the
purpose behind this move was an attempt "to imply a restriction

---

[41]Rutland, *Papers of Madison* 8: 473; Boyd, *Papers of Jefferson* 7: 119, 228. Before
this time, Madison appears to have been on friendly terms with Mercer (see, for example,
Rutland, *Papers of Madison* 8:239).

[42]Rutland, *Papers of Madison* 8: 437.

[43]Ibid., 8: 446; *JHD*, Dec. 14-15, 1785, pp. 92, 95. This view of serious opposition
to the bill is corroborated by Henry Fry, a delegate from Culpeper County and a staunch
Methodist, in his autobiography. Fry gave a detailed account of his attendance at this
session, but unfortunately most of it concerns his attempt to reform his fellow delegates
(Philip Slaughter, *Memoir of Col. Joshua Fry . . . with an Autobiography of His Son,
Rev. Henry Fry, and a Census of Their Descendants* [Richmond, 1880], p. 102).

[44]Francis Corbin, "The Corbin Family," *Virginia Magazine of History and Biography*
30 (1922): 315-18.

of the liberty defined in the Bill, to those professing his religion only."[45] That particular proposal was handily defeated, while another amendment, probably a very minor one, was approved by both the Committee of the Whole and by the House itself the following day.[46] Then, on the floor of the House, the opposition moved that the preamble be struck out entirely and the sixteenth article of the Declaration of Rights substituted in its place. This motion failed by a vote of 38 to 66, and the bill was ordered to be engrossed and receive a final reading.[47]

On the very next day, in a last-ditch effort to forestall the momentum of the bill, the opponents attempted to utilize the same tactics which Madison had enlisted the previous year against

[45]Jefferson reported this attempted amendment in his autobiography (Ford, *Writings of Jefferson* 1: 71). Madison did also, though in slightly different terms (Fleet, "Madison's 'Detached Memoranda,'" p. 556). From the context of both the preamble and the amendment, Jefferson's version seems the more accurate. However, both are in agreement as to the intention of the amendment. Jefferson wrote: "the insertion was rejected by a great majority, in proof that they meant to comprehend, within the mantle of it's protection, the Jew and the Gentile, the Christian and Mahometan, the Hindoo, and infidel of every denomination." However, both Madison and Jefferson were recalling this amendment after a long lapse of time. It is in no way mentioned in their correspondence, nor was it reported by others. Therefore, they may have been incorrect in attributing this intention to the proposers of the amendment, since it is not readily apparent how, in fact, the inclusion of these words would have in any way affected the latitude of the enabling clause. Finally, neither Madison nor Jefferson stated at what time or place in the course of debate this amendment was proposed. It seems likely that it would have come up in the Committee of the Whole since matters of this sort could be proposed and turned down without being recorded in the *Journal*. If it had been proposed on the floor of the House, there would have been a record of it.

With regard to the fate of the assessment bill, all of the petitions pertaining to this issue had been referred to the Committee of the Whole, but there is no record in the *Journal* that this issue was even discussed by that body or on the floor of the House. Grigsby, *Virginia Convention of 1788* 1: 124, suggested that it may have been proposed in the Committee of the Whole as an amendment to the bill for religious liberty. He based this possibility on a statement in Foote (*Sketches of Virginia*, p. 431) that the assessment bill was taken up by that committee, attacked by John Blair Smith, and then defeated by a margin of three votes. However, if this event did take place, it was not mentioned in the *Journal* or in any contemporary accounts. In addition, the substantial margins given to Jefferson's bill on each vote make Foote's statement even more dubious.

[46]*JHD*, Dec. 15-16, 1785, pp. 94-95. Madison told Jefferson at the end of the session that the bill had originally passed the House "without alteration," so this amendment must have been inconsequential (Rutland, *Papers of Madison* 8: 474).

[47]*JHD*, Dec. 16, 1785, p. 95.

the assessment. However, their motion to postpone further consideration of the bill until the next session was defeated. The engrossed bill was now taken up and passed by the lopsided majority of 74 to 20. The opposition had not yielded; it had collapsed. With many of the strongest supporters of the assessment either abstaining or absent from the House that day, the remnant who held firm for the establishment ideal was reduced to a pittance. Even Carter Braxton reversed himself and voted for the measure. However, it was not a simple matter of eastern versus western voting patterns. Counties solidly identified with the Tidewater interest were for the bill, while occasionally delegates from the West either opposed or stayed neutral on the measure (see Map 3). For Madison it must have been a heady triumph. In four days he had swept the House for Jefferson's bill. The problems were far from over, however, as the bill now went to the Senate.[48]

While the delegates waited for the upper house to consider the bill, they completed action on a measure which had been before them since the opening of the session. The Episcopal church had been released by the incorporation act of 1784 to attend to its own affairs and elect new vestrymen for church business. Nothing had been decided, however, concerning the secular functions of the vestry. Several of the religious petitions of 1785 took issue with this anomalous situation. An Essex County memorial had pointed out that the end of the old vestry system had left "the distressed part of our fellow Creatures . . . Destitute," while another petition from Amherst County requested that the legislators "make Provision for the Poor" since the vestries were now concerned only with the Episcopal church.[49] In early November, therefore, a bill was introduced "to provide for the poor of the several counties within the Commonwealth," but after its first two readings and subsequent referral to the Committee of the Whole, the matter was apparently left in abeyance.[50]

The committee had also received a bill in the revisal of the laws which pertained to this matter. Eventually the whole business was

[48]Ibid., Dec. 17, 1785, p. 96.

[49]RP, Nov. 2, Dec. 10, 1785.

[50]*JHD*, Nov. 3-4, 1785, pp. 21-22.

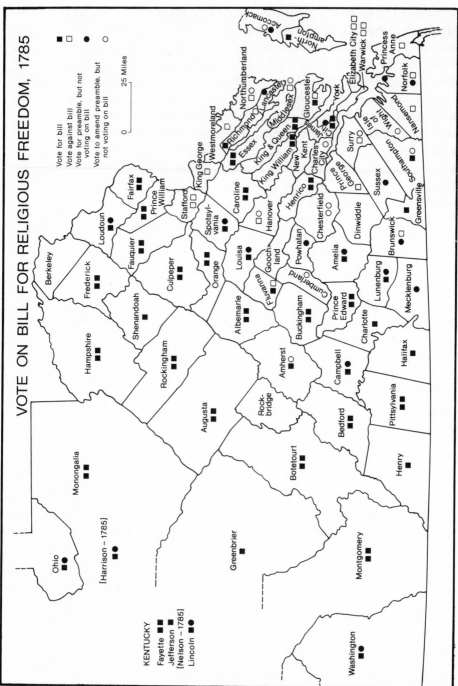

Map 3   Vote on Jefferson's Bill for Religious Freedom in the House of Delegates, 1785 (*JHD*, 1785)

handed over to a specially chosen committee which reported back to the House. Its work was accepted and passed by that body on December 23. Several days after the Christmas holiday, the Senate and House settled the question of a few amendments and the bill became law. Briefly, this legislation extended the system of over-seers of the poor which was already prevalent in the western region to all the counties of Virginia and transferred to them all of the secular functions which the vestries had previously held.[51] Thus a major link between church and state was formally dissolved, and the Episcopal vestries were transformed into purely ecclesiastical bodies.

While action on this bill was being completed, the delegates were informed that the Senate had passed an amendment to the bill for religious freedom. Although, as a purely revisory body, the upper house of the Assembly was extremely limited in its legisla-tive responsibilities, it could amend or reject bills passed by the House. During the previous decade, the senators had particularly asserted their powers in matters pertaining to religion and the state church. In comparison with the membership of the House, they formed a more aristocratic body, more oriented to the concept of an establishment. Senators tended to be wealthier, possess more extensive properties, and come from more prominent families than the average delegates.[52] Almost continually since the Revolution, the Speaker of the Senate had been Archibald Cary. Cary had been involved in government since 1748, and now at the ripe age of sixty-four he was a patriarch among the Virginia ruling class. "Old Iron," as he was familiarly known, was also a devout Episcopalian; and as a magistrate in Chesterfield County during the revivals among the Separate Baptists in the early 1770s, he had harassed and imprisoned their itinerant preachers. Now he lent his political

---

[51] For the bill as presented in the revisal, see Boyd, *Papers of Jefferson* 2: 419-23. For the action in the session of 1785, see *JHD*, Nov. 28, Dec. 22-23, Dec. 29-30, 1785, pp. 60, 104-5, 118-19. The text of the bill is found in Hening, *Statutes at Large* 12: 27-30.

[52] *JHD*, Dec. 29, 1785, p. 115; Jackson Turner Main, *The Upper House in Revolu-tionary America, 1763-1788* (Madison, Wis., 1967), pp. 125-31.

strength and prestige to the forces opposing Jefferson's bill.[53] Given its leadership and composition, as well as its past record, it should have been expected that the Senate would attempt to alter that proposal.

Shortly before the Christmas break, the upper house voted on two amendments. The first of these, which passed by a margin of 10 to 8, eliminated the preamble and substituted the sixteenth article of the Declaration of Rights. In effect, it reiterated the amendment requested by the opponents of the bill in the House. The second amendment proposed in the Senate would have simply scotched the final clause of the bill, which stated that although the legislature realized it lacked authority to bind the decisions of future assemblies, yet the rights elaborated in the statute belonged to the "natural rights of mankind" and any future attempt to repeal or limit the provisions of the bill would be a violation of those rights. The second amendment was defeated by the same majority which had passed the first one, two of the senators shifting positions. With the preamble having been changed but the rest of the bill unaltered, the proposed statute then passed its third reading in the upper house.[54]

The House and the Senate were now engaged in a test of strength which would last for several weeks. When the delegates received the bill with the Senate amendment on December 29, they promptly reinstated Jefferson's preamble by a vote of 56 to 35. Madison's allies had held their ground and, ironically, dispatched Francis Corbin to inform the upper house of their decision. Nine days passed before the Senate once again considered the matter. Then it insisted upon its amendment but suggested to the House that a "free conference" of representatives from both bodies be held on the issue. The delegates quickly concurred with this proposal, and Madison, Johnston, and James Innes of Williamsburg were appointed to meet with the Senate's managers.

[53]Cary was an intimate friend of Jefferson (*DAB*, s.v. "Cary, Archibald"; Meade, *Old Churches* 1: 455; Robert K. Brock, *Archibald Cary of Ampthill, Wheelhorse of the Revolution* [Richmond, 1937]).

[54]*Journal of the Senate of the Commonwealth of· Virginia* (Richmond, 1827; hereafter cited as *JS*), Dec. 23, 1785, p. 61.

Although Madison thought the Senate's objections to the preamble were "frivolous," the conference compromised on several
amendments and reported back to the respective constituencies.
A complicated series of amendments to the amendments followed
in first the House and then the Senate. Finally the whole matter
rested once again with the House of Delegates.[55]

The session was running out of time as the delegates considered
these proposals on January 16. The first two were relatively minor
deletions from the preamble, primarily relating to sentences considered too rationalistic or deistic in tone. The third amendment of
the Senate, however, struck from the preamble the statement that
"the religious opinions of men are not the object of civil government, nor under its jurisdiction." At this attempt to eliminate a
key tenet of the proponents of the bill, certain members of the
House gagged and revolted, most probably under the leadership of
Johnston. However, a roll-call vote passed the amendment by a
margin of 53 to 27. Even Madison supported its passage, for he
realized that without it the bill might not be enacted into law that
session. The bill for religious freedom now stood approved by both
houses. Two days after it was signed by Speaker Harrison, the
Assembly concluded its session on January 21. In one of its final
actions, the legislature approved sending a delegation to a conference on trade at Annapolis.[56] As individual liberty of conscience was definitively affirmed in Virginia, the movement to
increase the power and authority of the central government was
about to begin.

With the passage of the religious liberty bill, the decade-long
struggle to redefine the relationship between the government and
religion in the commonwealth had reached a new level of development. While the parameters of external observance and public
morality remained unsettled and thus susceptible to public legislation, the essential lines of the church-state arrangement had been

[55]*JHD*, Dec. 29, 1785, Jan. 9, Jan. 12, Jan. 13, Jan. 16, 1786, pp. 117, 134-35, 138,
139, 143; *JS*, Jan. 7, Jan. 9, Jan. 14, 1786, pp. 80, 81, 90; Rutland, *Papers of Madison*
8:474.

[56]*JHD*, Jan. 16, Jan. 19, Jan. 21, 1786, pp. 143, 148, 154; *JS*, Jan. 16, 1786, p. 92;
Rutland, *Papers of Madison* 8: 474.

determined. In essence, the bill set down restrictions; it told the government what it must not do. The state could not coerce conscience. It could not tell any man what he must or must not believe, nor require of him any religious practice or financial support. The possibility of a general assessment was definitely excluded, along with any civil discrimination on the basis of religious profession.

For Madison the enactment of the bill was a complete political triumph, marred only slightly by the amendments to the preamble. With obvious elation he informed his compatriot in Paris of the session's achievement and concluded: "I flatter myself that the enacted bill has in this country extinguished forever the ambitious hope of making laws for the human mind."[57] The taste of victory was sweet, and Madison was entitled to his bit of self-congratulation. Since the beginning of his public career he had firmly held to the belief that civil government's sole function with regard to religion was to preserve its free exercise among the people in a state. But the success of his crusade to establish this principle against the opposing values of those who favored the general assessment was only made possible in the last analysis by the political activities of the Presbyterians and Baptists. Madison had provided the political leadership for a cause which embraced very different forces, both in and out of the legislature. What Edmund Randolph later wrote about Jefferson applied equally well to Madison: "his opinions against restraints on conscience ingratiated him with the enemies of the establishment, who did not stop to inquire how far those opinions might border on skepticism or infidelity. Parties in religion and politics rarely scan with nicety the peculiar private opinions of their adherents."[58] Thus it was that although they started from widely separated philosophies about the nature of man and the value of organized religion in society, the rationalists and the religionists arrived at the same practical conclusions and joined forces. The combined political weight had won the battle.

[57] Rutland, *Papers of Madison* 8: 474.

[58] Randolph, *History of Virginia*, p. 183.

Jefferson too was highly gratified by the passage of the bill and took special pleasure in the admiration it aroused among his European friends and associates. It was comforting, he told Madison, to see "the standard of reason at length erected," and he was proud that his native Virginia had been the first to trust "the reason of man . . . with the formation of his own opinions."[59]

The boundaries of the act remained to be tested. During the previous session, the legitimacy of the act of incorporation of the Protestant Episcopal Church had been challenged by petitions from the Presbyterians and Baptists as well as several counties in the state. The Presbyterian convention thought that it had given their Episcopalian brethren "Peculiar distinctions & the Honour of an important name." Moreover, in granting that church the authorization to enact canons for government and church polity, the legislature had asserted a "Supremacy in Spirituals" over that church and transformed it into "the Church of the State." Most crucial of all, a grave injustice had been done in taking the property which had formerly belonged to the establishment and giving it to the Episcopal church. What had been purchased at common expense to all the citizens of the state should be devoted to the use of the general public.[60] During the October session of 1785, the House had in fact ordered a committee chaired by Wilson Cary Nicholas to draw up a bill to amend the incorporation act. However, though the bill received two readings, the Assembly adjourned before it could give the measure serious consideration.[61]

With the religious freedom bill now enacted into law, the fight against the incorporation act was renewed with fresh enthusiasm.

---

[59]Boyd, *Papers of Jefferson* 10: 604. For an earlier expression of Jefferson's reaction to the passage of the bill, see ibid., 10: 244. Not everyone approved of the bill. For an attack on the measure, see John Swanwick, *Considerations on an Act of the Legislature of Virginia, Entitled an Act for the Establishment of Religious Freedom* (Philadelphia 1786).

[60]The Presbyterian petition is found in RP, Nov. 2, 1785. For other petitions pertaining to the incorporation act, see ibid., Baptist petition, Nov. 17, 1785, Rockbridge County, Nov. 2, 1785, Chesterfield County, Dec. 9, 1785, James City County, Dec. 9, 1785. The primary thrust of most of these petitions was against that provision of the act which turned over the property to the exclusive use of the Episcopal church.

[61]*JHD*, Dec. 29, 1785, Jan. 14, Jan. 16, 1786, pp. 118, 141, 143.

During the summer of 1786 the Baptists held a meeting of their politically oriented General Committee and drafted a memorial to the Assembly attacking the act as "pregnant with evil and dangerous to religious Liberty." They asked that it be repealed and that the property of the former establishment be turned over for the common benefit of the people.[62] A variety of other petitions were also circulated against the act, principally in the central Piedmont and Tidewater counties.[63]

This year the Episcopalians were prepared to defend what they considered their legitimate rights. It was one thing to oppose public taxation for the support of religion, but quite another to launch an attack on the structure and property of a particular church. Even Edmund Randolph, who had argued against the assessment bill and privately sneered at the conservatism of the clergy, now changed his tune. "I cannot but consider the act of incorporation in the light of a compact," the next governor of Virginia wrote to Arthur Lee, "which legislative authority may dissolve by the arm of power, but not by the rules of justice and honour."[64] Though Randolph did not attend the May Convention of the Episcopal church in Richmond, the delegates there agreed with him.

The meeting opened with a sermon by the Reverend James Madison, who extolled the example which America now provided the world of "the first glorious instance, wherein religion and polity are no longer connected."[65] In addition to the important church business of ratifying the canons from the Philadelphia General Convention and nominating David Griffith to seek consecration as Virginia's first bishop, the Convention also spent time on a memorial to the Assembly. From the tone of this document, it is clear that the church leadership was both puzzled and hurt by the attempts to repeal the incorporation act. Their petition insisted that the act provided nothing for them which they would not gladly see extended to other denominations, and they wondered at

[62]RP, Nov. 1, 1786; Semple, *Rise of the Baptists in Virginia*, pp. 72-73.

[63]RP, Oct. 31-Dec. 7, 1786, passim.

[64]Conway, *Omitted Chapters in the Life of Randolph*, p. 164.

[65]Madison, *A Sermon Preached before the Convention, 1786*, p. 3.

the lack of understanding manifested by their opponents.[66] In a letter to William White shortly before the Assembly began its session that fall, Griffith expressed the concerns of his confreres: "We shall be again warmly attacked in the present session. The Presbyterians are Petitioning for a repeal of the incorporating Act, & the Baptists for the Sale of the Glebes & Churches. It would seem that nothing will satisfy these People but the entire destruction of the Episcopal Church."[67]

When the legislature settled down to business in the fall of 1786, the delegates discovered that the Episcopalians had not been reluctant to make their opinions known. After the May Convention had adjourned, a broadside had been sent to each parish requesting the membership to submit petitions to the Assembly against the repeal of the incorporation act.[68] At least thirty-six congregations responded to this plea, and their memorials streamed in to the legislature (see Map 4).[69] Though Griffith had been concerned that "many of our Ablest defenders & warmest friends" were not in the Assembly that session, the delegates showed no haste to move against the church.[70] Throughout November petitions on both sides of the question continued to "lie on the table." As the repeal forces mounted up their requests, it became obvious that their principal objective was the seizure of the church property and its application to public uses.[71] The Episcopalian standing committee, appointed by the Convention to represent the

[66]RP, Nov. 10, 1786; *Journal of a Convention, 1786,* pp. 12-18, in Hawks, *Contributions,* I, app.

[67]Oct. 20, 1786, Bishop William White Papers, Hist. Soc. Episcopal Church, Austin. Actually the Presbyterians did not submit a petition to the Assembly in 1786. They may well have believed that their former petition was sufficient and that the repeal bill which had been before the Committee of the Whole in 1785 would be taken up automatically.

[68]"In Convention, May 25, 1786," a broadside signed by John Buchanon, treasurer, and addressed to Rev. Lee Massey, Truro Parish, Fairfax, and Quaries to the Gentle Reader, Miscellaneous Papers, Protestant Episcopal Church in Virginia, VHS. The principal purpose of this broadside was to solicit funds for the expenses of having Griffith consecrated in England.

[69]RP, Oct. 31-Dec. 8, 1786, passim.

[70]Griffith to William White, Oct. 20, 1786, Bishop William White Papers, Hist. Soc. Episcopal Church, Austin.

[71]*JHD,* Nov. 2, 1786, p. 19; RP, Oct. 31–Dec. 7, 1786, passim.

168

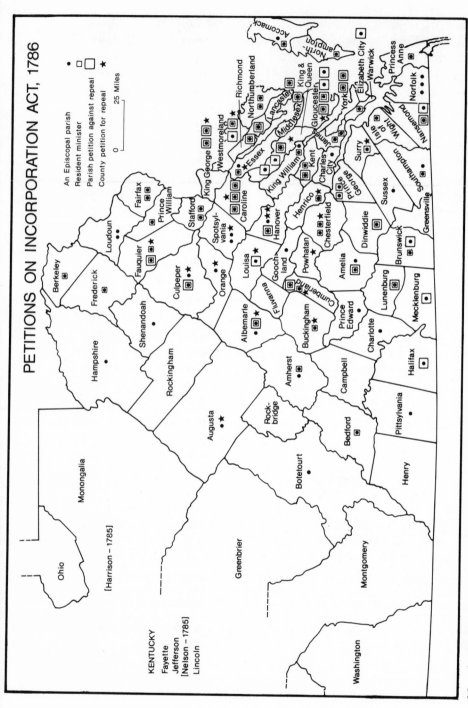

Map 4   Petitions on the Incorporation Act, 1786 (Brydon, *Virginia's Mother Church* 2: 608-12, with corrections from church records and newspapers listed in the Bibliography; RP, October-December 1786)

church's interests to the legislature, pointed this out in a special memorial to the House on December 5. In a forceful appeal to the rights of property, the committee argued that the possession of the churches and glebes was "a Right of which they cannot be deprived, but by violence, nor annihilating public Faith, disturbing the Principles of all Government, and shaking the Foundations of the State."[72] While Shays's Rebellion waxed to the north, this warning to the legislators carried added force. It came from men who were at least their peers; John Blair, John Page, and Hugh Nelson were the lay members of the standing committee and some of the most respected of the Virginia aristocracy. As Madison later noted in his report to Jefferson, the drive by the "other sects" against the property of the Episcopal church "involved the Legislature in some embarrassment."[73]

Immediately after the reception of this last memorial the House formed itself into the Committee of the Whole, discussed the religious petitions, and then formulated several resolutions. The first, and most important, stated: "That an act ought to be passed to empower all societies formed for the purposes of religion, to hold such property as they are now possessed of, to acquire property of any kind, and to dispose thereof in any manner that may be agreeable to the said societies." With the rights of property thus secured, the next two resolutions provided for the repeal of the incorporation act together with all past acts which in any way inhibited any religious society in the state from managing its own affairs. A committee to be chaired by Charles Mynn Thruston, the former Episcopalian minister, was ordered to prepare and bring in the necessary legislation.[74]

The main purpose of the bill was clearly identified in the original title presented by Thruston to the House shortly before

---

[72]RP, Dec. 5, 1786.

[73]Boyd, *Papers of Jefferson* 11: 153. Madison himself had introduced a bill from the revised code of laws entitled "for saving the property of the church heretofore by law established" at the beginning of the 1785 session and again in 1786 (*JHD*, Oct. 31, 1785, p. 14, Nov. 1, 1786, p. 16). The text of the bill may be found in Boyd, *Papers of Jefferson* 2: 553-55. It was never enacted into law. The two clerical members of the standing committee were Rev. James Madison and Rev. John Bracken.

[74]*JHD*, Dec. 5, 1786, p. 87.

Christmas. During the next two weeks, this bill, "to empower certain societies to hold lands, and for other purposes," was debated, discussed, and amended. Finally on January 6, 1787, it passed its third reading; by this time the title had been changed to "an act, to repeal the act, for incorporating the Protestant Episcopal Church, and for other purposes." This time the "other purposes" were of prime importance. The enacted bill was quite short, containing no preamble and only two brief clauses. The first repealed the incorporation act and simultaneously gave "to all religious societies the property to them respectively belonging" together with the authorization to appoint trustees to manage it. The other clause repealed any past laws which prevented "any religious society from regulating its own discipline."[75]

From the text of the bill, it is clear that a compromise had been reached which definitely favored the Episcopal church. Although their incorporation act had been repealed, the Episcopalians were now completely at liberty to organize their own church without reference to any future Assembly. In effect, they were given the same rights which the Baptists and Presbyterians had exercised from the beginning. At the same time, these latter groups could now organize for the management of whatever property they possessed. However, the most important provision of the bill was the thoroughly conservative stand taken by the delegates on the issue of property rights. While revoking the incorporation act as a sop to the former dissenters, they retained its most crucial provision. They kept the church lands intact and made it clear that the Episcopalians would not be deprived of them.[76]

The legislature reiterated this decision in the session of the following year. At their convention in the summer of 1787, the Presbyterians drafted a memorial to the Assembly once again asking that the property be sequestered since the Episcopal church

[75]Ibid., Dec. 23, Dec. 29, 1786, Jan. 5-6, Jan. 9-10, 1787, pp. 120, 129-30, 142, 148-51. The Senate at first wished several amendments but later rescinded them in the face of opposition in the House. The text of the bill is in Hening, *Statutes at Large* 12:266-67.

[76]Hamilton James Eckenrode, *Separation of Church and State in Virginia: A Study in the Development of the Revolution* (rept. New York, 1971), p. 129, called the repeal of the incorporation act a "radical triumph." However, in light of the affirmation of the church's property rights, this assessment appears incorrect.

had "not the least shadow of a claim" to it. They based their case on the argument that there existed no intrinsic connection between that church and the former Church of England established in Virginia. The two were as different, the memorial asserted, as the English church was from the "church of Rome." Since the property of the former establishment had been purchased at the common expense of all the citizens, it was highly unjust for the legislature to assign all the glebes and churches to this one "infant church." The Presbyterians insisted that the glebes should be sold and the money distributed among the various religious groups in each parish on the basis of their tithes, while the church buildings and plate could be made available for the use of those who had paid for them.[77]

The House delayed for more than a month before considering this memorial in the Committee of the Whole. When that body failed to reach any resolution on the matter, a motion was made that at least those glebes which had no incumbent minister could be sold for public purposes, provided that a majority of the parishioners approved of the sale. However, this rather modest implementation of the Presbyterian petition was decisively rejected by a vote of 62 to 45. Even delegates such as George Mason and George Nicholas who were noted for their Jeffersonian convictions failed to support the proposal. Despite their commitment to separation of church and state, they would not be party to the dismemberment of their church.[78]

During the next decade the Baptists took up the cause and repeatedly petitioned the legislature to seize the church property. The religious revivals of 1787 and 1788 had boosted that denomination and the Methodists to the point that by the end of the century they were the principal religious bodies in the state. Meanwhile, the Episcopal church suffered a comparable decline. Even then, it was not until 1799 that the legislature moved against the church property and 1802 before it finally authorized the seizure

[77] RP, Oct. 31, 1787.

[78] *JHD*, Dec. 4, 1787, p. 82. There is no indication that Madison would have supported this proposal, though from 1789 to 1799 he led the fight to seize the glebes. In 1787 his closest associates, including James Monroe, voted against it.

and sale of the glebes.[79] By that time Madison, now functioning as the Republican leader in Congress, had persuaded those party members resisting the confiscation of church property in the Virginia Assembly to drop their opposition and yield to the special interests of the Baptists in order to woo that numerically powerful bloc of voters into Republican ranks.[80] Thus the final settlement of the glebe question was determined not by abstract principles of separation of church and state but by the necessities of practical politics.

[79]Brydon, *Virginia's Mother Church* 2: 474-535, traces the decline of the church and loss of the glebes in some detail. For the Baptist petitions, see RP, 1789-97, passim.

This legislative act of 1802 was challenged in the state courts and eventually upheld by the State Supreme Court of Appeals in a split decision. However, if Edmund Pendleton had lived to give the decision, it would have been ruled unconstitutional. He had prepared an opinion so ruling, but he died the night before he could render the verdict, and his successor, St. George Tucker, voted to uphold the act (Mays, *Pendleton* 2: 340-45).

The growth of the Baptists and Methodists is traced in Wesley M. Gewehr, *The Great Awakening in Virginia, 1740-1790* (Durham, N.C., 1930), pp. 167-86. For the revivals, see John B. Boles, *The Great Revival: 1787-1805: The Origins of the Southern Evangelical Mind* (Lexington, Ky., 1972). For a general review of religion and religious denominations in Virginia during the succeeding period, see Richard Beale Davis, *Intellectual Life in Jefferson's Virginia, 1790-1830* (Chapel Hill, N.C., 1964), pp. 121-46.

[80]Richard R. Beeman, *The Old Dominion and the New Nation, 1788-1801* (Lexington, Ky., 1972), pp. 93-95, 198-99. However, Beeman states that a major motive in the drive against the glebes was also the fact that "the Episcopal Church was not using its lands for the purpose for which they were designed—the care of the poor; the job needed to be handled by a more efficient agency" (ibid., p. 93). Such was not the case; the glebe lands were for the support of the minister.

Conclusion
The Evangelical Contribution

THE passage of Jefferson's bill establishing religious liberty and the repeal of the incorporation act the following year finally provided Virginia with a respite from the religious controversies which had troubled the state for more than a decade. The Old Dominion, with however much hesitation, had chosen a genuinely revolutionary course of action. It granted absolute liberty of conscience, the right to believe as one wished and to practice that belief without any civil disabilities. The state church was disestablished, and all religious groups were placed on an equal basis. Finally, church and state were separated in the sense that there no longer existed any organic connection between the two.

The significance of this development is all the more revealing in light of the alternatives which were rejected. In defining the role of religion in society, Virginia had broken with the models provided by Great Britain and the other states in the American confederation. It had not been at all apparent at the beginning of the Revolution that the relationship between church and state in Virginia would be much different than it had been in the colonial period. Since the vast majority of delegates to both the Revolutionary convention and the early state assemblies were members of what had been the Church of England, it was distinctly possible that they would regroup themselves and their fellow adherents into a Church of Virginia while simultaneously extending a liberal toleration to dissenters. As it was, the sixteenth article of the Declaration of Rights had not intended a wall of separation between church and state, and the delegates in 1776 made it abundantly clear that no such eventuality was desired. Liberty of conscience for them meant freedom of religious belief and practice as well as voluntary support of the churches. For the Episcopalians, the latter principle was affirmed three years later by the Assembly of 1779.

Even more likely was the possibility that the legislature would chose a position adopted by other states in similar circumstances and institute a multiple establishment of Christianity. This was a decided advance over a single establishment as it was conducive to a pluralistic society, would conciliate as many citizens as possible to the cause of the Revolution, and recognized the importance of organized religion as a prop to civil government and a force to maintain republican virtue. In 1779, amid the turmoil of war, the Assembly had dallied with the possibility of such a measure, the bill "concerning religion," which was closely modeled on a provision in the new South Carolina Constitution.

The very least that might have been expected was that Virginia would have instituted some general test of Christianity for office-holding and voting privileges. Such measures were passed by every other state in the new nation except Rhode Island.[1]

But Virginia chose otherwise, and the result is best explained in terms of the forces which allied to produce it. Certainly the leadership of Madison and Jefferson was crucial to the outcome. From the beginning of the controversy, these two men assumed the intellectual and political direction of the struggle to guarantee complete religious freedom by statutory law. For both of them religion was an entirely personal matter between man and his Creator, a natural right antecedent to the formation of society and thus incapable of direction either by state or church. Jefferson's contribution is obvious in his draft of the bill establishing religious freedom, and he prized that contribution enough to order it engraved on his tombstone. Madison's role was even more significant, since it was his political acumen which directed the struggle against any kind of establishment and his pen which composed the "Memorial and Remonstrance," the most comprehensive statement opposing the assessment and supporting the religious liberty bill. Without Madison on hand in Richmond, Jefferson would have been as powerless to prevent the assessment from Paris as Richard Henry Lee was to advance it from Philadelphia.

[1] Stokes, *Church and State* 1: 444.

But the role of Madison and Jefferson and the liberal elements who gathered under their banner can be overplayed, just as the significance of the "Memorial and Remonstrance" as representative of the sentiments of Virginians can be overemphasized. To do so is to distort the meaning of what happened.[2] Despite the best efforts of Madison's allies to circulate the memorial, less than one fifth of those who signed petitions against the assessment in 1785 put their names beneath his composition. The key to understanding the nature of the religious settlement in Virginia rests with the dissenters, the members of the evangelical churches, for they wrote and signed the overwhelming majority of the memorials which engulfed the legislature that year; and their representatives provided the votes in the Assembly which determined the outcome. Had the evangelicals, and particularly the Presbyterians, opted for the assessment bill, Virginia would have had a multiple establishment of religion instead of Jefferson's bill.

Although the reasons for their choice are complex, the evangelicals were at least partially motivated by a strong animosity toward what had been the state church. No one can read the newspapers and religious petitions for the decade between 1776 and 1786 without noting the extraordinary invective hurled back and forth between establishment and antiestablishment forces. The persecution and discrimination suffered by dissenters before the Revolution had furnished ample reasons to end all of the privileges and controls once vested in the establishment, and the slow pace at which the legislature moved only increased antagonism. The general assessment bill of 1784, though presented as a plan to promote the morality necessary for a republic by assisting all of the religious bodies in the state, was viewed by the former dissenters as a ploy to patch up a rapidly declining Episcopal church.

---

[2]Madison's own recollections more than thirty years after the controversy are a case in point; he wrote: "The memorial & remonstrance against it was drawn up ... and printed Copies of it circulated thro' the State, to be signed by the people at large. It met with the approbation of the Baptists, the Presbyterians, the Quakers, and the few Roman Catholics, universally; of the Methodists in part; and even of not a few of the Sect formerly established by law. When the Legislature assembled, the number of Copies & signatures prescribed displayed such an overwhelming opposition of the people, that the proposed plan of a general assessment was crushed under it" (Fleet, "Madison's 'Detached Memoranda,'" 555-56).

Since it was offered for consideration at the same time as the passage of the incorporation act for that church, the real purpose of the assessment seemed all the more transparent. Though they were later to protest that the Episcopalians belonged to an "infant church" with no connection to the former establishment, they knew differently in 1785; and for that Episcopal church, the other religious bodies in Virginia felt little sympathy.

Even more important, however, were the avowedly religious reasons presented by the evangelicals, and especially their desire to maintain as the most widely circulated petition urged, the "Spirit of the Gospel." This was clearly preeminent in the considerations of the Baptists. Among all the religious groups represented in Virginia, they had presented the most steadfast opposition to any form of church-state connection. Virtually every year from the beginning of the Revolution, the delegates to the Assembly could expect to receive one or more Baptist memorials protesting against the residual privileges of the establishment and insisting that all churches be treated on an equal basis before the state. Although their petitions were generally brief documents and lacked the extensive arguments of the Presbyterians, they are remarkable for their consistency and place the Virginia Baptists squarely in the tradition of Roger Williams and Isaac Backus. Requesting no favors from civil government, they wanted what may be fairly termed a separation of church and state based on the distinctive difference between these two spheres of man's activity and the need to maintain a pure church. For the Baptists, the church was a spiritual body, wholly competent in its own area of responsibility and subject to corruption when mingled with or influenced by the state. Religion in terms of both adherence and financial support should be entirely voluntary. Thus they set themselves against a multiple establishment or any system which would bring religion into a formal relationship with civil government.

The role of the Presbyterians was even more critical to the outcome, for they were the most numerous members of the evangelical bloc of delegates in the Assembly and held social and economic power second only to the Episcopalians. Madison was justifiably nervous over a possible combination of these two groups, for the decision of the Presbyterians not to support a multiple establishment and to vote instead for Jefferson's bill was the result of an evolution of thought rather than a consistent position maintained throughout the period. Unlike the Baptists who had urged the passage of the bill for religious freedom when it was first published in 1779, the Presbyterians withheld formal approbation until 1785. They had inherited a churchly tradition of religious freedom which was not necessarily opposed to the concept of state aid for religion. Although their colonial forebears had rejected those portions of the Westminister Confession which asserted the coercive authority of magistrates in matters of church and conscience, they did not advocate separation of church and state. During the Revolution as the relationship between civil government and the churches was redefined, two groups emerged within the ministry and membership of the Presbyterian church in Virginia. One favored state support for religion on a nonpreferential basis; the other opposed this policy. Ultimately these two groups coalesced because they saw in the incorporation act and the assessment proposal a threat to two basic principles: the right of all religious groups to equality of treatment by the state and the noninterference of civil government in the affairs of the church.

A consistent theme in all their petitions from 1776 to 1786 was the insistence that liberty of conscience demanded that the state treat all religious groups equally. Their determination to press for this equality led them to attack repeatedly the unjust preeminence and special prerogatives granted to the Episcopal church by the marriage, vestry, and property laws; and the incorporation act only served to heighten their suspicion. Liberty of conscience also meant that the church had to be entirely free from civil control, and this too the Presbyterians had insisted upon from the beginning. The government had no business intruding in the internal affairs of any religious body; it had no authority to set forms of doctrine, establish modes of worship, or dictate church polity. But the distinctions were carefully drawn. Thus the Presbytery in 1784 and 1785 did not object to a general incorporation of religious bodies for the purpose of holding and managing their property. What they minded was the function which the legislature assumed in defining the outlines of church organization for the Episcopalians. This tampering with "Spirituals" made the incorporation act doubly unacceptable.

The relationship between ministers and laity was another delicate issue, one which the Presbytery had noted in 1784 when it pointed out that the clergy should not be incorporated separately from the lay members of the church. Within Presbyterian polity, there existed a balance between the Presbytery which certified and assigned the ministers to the various congregations and the members of these congregations who elected the ministers and paid their salaries. An assessment would introduce civil government as an alien force in this equation, rendering the clergy independent of the laity. For this reason, state aid in the form of a tax assessment was particularly unappealing to the laity. Other evangelical groups, however different in polity, agreed; and they all insisted that a shortage of clergy was preferable to filling up the ranks of the ministry with men more interested in salary benefits than the cure of souls.

Thus there were certain features of church-state thought which were common to Baptists and Presbyterians, as well as shared by the smaller groups of Methodists, Quakers, Lutherans, and Mennonites. All wished to safeguard the free exercise of conscience so recently won; all viewed religion as voluntary and prior in its rights to the claims of civil society; all were concerned that the incorporation of the Protestant Episcopal Church and the proposed assessment might be a prelude to the revival of the former establishment and a possible renewal of the restrictions they had suffered before the Revolution. In the process of relating these positions to the Assembly, the evangelicals articulated a consistent theory of religious liberty with a scriptural basis and ecclesiological perspective which marked it off as distinctively different from that presented by the rationalists.

The evangelicals grounded their position in support of religious liberty on the nature of the relationship between God and the individual believer. Every man had to be free to respond in faith and worship as God would draw him. The intervention of the state in any fashion hindered the purity of that relationship and was unwarranted interference in God's work. Inherent in the individual's religious liberty was the right of the church, the collective body of believers founded by Jesus Christ, to organize, to worship, and to preach the Gospel without the control or supervision of the state. The authority of the church came from Jesus Christ, not from men. Thus both conscience and church were antecedent in their rights to any claims made by civil government.

The church needed neither the state nor civil society to assist its work or ensure its continuation. Conversions to a religious life were to be effected in the manner of Christ: through the peaceful persuasion of the Gospel rather than the coercive laws of the state; and his promises precluded any possibility that the church would cease to exist if governmental support was withheld. As the evangelicals quoted their Bibles to the legislature, they sharply distinguished the kingdom of God, identified with Christ's church, from the world in which it operated. The first was holy and pure, the other corrupt and evil.

Their scriptural exegesis found reinforcement in an interpretation of history which portrayed the first three centuries of the Christian era as a halcyon time when the church was pure, its ministers devout and competent, and the sweep of Christianity complete. Constantine, by placing the church and state in unholy alliance, had compromised this success as well as the integrity of the Gospel; and from that time forward dated the evils, corruptions, and sufferings of both religion and society. Only now, with the removal of the state from any formal relationship with the church, the evangelicals saw a glorious opportunity to restore primitive Christianity in a way that had eluded the sixteenth-century reformers and to preach Christ's Gospel as he had intended.

Both the evangelicals and the rationalists emerged from this period of controversy in Virginia with clearly developed theories of religious liberty that agreed on a number of conclusions. Both supported freedom of religious conscience, the voluntary nature of religion, and man's relationship to God as prior to the authority of the state. Both wanted the churches separated in some fashion from civil government. But each had a distinctive perspective, for while the rationalists emphasized natural rights, the use of reason in pursuit of truth, and the unhappy influence of religious persecution on man's development, the evangelicals stressed the need for man to be free to respond to God's call, the scriptural commands and teachings of Christ, and the historical opportunity to recapture the condition of primitive Christianity. Each side drew upon the other to enhance their arguments. Thus Madison's "Memorial and Remonstrance" clearly shows the influence of the religious petitions drawn up by the evangelicals, while their petitions incorporate references to natural rights and the purposes of government.

But the differences in emphases were significant for the future of the religious settlement in Virginia. Believing that religion was a strictly private affair, the rationalists wanted the state, and by implication society at large, separated from the churches' influence. Those values and morals necessary to a successful republic could best be communicated and maintained through an extensive system of education. Hence Jefferson's enthusiasm for the bill in his revisal "for the more general diffusion of knowledge," which he considered "by far the most important bill in our whole code."[3] The evangelicals disagreed. They were concerned about the future of the church, and wanted it separated from the state precisely so that it might freely influence society and permeate it with the Gospel message. The concept that religious belief and practice were totally beyond the ken of the state was never fully accepted by the soon-to-be dominant religious bodies of Presbyterians, Baptists, and Methodists. Willing to embrace Jefferson's legislation in terms of the freedom it guaranteed their own activities and the coup de grace it administered to what had once been an overbearing established church, they did not accept its author's philosophy on separation of church and state. What the law stated was of much less importance than what it enabled them to do. It served their purposes.

The intent of the evangelicals was not a complete separation of church and state in rationalist terms nor the total privatization of religion. In contrast to Jefferson and Madison, they did not envision or desire a secular state but the salvation of a Christian

[3]Boyd, *Papers of Jefferson* 10: 244; for the complete text of the bill, see ibid., 2: 526-35. One of the best studies of this somewhat unnatural alliance between rationalism and pietism was made by Sidney E. Mead in *The Lively Experiment: The Shaping of Christianity in America* (New York, 1963), pp. 38-54; but I believe that Mead underestimated the importance of evangelical thought on religious freedom.

America through the Gospel message. Jefferson's bill gave them the opportunity to preach the word without hindrance from civil government. For their work they required no assessment; revivals and itineracy sufficed. And before Jefferson had returned to Monticello from the White House they would capture a dual prize in the suppression of the glebes and the decline of the "baneful influence" of rational religion. They would also begin the process of imposing their own religious values on the legislation of the state, for the new majority of religious bodies endorsed the legal statement of 1786 in terms of their own freedom but at the same time pressed for laws designed to enforce a style of public morality and life dictated by and expressive of their own particular religious beliefs.

Even as the evangelicals protested against the assessment and incorporation bills, their petitions expressed a desire for the members of the Assembly to "recommend religion" by the quality of their lives and pass laws to "Punish the Vices, and Immoralities of the times."[4] While the Presbytery asked for "wholesome Laws" and insisted on the "happy influence" of religion upon "the morality of the Citizens," the Baptists pointed out that the legislature would do "its part in favour of Christianity" by "supporting those Laws of Morality, which are necessary for Private and Public happiness."[5]

The Assembly responded. At the same time as it passed the bill establishing religious liberty, the legislature did not commit itself to a total withdrawal of government from religion. Rather, this same session of the Assembly approved another law which foreshadowed the church-state arrangement that would prevail for the next century and a half. It compelled the observance of Sunday as a day of rest. Any person found working on the Sabbath or employing his apprentices, slaves, or servants on that day, "except it be in the ordinary household office of daily necessity, or other work of necessity or charity," would be fined ten shillings.[6] This

---

[4]RP, Cumberland County, Oct. 26, 1785.

[5]Ibid., Oct. 24, 1776, Nov. 12, 1784, Nov. 3, 1785.

[6]Hening, *Statutes at Large* 12: 337. Though the majority of Baptists would take their cue from Isaac Backus of New England and support such legislation (see McLoughlin, "Isaac Backus and the Separation of Church and State," pp. 1407-13),

legislation inaugurated a series of so-called blue laws which would keep government firmly enmeshed in the business of religion. Ostensibly designed for the benefit of the whole community, and without reference to particular creeds or religious systems, they were in reality meant to impose the beliefs and values of the dominant Protestant churches upon the inhabitants of the state. Thus Virginia, like many other states in similar circumstances, managed to legislate virtue and retain a type of functional establishment.[7]

In this enterprise the evangelicals could join forces with advocates of the assessment, for the latter had argued throughout the preceding decade that since institutional religion was important for the sustanance of a republic, the government ought to protect and nurture religious ideals and values for the sake of the whole society. This had been a major reason for their support of the assessment bill; and though disappointed by its failure, they did not relinquish their commitment to a program of civil support for religion. Evangelicals and traditional religionists shared a belief that religion had an important place in American life which ought to be publicly acknowledged, that the fabric of society and the survival of the republican experiment depended on something more than the light of pure reason. They expected that government, in caring for the general welfare, would institutionalize certain Christian norms and values. Despite the defeat of the assessment bill and the passage of the statute for religious freedom, their viewpoint reflected the real consensus of Virginians and inspired the moral legislation of the next century.

John Leland, a leading Virginia preacher after 1785, was a major exception. For his position, see L. F. Greene, ed., *The Writings of John Leland* (rept. New York, 1969), p. 119; and L. H. Butterfield, "Elder John Leland, Jeffersonian Itinerant," *Proceedings of the American Antiquarian Society* 62 (1952): 236-39.

[7] For an analysis of this development, see Robert T. Handy, *A Christian America: Protestant Hopes and Historical Realities* (New York, 1971), and Elwyn A. Smith, "The Voluntary Establishment of Religion," in Smith, ed., *The Religion of the Republic* (Philadelphia, 1971), pp. 154-82.

APPENDIXES

BIBLIOGRAPHY

INDEX

Documents, 1779–1786

1. "A Bill concerning Religion," 1779

FOR the encouragement of Religion and virtue, and for removing all restraints on the mind in its inquiries after truth, *Be it enacted by the General Assembly,* that all persons and Religious Societies who acknowledge that there is one *God,* and a future State of rewards and punishments, and that *God* ought to be publickly worshiped, shall be freely tolerated.

The Christian Religion shall in all times coming be deemed, and held to be the established Religion of this Commonwealth; and all Denominations of Christians demeaning themselves peaceably and faithfully, shall enjoy equal privileges, civil and Religious.

To accomplish this desirable purpose without injury to the property of those Societies of Christians already incorporated by Law for the purpose of Religious Worship, and to put it fully into the power of every other Society of Christians, either already formed or to be hereafter formed to obtain the like incorporation, *Be it farther enacted,* that the respective Societies of the *Church of England* already formed in this Commonwealth, shall be continued Corporate, and hold the Religious property now in their possession for ever.

Whenever free male Persons not under twenty one Years of Age professing the Christian Religion, shall agree to unite themselves in a Society for the purposes of Religious Worship, they shall be constituted a Church, and esteemed and regarded in Law as of the established Religion of this Commonwealth, and on their petition to the General Assembly shall be entitled to be incorporated and shall enjoy equal Privileges with any other Society of Christians, and all that associate with them for the purpose of Religious Worship, shall be esteemed as belonging to the Society so called.

Every Society so formed shall give themselves a name or denomination by which they shall be called and known in Law. *And it is farther enacted,* that previous to the establishment and incorporation of the respective Societies of every denomination as aforesaid, and in order to entitle them thereto, each Society so Petitioning shall agree to and subscribe in a Book the following five Articles, without which no agreement or Union of Men upon pretence of Religious Worship shall entitle them to be incorporated and esteemed as a Church of the Established Religion of this Commonwealth.

First, That there is one Eternal God and a future State of Rewards and Punishments.

Secondly, That God is publickly to be Worshiped.

Thirdly, That the Christian Religion is the true Religion.

Fourthly, That the Holy Scriptures of the old and new Testament are of divine inspiration, and are the only rule of Faith.

Fifthly, That it is the duty of every Man, when thereunto called by those who Govern, to bear Witness to truth.

And that the People may forever enjoy the right of electing their own Teachers, Pastors, or Clergy; and at the same time that the State may have Security for the due discharge of the Pastoral Office by those who shall be admitted to be Clergymen, Teachers, or Pastors, no Person shall officiate as Minister of any established Church who shall not have been chosen by a Majority of the Society to which he shall be Minister, or by the Persons appointed by the said Majority to chose and procure a Minister for them, nor until the Minister so chosen shall have made and subscribed the following declaration, over and above the aforesaid five Articles, to be made in some Court of Record in this Commonwealth, viz.:

"That he is determined by *God's* Grace out of the Holy Scriptures to instruct the people committed to his charge, and to teach nothing (as required of necessity to eternal Salvation) but that which he shall be persuaded may be concluded and proved from the Scriptures; that he will use both publick and private admonitions, with prudence and discretion, as need shall require, and occasion shall be given; that he will be diligent in prayers and in reading the Holy Scriptures, and in such Studies as lead to the knowledge of the same; that he will be diligent to frame and fashion himself and his Family according to the doctrines of Christ, and to make both himself and them, as much as in him lieth, wholesome examples and patterns to the flock of Christ; and that he will maintain and set forward, as much as he can, peace and love among all people, and especially among those that are or shall be committed to his charge."

No Person whatsoever shall speak any thing in their Religious Assemblies disrespectfully or Seditiously of the Government of this State.

And that permanent encouragement may be given for providing a sufficient number of ministers and teachers to be procured and continued to every part of this Commonwealth, *Be it farther enacted,* that the sum of pounds of Tobacco, or such rate in Money, as shall be Yearly settled for each County by the Court thereof, according to the Current Price, shall be paid annually for every Tithable by the Person enlisting the same, for and towards the Support of Religious Teachers and places of Worship in manner following: Within   Months after the passing of this Act every freeholder, Housekeeper, & person possessing Tithables, shall enroll his or her name with the Clerk of the County of which he or she shall be an Inhabitant, at the same time expressing to the Support of what Society or denomination of Christians he or she would chose to contribute; which enrollment shall be binding upon each such Person, untill he or she shall in like manner cause his or her name to be enrolled in any other Society.

The Clerk of each County Court shall Annually before the day of   , deliver to the Trustees of each Religious Society, a list of the several names enrolled in his office as Members of such Society, with the number of Tithables belonging to each, according to the List taken and returned that Year. Whereupon such Trustees respectively shall meet and determine how the Assessment aforesaid upon such Tithables shall be laid out for the support of their teachers or places of Worship, according to the true intent of this Act; and having entered such disposition in a Book to be kept for that purpose, shall deliver a Copy thereof to the Sheriff, together with the List of Tithables so received from the Clerk, and such Sheriff shall on or before the   day of   , then next following, Collect, Levy, or Distrain for the amount of such Assessment, which he shall account for and pay to the several Persons to whom he shall have been directed to pay it by the Trustees of each respective Society, deducting Insolvents and Six *per Centum* for Collection.

If any Person shall fail to enlist his Tithables, the Sheriff shall nevertheless Collect or distrain for the Assessment aforesaid in like manner as if he or she had done so, and pay the same to that Religious Society of which he or she shall be enrolled as a Member. And should any Person liable to this Assessment fail to procure himself to be enrolled according to this Act, or to make his Election at the time of paying his Assessment to the Sheriff, the Sheriff shall nevertheless Levy in like manner the Assessment for his or her Tithables, and lay an Account upon Oath of all Tobacco or Monies so Collected before his Court in the Month of   Annually; or if no Court be then held, at the next Court which shall be here thereafter, who shall apportion the same between the several Religious Societies in the Parish in which such Person or Persons shall reside, according to the amount of the Assessment for each to be paid to the Order of such Trustees for the purposes of this Act. And every Sheriff shall Annually before the   day of   , enter into Bond, with sufficient Security to be approved by the County Court, for the faithful Collection and disbursement of all Tobacco or monies received in consequence of this Act; and the Trustees of any Religious Society, or any Creditor to whom Money may by them be Ordered to be paid, on motion in the County Court, having given him ten days previous notice thereof, may have Judgment against any delinquent Sheriff and his Securities, his or their Executors or Administrators, for what shall appear to be due from him to such Society or Creditor, or may bring suit on the Bond given by the Sheriff; and the Bond shall not be discharged by any Judgment had thereon, but shall remain as a Security against him, and may be put in Suit as often as any breach shall happen, until the whole Penalty shall have been Levied.

And if any Society or Church so established, shall refuse to appoint some Person to receive their Quota of the Assessment from the Sheriff, the Money shall remain in his hands for one Year; and if then no person properly appointed shall apply for such Money, the same shall by the County Court be equally apportioned between the several Religious Societies in the parish in which such person or persons shall reside, in proportion to the amount of the Assessment for each Society.

The Clerks of the respective County Courts shall be entitled to the same fees for making out and delivering the lists of Tithables required by this Act as they are entitled to for the like services in other cases.

And be it farther enacted, that so much of an Act of Assembly passed in the Year 1748, intituled "An Act for the Support of the Clergy, and for the regular Collecting and paying the Parish Levies," as respects the Levying, Collecting, and payment of the Salaries of the Clergy of the *Church of England* which has been suspended by several Acts of the General Assembly; and also so much of an Act intituled *"ministers to be inducted,"* as required Ordination by a *Bishop* in *England,* be and the same are hereby Repealed.

Source: A "bill concerning religion," Oct. 25, 1779, in House of Delegates Bills, Resolutions, etc., Box 3, Rough Bills, Oct. 1779, VSL. This is the final draft of the proposed bill.

2. A Bill "Establishing a Provision for Teachers of the Christian Religion," 1784

WHEREAS the general diffusion of Christian knowledge hath a natural tendency to correct the morals of men, restrain their vices, and preserve the peace of society, which cannot be effected without a competent provision for learned teachers, who may be thereby enabled to devote their time and attention to the duty of instructing such citizens, as from their circumstances and want of education, cannot otherwise attain such knowledge; and it is judged that such provision may be made by the Legislature, without counteracting the liberal principle heretofore adopted and intended to be preserved by abolishing all distinctions of preeminence amongst the different societies or communities of Christians;

Be it therefore enacted by the General Assembly, That for the support of Christian teachers,   per centum on the amount, or   in the pound on the amount, or   in the pound on the sum payable for tax on the property within this Commonwealth, is hereby assessed, and shall be paid by every person chargeable with the said tax at the time the same shall become due; and the Sheriffs of the several Counties shall have power to levy and collect the same in the same manner and under the like restrictions and limitations, as are or may be prescribed by the laws for raising the revenues of this State.

And be it enacted, That for every sum so paid, the Sheriff or Collector shall give a receipt, expressing therein to what society of Christians the person from whom he may receive the same shall direct the money to be paid, keeping a distinct account thereof in his books. The Sheriff of every County, shall, on or before the   day of   in every year, return to the Court upon oath, two alphabetical lists of the payments to him made, distinguishing in columns opposite to the names of the persons who shall have paid the same, the society to which the money so paid was by them appropriated; and one column for the names where no appropriation shall be made. One of which lists, after being recorded in a book to be kept for that purpose, shall be filed by the Clerk in his office; and the other shall by the Sheriff be fixed up in the Court-house, there to remain for the inspection of all concerned. And the Sheriff, after deducting a five per centum for the collection, shall forthwith pay to such persons or persons as shall be appointed to receive the same by the Vestry, Elders, or Directors, however denominated of each such society, the sum so stated to be due to that society; or in default thereof, upon the motion of such person or persons to the next or any succeeding Court, execution shall be awarded for the same against the Sheriff and his security, his and their executors or administrators; provided that ten days previous notice be given of such motion. And upon every such execution, the Officer serving the same shall proceed to immediate sale of the estate taken, and shall not accept of security for payment at the end of three months, nor to have the goods forthcoming at the day of sale, for his better direction wherein, the Clerk shall endorse upon every such execution that no security of any kind shall be taken.

And be it further enacted, That the money to be raised by virtue of this act, shall be by the Vestries, Elders, or Directors of each religious society, appropriated to a provision for a Minister or Teacher of the Gospel of their denomination, or the providing places of divine worship, and to none other use whatsoever; except in the denominations of Quakers and Menonists, who may receive what is collected from their members, and place it in their general fund, to be disposed of in a manner which they shall think best calculated to promote their particular mode of worship.

And be it enacted, That all sums which at the time of payment to the Sheriff or Collector may not be appropriated by the person paying the same, shall be accounted for with the Court in manner as by this Act is directed; and after deducting for his collection, the Sheriff shall pay the amount thereof (upon account certified by the Court to the Auditors of Public Accounts, and by them to the Treasurer) into the Public Treasury, to be disposed of under the direction of the General Assembly, for the encouragement of seminaries of learning within the Counties whence such sums shall arise, and to no other use or purpose whatsoever.

Source: Va. Journal and Alexandria Advertiser, Mar. 17, 1785.

3. A Bill "for Establishing Religious Freedom"

Well aware that the opinions and belief of men depend not on their own will,
but follow involuntarily the evidence proposed to their minds;[1] that Almighty
God hath created the mind free, *and manifested his supreme will that free it*
shall remain by making it altogether insusceptible of restraint; that all
attempts to influence it by temporal punishments, or burthens, or by civil
incapacitations, tend only to beget habits of hypocrisy and meanness, and are
a departure from the plan of the holy author of our religion, who being lord
both of body and mind, yet chose not to propagate it by coercions on either,
as was in his Almighty power to do, *but to extend it by its influence on*
reason alone; that the impious presumption of legislators and rulers, civil as
well as ecclesiastical, who, being themselves but fallible and uninspired men,
have assumed dominion over the faith of others, setting up their own opinions
and modes of thinking as the only true and infallible, and as such endeavoring
to impose them on others, hath established and maintained false religions
over the greatest part of the world and through all time: That to compel a
man to furnish contributions of money for the propagation of opinions which
he disbelieves *and abhors*, is sinful and tyrannical; that even the forcing him
to support this or that teacher of his own religious persuasion, is depriving
him of the comfortable liberty of giving his contribution to the particular
pastor whose morals he feels most persuasive to righteousness; and is with-
drawing from the ministry those temporary rewards, which proceeding from
an approbation of their personal conduct, are an additional incitement to
earnest and unremitting labours for the instruction of mankind; that our civil
rights have no dependence on our religious opinions, any more than our
opinions in physics or geometry; that therefore the prescribing any citizen as
unworthy the public confidence by laying upon him any incapacity of being
called to offices of trust and emolument, unless he profess or renounce this
or that religious opinion, is depriving him injuriously of those privileges and
advantages to which, in common with his fellow citizens, he had a natural
right; that it tends only to corrupt the principles of that *very* religion it is
meant to encourage, by bribing, with a monopoly of worldly honours and
emoluments, those who will externally profess and conform to it; that though
indeed these are criminal who do not withstand such temptation, yet neither
are those innocent who lay the bait in their way; *that the opinions of men*
are not the object of civil government, nor under its jurisdiction; that to
suffer the civil magistrate to intrude his powers into the field of opinion and
to restrain the profession or propagation of principles on supposition of their
ill tendency is a dangerous falacy, which at once destroys all religious liberty,
because he being of course judge of that tendency will make his opinions the

---

[1]The italicized sections were omitted by amendments during the 1785 session. The
final bill began: "Whereas, Almighty God hath . . ."

rule of judgment, and approve or condemn the sentiments of others only as they shall square with or differ from his own; that it is time enough for the rightful purposes of civil government for its officers to interfere when principles break out into overt acts against peace and good order; and finally, that truth is great and will prevail if left to herself; that she is the proper and sufficient antagonist to error, and has nothing to fear from the conflict unless by human interposition disarmed of her natural weapons, free argument and debate; errors ceasing to be dangerous when it is permitted freely to contradict them.

We the General Assembly of Virginia do enact[2] that no man shall be compelled to frequent or support any religious worship, place, or ministry whatsoever, nor shall be enforced, restrained, molested, or burthened in his body or goods, nor shall otherwise suffer on account of his religious opinions or belief; but that all men shall be free to profess, and by argument to maintain, their opinion in matters of religion, and that the same shall in no wise diminish, enlarge, or affect their civil capacities.

And though we well know that this Assembly, elected by the people for the ordinary purposes of legislation only, have no power to restrain the acts of succeeding Assemblies, constituted with powers equal to our own, and that therefore to declare this act irrevocable would be of no effect in law; yet we are free to declare, and do declare, that the rights hereby asserted are of the natural rights of mankind, and that if any act shall be hereafter passed to repeal the present, or to narrow its operation, such act will be infringement of natural right.

Source: The text of this act as presented in the 1785 Assembly may be found in *Report of the Committee of Revisors Appointed by the General Assembly of Virginia in 1776* (Richmond, 1784). The text of the act as passed by the legislature is in Hening, *Statutes at Large* 12: 84-86. For comments and critiques of various editions of the bill, see Boyd, *Papers of Jefferson* 2: 547-53.

[2] The wording here was changed to "Be it enacted by the General Assembly, . . ."

Division on Religious Questions

in the House of Delegates, 1784–1785

The following divisions are based on the roll-call votes taken in the House on the assessment and incorporation issues in the session of 1784 and Jefferson's bill for establishing religious freedom in the session of 1785. Where information is available, the delegate's position is stated in terms of his religious background and affiliation, education, and participation in church activities.

Delegates Favoring Church-State Relationship

These legislators supported the religious bills introduced in the 1784 Assembly. In the session of 1785 they favored the substitution of the sixteenth article of the Declaration of Rights in place of Jefferson's preamble. If a particular delegate voted against Jefferson's bill itself, that fact is noted.

Anderson, Garland ('84, '85), Hanover County. A wealthy farmer and vestry-man, Anderson (1742-1811) voted against Jefferson's bill. He differs from the general pattern, however, in that he voted against the incorporation bill though he had supported it as a resolution. In 1787 he served as a lay delegate from St. Martin's Parish to the church Convention (W. P. Anderson, *The Early Descendants of William Overton and Elizabeth Waters of Virginia, and Allied Families* [Cincinnati, 1938], pp. 18-19).

Ball, James, Jr. ('84, '85), Lancaster County. A vestryman of Christ Church, Ball (1755-1825) represented that parish in the church conventions of 1785, 1790, 1791, and 1796. In 1786 he signed a petition in favor of retaining the incorporation act, and the following year he voted against the sale of any glebes (RP, Nov., 1786; Horace Edwin Hayden, *Virginia Genealogies* [rept. Baltimore, 1959], p. 111).

Bland, Edward ('84, '85), Prince George County, was the son of Richard Bland (1710-1776) who had been very active in church-state affairs on the eve of the Revolution. Edward (b. 1746) voted against Jefferson's bill. In 1790 he served as a lay delegate from Martin's Brandon Parish to the church Convention (Genealogical notes on Bland Family in VHS).

Cary, Wilson Miles ('84, '85), Warwick County. Like his distant cousins Archibald Cary in the Senate and Richard Cary, Jr., in the House, Wilson Miles Cary (1734-1817) strongly opposed Jefferson's bill. Educated at

William and Mary and devoutly attached to the Episcopal church, Cary attended church conventions in 1785, 1786, 1789, and 1797 as a delegate from Elizabeth City Parish. In 1786 he also signed a petition against the repeal of the incorporation act (RP, Dec. 4, 1786; Tyler, *Encyclopedia* 1: 206; [Fairfax Harrison], *The Virginia Carys: An Essay in Genealogy* [New York, 1919], pp. 108-10).

Claiborne, Thomas ('84, '85), Brunswick County. An Episcopal church leader, Claiborne (1749-1812) served as a lay delegate to the Convention of 1785 from Meherrin Parish. That same year he cast the first vote against Jefferson's bill when the roll was called. For a sketch of his public life, see *Biographical Directory of the American Congress, 1774-1961* (Washington, D.C., 1961), p. 694.

Corbin, Francis ('84, '85), Middlesex County. Corbin (1759-1821) was a leader of the assessment forces and voted against the bill for religious freedom. A wealthy planter and lawyer, educated in England, he was made rector of William and Mary in 1790. Two years later he served as a lay delegate from Christ Church Parish to the Episcopal Convention (Corbin, "The Corbin Family," pp. 315-18).

Cropper, John ('84, '85), Accomack County. An officer in the Revolution and close friend of Washington, Cropper (1755-1821) was a leading Episcopalian layman. He served in the vestry of St. George's Parish both before and after the incorporation act, attended the church Convention in 1786, and the following year took charge of recruiting a minister for the parish. But despite his warm attention toward his church, Cropper was no bigot. From time to time he attended Methodist services and was intrumental in finding a place for their ministers to preach after the break with the Episcopal church (John Cropper Papers, VHS; St. George's Parish Vestry Book, 1763-87; VSL; Ralph T. Whitelaw, *Virginia's Eastern Shore: A History of Northhampton and Accomack Counties* [Gloucester, Mass., 1968], 2: 1041-43.

Garrard, William ('85), Stafford County. Garrard voted against Jefferson's bill in 1785. William (c. 1760-1836) did so despite his older half brother James Garrard's support for the measure. For a brief sketch of his life, see Anna Russell Des Cognets, *Governor Garrard of Kentucky, His Descendants and Relatives* (Lexington, KY., 1898), p. 108.

Harrison, Benjamin ('84, '85). After his term as governor ended in November 1748, Harrison (1726-1791) resumed his seat from Charles City County. The following year he was elected from Surry County. Harrison supported the religious bills, though perhaps with less fervor than his brother and son. For a sketch of his life, see *DAB*.

Harrison, Carter Bassett ('84, '85), Surry County. A strong Episcopalian, Carter Harrison (c. 1758-1808) was a delegate from Southwark Parish to the Convention of 1785, and voted against Jefferson's bill (Tyler, *Encyclopedia* 2: 112).

Harrison, Carter Henry ('84, '85), Cumberland County. The brother of the governor and like the rest of the family a graduate of William and Mary, he had no use for the dissenters. Late in life Harrison (c. 1726-1794) rallied in vain in defense of the establishment. A brief sketch of his life is in Stanard, "Harrison of James River," pp. 183-87.

Henry, Patrick ('84), Henry County. Henry (1736-1799) requires no sketch.

Jones, Joseph ('84, '85), Dinwiddie County. A wealthy planter and officer of the Virginia militia, Jones (1749-1824) favored the establishment scheme. He also voted against the sale of any of the glebes in 1787 (Tyler, *Encyclopedia* 2: 143).

Jones, Joseph ('84), King George County. Despite his close friendship with Madison and Jefferson, Jones (1727-1805) favored both the assessment and incorporation. Like the other Joseph Jones (from Dinwiddie), he served on the drafting committee for the assessment bill. However, in 1786 he signed a petition requesting the repeal of the incorporation (RP, Nov. 30, 1786; *DAB*).

King, Miles ('84, '85), Elizabeth City County. King (1747-1814) was a merchant and later mayor of Norfolk. He voted against Jefferson's bill in 1785 and also against the sale of the glebes in 1787. A survey of his life may be found in the "King Family of Virginia," *William and Mary Quarterly*, 1st ser., 16 (1907): 108-10.

Lee, Richard ('84, '85), Westmoreland County. Known as the "old squire" from Lee Hall, Richard Lee (1726-1795) was a cousin to Richard Henry Lee and the uncle of Henry "Light Horse Harry" Lee and Richard Bland Lee, all of whom were members of the House during this period. Devoted to the old church, Richard Lee was a perennial vestryman of Cople Parish and voted against Jefferson's bill for religious freedom (Meade, *Old Churches* 2: 153; Cazenove Gardner Lee, Jr., *Lee Chronicle: Studies of the Early Generations of the Lees of Virginia,* ed. Dorothy Mills Parker [New York, 1957], pp. 348-49).

Markham, Bernard ('84, '85), Chesterfield County. A devoted Episcopalian, Markham (1737-1802) was a vestryman of Manchester Parish and operated a lottery for the benefit of the church in 1784. For a brief sketch of his life, see Mrs. Flournoy Rivers, "The Markham Family of Virginia," *Virginia Magazine of History and Biography* 5 (1897): 205.

Marshall, John ('84), Fauquier County. Though Beveridge stated that Marshall "took only a languid interest in the religious struggle," the future chief justice strongly favored the assessment proposal. He voted for the incorporation act and against Madison's motion to postpone the assessment vote. He was also during this period a generous benefactor to the Episcopal church (Albert J. Beveridge, *The Life of John Marshall* [Boston, 1919], 1: 179-80, 187, 222; Herbert A. Johnson, ed., *The Papers of John Marshall* [Chapel Hill, N.C., 1974], 1: 131).

Mercer, John Francis ('85), Stafford County. Mercer (1795-1821) solidly opposed his former law teacher's bill for religious freedom. From an old

Anglican family, Mercer had a long political career before him in Maryland (*DAB*).

Page, John ('85), Gloucester County. Page (1743-1808) was a liberal Episcopalian in theology but a conservative in matters of church and state. A lay delegate to the church conventions of 1785, 1786, and 1787, Page voted against his friend Jefferson's bill in 1785 and the following year signed a petition from Abingdon Parish opposing the repeal of the incorporation act (RP, Oct. 31, 1786; *DAB*).

Pendleton, James ('84), Culpeper County. A casualty of the 1785 elections, Pendleton (1735-1793) was returned to the House in 1787 to vote against the sale of the glebes. He served as a vestryman of St. Mark's Parish and in 1785 was a lay delegate to the church Convention (Rutland, *Papers of Madison* 8: 272-73; Slaughter, *St. Mark's Parish*, p. 20).

Riddick, Willis ('84, '85), Nansemond County. A member of the vestry of Upper Parish both before and after the incorporation act, Riddick (1725-1800) was a senior member of the legislature and strong defender of the church establishment. He was a lay delegate to the Convention of 1785, and the following year he signed a petition against the repeal of the incorporation act. He voted against Jefferson's bill (RP, Oct. 31, 1786; William L. Hall, ed., *The Vestry Book of the Upper Parish, Nansemond County, Virginia, 1743-1793* [Richmond, 1949], pp. 250, 255, 257). For a sketch of his life, see Joseph B. Dunn, *The History of Nansemond County, Virginia* (n.p., 1907), pp. 43-44.

Smith, Thomas ('84, '85), Gloucester County. A former student at William and Mary and a vestryman of Kingston Parish both before and after the incorporation act, Smith was the parish delegate to the Convention of 1785. Though he supported the religious bills in 1784 and the amendments to the preamble in 1785, he also voted for Jefferson's bill. The following year he signed a petition against the repeal of the incorporation act (which he had helped to draft), and in 1787 he opposed the sale of the glebes (C. G. Chamberlayne, ed., *The Vestry Book of Kingston Parish, Mathews County, Virginia, 1679-1796* [Richmond, 1929], pp. 118, 120; RP, Oct. 31, 1786; Tyler, *Encyclopedia* 2: 360).

Tazewell, Henry ('84), Williamsburg. An extremely wealthy and influential lawyer, Tazewell (1753-1799) served on the drafting committees for both the assessment and incorporation acts. He supported both measures but was removed from the House in 1785 by election to the bench of the General Court. For a further sketch of his life, see *DAB*.

Thornton, William ('84, '85), King George County. Thornton voted against the bill for religious freedom despite the fact that he was George Mason's son-in-law (W. G. Stanard, "Thornton Family," *William and Mary Quarterly*, 1st ser., 25 [1916]: 124).

Turberville, George Lee ('85), Richmond County. From one of the wealthiest families in the state, young Turberville (1760-1798) was a staunch Episcopalian and voted against Jefferson's bill (Tyler, *Encyclopedia* 2: 154-55).

Tyler, John ('84, '85), Charles City County. A member of the Episcopal
  church, Tyler (1747-1813) represented Westover Parish in the Convention
  of 1785. While serving as Speaker he did not vote on the religious questions, but in 1785 he supported the amendments to the preamble of the
  bill for religious freedom (*DAB*).
Walke, Anthony ('85), Princess Anne County. A member of the vestry of
  Lynnhaven Parish and a devout churchman, Walke (1726-1794) voted
  against Jefferson's bill. Two years later he took orders and was inducted
  into Lynnhaven Parish as its minister (George Carrington Mason, ed., *The
  Colonial Vestry Book of Lynnhaven Parish, Princess Anne County, Virginia, 1723-1788* [Newport News, Va., 1949], pp. 117, 119; Meade, *Old
  Churches* 1: 249).
Westwood, Worlich ('85), Elizabeth City County. Westwood served as a
  vestryman before the disestablishment of the church, voted against the
  bill for religious freedom, and in 1786 signed a petition opposing the
  repeal of the incorporation act (RP, Dec. 4, 1786; Tyler, *Encyclopedia*
  1: 357).
Wills, John S. ('84, '85), Isle of Wight County. An Episcopalian, Wills represented Newport Parish at the Convention of 1786 (Tyler, *Encyclopedia*
  1: 361).
Wray, George ('84), Elizabeth City County. Wray served on the committee to
  draft the assessment bill. He also served as a lay delegate to the Convention
  of 1785 from Elizabeth City Parish and the following year signed a petition against the repeal of the incorporation bill (RP, Dec. 4, 1786).

Other delegates who tended to side with this group included *John Allen* of
Surry ('84), the brother-in-law of Carter Bassett Harrison and a devoted
Episcopalian in his own right; *Philip Barbour* ('84), serving a single term in
the House from Jefferson County in Kentucky; *Edward Carrington* ('84, '85),
from Cumberland County, who was an active member of Southam Parish;
William Curtis ('84, '85), from Middlesex County; *Littleton Eyre* ('84), from
Northampton on the Eastern Shore and a William and Mary graduate; and
John Thornton ('85), from Northumberland County.

Three other delegates voted against Jefferson's bill for religious freedom:
John Gordon ('85), from Northumberland and lay delegate to the Episcopal
Convention in 1795; *Daniel Sanford* ('84, '85), from Norfolk County; and
Elias Wills ('85), from Fluvanna County.

Delegates Opposing Church-State Relationship

These legislators opposed the assessment and incorporation acts in 1784, and
in the 1785 session they voted for Jefferson's bill and against the attempts to
change the preamble to the sixteenth article of the Declaration of Rights.
Members sharing these positions divided into two groups: those with

Episcopalian-rationalist backgrounds and those with dissenter (predominantly Presbyterian) backgrounds. Although these categories are not absolute, they demonstrate the need for an alliance between the two groups in order to assure the defeat of the assessment and the passage of the bill establishing religious freedom.

Episcopalian-Rationalist Group

Breckinridge, John ('84), Montgomery County. Breckinridge later became a staunch Presbyterian, and three of his sons were ministers. For a further sketch of his life, see *DAB*.

Bullitt, Cuthbert ('85), Prince William County. Bullitt (c. 1740-1791) was an extremely wealthy planter and lawyer. A graduate of William and Mary, he was married to the daughter of an Episcopalian clergyman and served in the vestry of Dettingen Parish for many years before the incorporation act. However, he was not reelected to the vestry in the spring of 1785 (Dettingen Parish Vestry Book, 1745-1802, photostat, VSL; Tyler, *Encyclopedia* 2: 6).

Cabell, Samuel Jordan ('85), Amherst County. The son of the liberal Episcopalian Col. William Cabell, Samuel J. Cabell (1756-1818) had attended William and Mary. For a sketch of his later career, see *DAB*.

Carter, Edward ('84), Albemarle County. A member of one of the richest families in Virginia, this Edward Carter (b. 1750) was probably the son of Edward Carter of Blenheim. In 1786 he signed a petition for the repeal of the incorporation act (RP, Nov. 24, 1786; George Selden Wallace, *The Carters of Blenheim* [Huntington, Va., 1955], pp. 1-3, 69).

Eggleston, Joseph ('85), Amelia County. Despite the fact that he was a vestryman of the church after its disestablishment and, in Meade's terms, a "devout Episcopalian," Eggleston (1754-1811) took Madison's side in the session of 1785. However, a year earlier he had signed a proassessment petition from Powhatan County, and in 1787, like Mason and George Nicholas, he voted against the sale of any glebe lands (Meade, *Old Churches* 2: 21-22; RP, June 4, 1784).

Gatewood, William ('84, '85), Essex County. Although he had signed a proassessment petition in 1779, Gatewood voted against the religious bills in 1784. An Episcopalian, he represented South Farnham Parish in the conventions of 1792 and 1793 (RP, Oct. 22, 1779).

Hawes, Samuel, Jr. ('84, '85), Caroline County. Despite the fact that his father was a vestryman of St. Margaret's Parish and a lay deputy to the Convention of 1785, young Hawes (1754-1788) solidly supported Madison in 1784 and 1785 (Elizabeth Hawes Ryland, "Hawes Family of Caroline Co., Va.," *William and Mary Quarterly*, 2d ser., 15 [1935]: 143-44).

Innes, James ('85), Williamsburg. The son of an Episcopal clergyman, Innes

(1754-1798) became a prominent lawyer and politician (Grigsby, *Virginia Convention of 1788* 1: 324-26; Tyler, *Encyclopedia* 2: 149).

Madison, James ('84, '85), Orange County. Requires no sketch.

Nicholas, Wilson Cary ('84, '85), Albemarle County. The son of one of the most prominent and devoted members of the established church, Nicholas (1761-1820) began his highly successful political career by opposing both the assessment and incorporation acts (*DAB*).

Roane, Spencer ('84), Essex County. Though a member of the Episcopal church and a delegate from South Farnham Parish to the Convention of 1785, Roane (1762-1822) opposed both the assessment and incorporation bills (*DAB*).

Simms, Charles ('85), Fairfax County. A lawyer, Simms (1755-1819) was listed in 1785 as a subscriber to Christ Church in Fairfax Parish. That same year he advised David Griffith and the vestry that they possessed the right under the incorporation act "to let and dispose of the pews in the Church . . . in any manner that they shall think most conducive to the interest and prosperity of that Church" (Fairfax Parish, Christ Church, Alexandria, Vestry Book and Records, 1765-1928, microfilm, VSL).

Strother, French ('84, '85), Culpeper County. Although an active member of the church before the disestablishment, Strother (1733-1800) even supported the sale of the glebes in 1787 (Slaughter, *St. Mark's Parish*, pp. 83-84).

Stuart, David ('85), Fairfax County. His father and grandfather had been ministers of the Church of England. Stuart (b. 1753) attended William and Mary, belonged to the vestry of Christ Church in 1787, and voted against the sale of any glebe lands that year (Fairfax Parish, Christ Church, Alexandria, Vestry Books and Records, 1765-1928, microfilm, VSL; Grigsby, *Virginia Convention of 1788* 2: 373).

Thruston, Charles Mynn ('85), Frederick County. Ordained as an Anglican minister in 1765, Thruston (1738-1812) served parishes in Gloucester and Frederick counties. He left the ministry during the Revolution to serve as an officer in the Continental army. Though he attended services and was elected to the vestry of Frederick Parish in 1785, his rector, Rev. Alexander Balmain, complained that Thruston refused to contribute to the parish subscription (Alexander Balmain's Memorandum Book, photostat, Swem Lib., College of William and Mary; Tyler, *Encyclopedia* 1: 342).

Other Episcopal vestrymen in the House who sided with this group on the religious liberty bill included *Samuel Garland* ('85), from Lunenburg County; *William Harrison* ('85), of Pittsylvania County; *Meriwether Smith* ('85), from Essex County; and *Nathaniel Wilkinson* ('84, '85), of Henrico County, who, despite his total opposition to the assessment and incorporation bills, was elected to the vestry of Henrico Parish in Richmond in 1785.

Dissenter (Predominantly Presbyterian) Group

Bibb, Richard ('84, '85), Prince Edward County. Bibb was studying for the Anglican ministry at William and Mary when the Revolution broke out. He left college to enter the army and after the war became a Methodist and later one of their preachers (Charles William Bibb, comp., *The Bibb Family in America, 1640-1940* [Baltimore, 1941], pp. 66-67).

Bowyer, Michael ('84, '85), Augusta County. Although a Presbyterian, Bowyer served as a vestryman for Augusta Parish from 1771 to 1777 and as a churchwarden for one of these years. As early as 1776 he had signed a petition asking relief for dissenters. He and his brother *John Bowyer* ('84, '85), Rockbridge County, both favored complete disestablishment (RP, Nov. 9, 1776; Beverly Ruffin, *Augusta Parish, Virginia, 1730-1780* [Verona, Va., 1970], p. 61; Evelina Gleaves Cohen, *Family Facts and Fairy Tales* [Wynnewood, Pa., 1953], pp. 1-2).

Clendinen, George ('84, '85), Greenbrier County. Born in Northern Ireland, Clendinen (1746-1797) was probably a Presbyterian. However, in 1779 he was married by a Baptist minister on the frontier. He voted against the sale of the glebes in 1787 (see John Edmund Stealey III, "George Clendinen and the Great Kanawha Valley Frontier: A Case Study of the Frontier Development of Virginia," *West Virginia History* 21 [1966]: 278-95).

Fry, Henry ('85), Culpeper County. The son of Joshua Fry, the boon companion of Jefferson's father, Henry Fry (1738-1823) had been raised in the Church of England. However, he underwent a conversion experience; and after a brief period with the Baptists, he enlisted as a "substitute" Methodist preacher during the Revolutionary period. His nephew *Joshua Fry* ('85), Albemarle County, also was in the legislature that year and supported Jefferson's bill (Slaughter, *Autobiography of Henry Fry*).

Garrard, James ('85), Fayette County, Kentucky. Garrard was the half brother of *William Garrard* of Stafford County. James (1749-1822) entered the Baptist ministry and then, during his second term as governor of Kentucky, became a Unitarian (Des Cognets, *Governor Garrard of Kentucky*, pp. 9, 12-13).

Johnston, Zachariah ('84, '85), Augusta County. Johnston (1742-1800) was the principal Presbyterian leader in the House. He also voted for the sale of the glebes in 1787. For a sketch of his life, see *DAB*.

Logan, Benjamin ('84, '85), Lincoln County, Kentucky. An Indian fighter baptized a Presbyterian, Logan (1743-1802) signed a call in 1773 to the Reverend Charles Cummings to become the pastor of his settlement (Charles Gano Talbert, *Benjamin Logan, Kentucky Frontiersman* [Lexington, Ky., 1962], p. 258; Joseph A. Waddell, ed., *Annals of Augusta County, Virginia, from 1726 to 1871* [2d ed., Bridgewater, Va., 1950], p. 318).

Moore, Andrew ('85), Rockbridge County. Moore had studied law under

George Wythe in Williamsburg. A Scotch-Irish Presbyterian, he (1752-1821) was a trustee of Liberty Hall Academy and an associate of William Graham. For a sketch of his political career, see Tyler, *Encyclopedia* 2: 88-89.

Pickett, William ('84, '85), Fauquier County. His older brother was a liberal Episcopalian, but two other brothers were Baptist ministers, and his sister married a Baptist minister. Pickett (b. 1742) was probably a Baptist himself (Stella Pickett Hardy, "The Pickett Family," *Fauquier Historical Society Bulletin,* 1st ser. [1921-24] : 207-15).

Russell, William ('84, '85), Washington County. Russell (1735-1793) attended William and Mary and later became a Methodist. He married Patrick Henry's sister in 1783, and when Francis Asbury visited them in 1788, he found them "a most kind family in deed and truth" (Clark, *Journal of Asbury* 1: 570; Tyler, *Encyclopedia* 2: 243).

Stuart, Archibald ('84, '85), Botetourt County. A Scotch-Irish Presbyterian, Stuart (1757-1832) was heavily influenced by William Graham at Liberty Hall. Later, while attending William and Mary, he lived in the home of the future Episcopal bishop, James Madison. He voted for the sale of the glebes in 1787 (Archibald G. Robertson, "Judge Archibald Stuart," an address delivered at the annual meeting of the Augusta County Historical Society, May 15, 1968; VHS; see also sketches in Grigsby, *Virginia Convention of 1788* 2: 9-14, and *DAB*).

Trigg, John ('84, '85), Bedford County. Trigg (1748-1804) was probably a Presbyterian. He received "a liberal schooling" and voted for the sale of the glebes in 1787 (*Biographical Directory of American Congress,* p. 1728).

Zane, Isaac ('84, '85), Shenandoah County. Perhaps the only Quaker in the House of Delegates, Zane also supported the sale of the glebes in 1787 (Roger W. Moss, Jr., "Isaac Zane, Jr., a 'Quaker for the Times,' " *Virginia Magazine of History and Biography* 77 [1969] : 291-306).

Other delegates from the western counties who associated themselves with this position and were probably Presbyterians included *Gawin Hamilton* ('84, '85) and *John Hopkins* ('84, '85), both of Rockingham County; *John Hays* ('84), from Rockbridge County; *Ralph Humphreys* ('84, '85), from Hampshire County; *James Montgomery* ('84) from Washington County; and *Daniel Trigg* ('85) and *Robert Sayers* ('84, '85) both from Montgomery County.

Bibliography

Primary Sources

Official Records

Hening, William Waller, ed. *The Statutes at Large: Being a Collection of All the Laws of Virginia, from the First Session of the Legislature in the Year 1619.* 13 vols. Richmond, 1809-28.

Journals of the House of Delegates of Virginia, 1776-1787. Richmond, 1827-28.

Journals of the Senate of the Commonwealth of Virginia, 1785-1786. Richmond, 1827.

Report of the Committee of Revisors Appointed by the General Assembly of Virginia in 1776. Richmond, 1784.

Thorpe, Francis Newton, ed. *The Federal and State Constitutions.* 7 vols. Washington, D.C., 1909.

Church Records, Published and Unpublished

Bell, Landon C., ed. *Cumberland Parish Vestry Book, 1746-1816.* Richmond, 1930.

Black Creek Church (Baptist), Southampton County, Records, 1776-1804. Photostat. Virginia State Library, Richmond.

Broad Run Baptist Church, Fauquier County, Records, 1762-1873. Photostat. Virginia State Library, Richmond.

Camden Parish, Pittsylvania County, Vestry Book, 1767-1852. Photostat. Virginia State Library, Richmond.

Chamberlayne, C. G., ed. *The Vestry Book of Kingston Parish, Mathews County, Virginia, 1679-1796.* Richmond, 1929.

Dettingen Parish, Prince William County, Vestry Book, 1745-1802. Photostat. Virginia State Library, Richmond.

Fairfax Parish, Christ Church, Alexandria, Vestry Book and Records, 1765-1928. Microfilm, Virginia State Library, Richmond. (Original in Library of Congress.)

Hall, William L., ed. *The Vestry Book of the Upper Parish, Nansemond County, Virginia, 1743-1793.* Richmond, 1949.

Mason, George Carrington, ed. *The Colonial Vestry Book of Lynnhaven Parish, Princess Anne County, Virginia, 1723-1788.* Newport News, Va., 1949.

Mill Swamp Baptist Church, Isle of Wight County, Records, 1777-90. Photostat. Virginia State Library, Richmond.

Minutes of Hanover Presbytery, 1755-86. Microfilm. Union Theological Seminary, Richmond.

St. George's Parish, Accomack County, Vestry Book, 1763-87. Photostat. Virginia State Library, Richmond.

St. John's Church (Protestant Episcopal), Richmond, Vestry Book, 1785-1887. Virginia Historical Society, Richmond.

Tinkling Springs Church (Presbyterian), Augusta County, Records, 1741-93. Photostat. Virginia State Library, Richmond.

Published Sources

Adair, Douglass, ed. "James Madison's Autobiography." *William and Mary Quarterly,* 3d ser., 2 (1945): 191-229.

Adams, Charles F., ed. *The Works of John Adams.* 10 vols. Boston, 1850-56.

Ballagh, James Curtis, ed. *The Letters of Richard Henry Lee.* 2 vols. Rept. New York, 1970.

Blackstone, W[illiam]. *Commentaries on the Laws of England.* 4 vols. London, 1769.

Boucher, Jonathan. *A View of the Causes and Consequences of the American Revolution: In Thirteen Discourses, Preached in North America between the Years 1763 and 1775.* Rept. New York, 1967.

Boyd, Julian P., ed. *The Papers of Thomas Jefferson.* 19 vols to date. Princeton, N.J., 1950—.

Clark, Elmer T., J. Manning Potts, and Jacob S. Payton, eds. *The Journal and Letters of Francis Asbury.* 3 vols. Nashville, 1958.

Dexter, F. B., ed. *The Literary Diary of Ezra Stiles.* 3 vols. New York, 1901.

Fleet, Elizabeth, ed. "Madison's 'Detached Memoranda.'" *William and Mary Quarterly,* 3d ser., 3 (1946): 534-68.

Ford, Paul Leicester, ed. *The Works of Thomas Jefferson.* 12 vols. New York, 1904-5.

"A Freeman of Virginia," *The Freeman's Remonstrance against an Ecclesiastical Establishment: Being Some Remarks on a Late Pamphlet Entitled the Necessity of an Established Church in Any State.* Williamsburg, 1777.

Greene, L. F., ed. *The Writings of John Leland.* Rept. New York, 1969.

Hawks, Francis L. *Contributions to the Ecclesiastical History of the United States of America.* 2 vols. New York, 1836-39.

Hill, William. *Autobiographical Sketches of Dr. William Hill... and Biographical Sketches... of the Reverend Dr. Moses Hoge of Virginia.* Rept. Richmond, 1968.

Hutchinson, William T., and William M. E. Rachal, eds., vols. 1-7. Robert A. Rutland and William M. E. Rachal, eds., vols. 8-10. *The Papers of James Madison.* 10 vols. to date. Chicago, 1962—.

"In Convention, May 25, 1786." Broadside signed by John Buchanan, Treasurer. Addressed to Rev. Lee Massey, Truro Parish, Fairfax, and Quaries to the Gentle Reader. Miscellaneous Papers, Protestant Episcopal Church in Virginia. Virginia Historical Society, Richmond.

Jarratt, Devereux. *The Life of the Reverend Devereux Jarratt, Rector of Bath Parish, Virginia, Written by Himself in a Series of Letters Addressed to the Rev. John Coleman.* Rept. New York, 1969.

Jefferson, Thomas. *Notes on the State of Virginia.* Ed. William Peden. Chapel Hill, N.C., 1955.

Johnson, Herbert A. ed., *The Papers of John Marshall.* 1 vol. to date. Chapel Hill, N.C., 1974—.

"Journal of the President and Masters or Professors of William and Mary College." *William and Mary Quarterly,* 1st ser., 15 (1907): 164-74, 264-69; 16 (1907): 73-80.

Joyce, John, to Robert Dickson, Mar. 25, 1785. *Virginia Magazine of History and Biography* 23 (1915): 407-14.

Kraus, Michael. "Charles Nisbet and Samuel Sanhope Smith—Two Eighteenth Century Educators." *Princeton University Library Chronicle* 6 (1944): 17-36.

Locke, John. *Epistolia de Tolerantia: A Letter on Toleration.* Ed. Raymond Klibansky and J. W. Gough. Oxford, 1968.

——. *Two Treatises on Government.* Ed. Peter Laslett. London, 1967.

Madison, James. *A Sermon Preached before the Convention of the Protestant Episcopal Church in the State of Virginia, on the Twenty Sixth of May, 1786.* Richmond, 1786.

Mays, David John, ed. *The Letters and Papers of Edmund Pendleton, 1734-1803.* 2 vols. Charlottesville, 1967.

Munford, Robert. *The Candidates; or, the Humours of a Virginia Election.* Ed. J. B. Hubbell and Douglass Adair. *William and Mary Quarterly,* 3d ser., 5 (1948): 217-57.

Randolph, Edmund. *History of Virginia.* Ed. Arthur H. Shaffer. Charlottesville, 1970.

Rutland, Robert A., ed. *The Papers of George Mason.* 3 vols. Chapel Hill, N.C., 1970.

Schoepf, Johann David. *Travels in the Confederation, 1783-1784.* 2 vols. Trans. and ed. Alfred J. Morrison. Philadelphia, 1911.

"Selections and Excerpts from the Lee Papers." *Southern Literary Messenger* 27 (1858): 324-32.

Slaughter, Philip. *Memoir of Col. Joshua Fry . . . with an Autobiography of His Son, Rev. Henry Fry, and a Census of Their Descendants.* Richmond, 1880.

Swanwick, John. *Consideration on a Act of the Legislature of Virginia, Entitled An Act for the Establishment of Religious Freedom.* Philadelphia, 1786.

Waddell, Joseph A., ed. *Annals of Augusta County, Virginia, from 1726 to 1871.* 2d ed. Bridgewater, Va., 1950.

Unpublished Sources

Alexander Balmain's Memorandum Book. Photostat. Earl Gregg Swem Library, the College of William and Mary in Virginia.

Robert Beverley Letterbook. Library of Congress.

A "bill concerning religion," Oct. 25, 1779, in House of Delegates Bills, Resolutions, etc., Box 3, Rough Bills, Oct. 1779. Virginia State Library, Richmond.

Bland Family. Genealogical notes. Virginia Historical Society, Richmond.

Breckinridge Family Papers. Library of Congress.

Thomas Coke, Sermon. Methodist Church Papers. Duke University Library, Durham, N.C.

John Cropper Papers. Virginia Historical Society, Richmond.

Edward Dromgoole Papers. Microfilm. Southern Historical Collection, University of North Carolina Library, Chapel Hill, N.C., 1966.

David Griffith Papers, 1760-1789. Virginia Historical Society, Richmond.

Thomas Haskins's Journal, 1782-85. Library of Congress.

Herndon Family Papers. Typescript. University of Virginia Library, Charlottesville.

Zachariah Johnston Papers. Virginia State Library, Richmond.

Arthur Lee Papers. Houghton Library, Harvard University, Cambridge, Mass.

Lee Family Papers, 1742-95. Microfilm. University of Virginia Library, Charlottesville.

Bishop James Madison Papers, 1781-1840. Virginia Historical Society, Richmond.

John Marshall Papers. Library of Congress.

Miscellaneous Letters, Protestant Episcopal Church in U.S.A., Virginia (Diocese) Papers, 1760-1972. Virginia Historical Society, Richmond.

George Nicholas, "Memoir of Wilson Cary Nicholas." Virginia Historical Society, Richmond.

Wilson Cary Nicholas Papers. Virginia Historical Society, Richmond.

Notebook of John Page. Earl Gregg Swem Library, the College of William and Mary in Virginia.

Robert Preston Papers. Virginia Historical Society, Richmond.

Religious Petitions, 1774-1802, presented to the General Assembly of Virginia. Microfilm. Virginia State Library, Richmond.

Thomas Rutherfoord Letterbook, 1784-86. Virginia Historical Society, Richmond.

William Short Papers. Library of Congress.

Archibald Stuart Papers. Earl Gregg Swem Library, the College of William and Mary in Virginia.

Tucker-Coleman Papers. Earl Gregg Swem Library, the College of William and Mary in Virginia.

Virginia, Executive Papers, 1784-85. Virginia State Library, Richmond.

Bishop William White Papers. Archives and Historical Collections of the Episcopal Church. Historical Society of the Episcopal Church, Austin, Texas.

Newspapers

Virginia Gazette (Purdie). Williamsburg, 1776-79.

Virginia Gazette (Dixon & Hunter). Williamsburg, 1776-78.

Virginia Gazette (Dixon & Nicholson). Williamsburg, 1778-79.

Virginia Gazette (Clarkson & Davis). Williamsburg, 1779.

Virginia Gazette, and Independent Chronicle. Richmond, 1783.

Virginia Gazette and Weekly Advertizer. Richmond, 1784-86.

Virginia Gazette, or the American Advertizer. Richmond, 1783-86.

Virginia Journal and Alexandria Advertizer, 1785.

Secondary Sources

Books

Anderson, W. P. *The Early Descendants of William Overton and Elizabeth Waters of Virginia, and Allied Families.* Cincinnati, 1938.

Beeman, Richard R. *The Old Dominion and the New Nation, 1788-1801.* Lexington, Ky., 1972.

Benedict, David. *A General History of the Baptist Denomination in America, and Other Parts of the World.* 2 vols. Boston, 1813.

Beveridge, Albert J. *The Life of John Marshall.* 4 vols. Boston, 1919.

Bibb, Charles William, comp. *The Bibb Family in America, 1640-1940.* Baltimore, 1941.

Biographical Directory of the American Congress, 1774-1961. Washington, D.C., 1961.

Boles, John B. *The Great Revival, 1787-1805: The Origins of the Southern Evangelical Mind.* Lexington, Ky., 1972.

Brant, Irving. *James Madison.* 6 vols. Indianapolis, 1941-61.

Bridenbaugh, Carl. *Mitre and Sceptre: Transatlantic Faiths, Ideas, Personalities, and Politics, 1689-1775.* New York, 1962.

Brock, Robert K. *Archibald Cary of Ampthill, Wheelhorse of the Revolution.* Richmond, 1937.

Brown, Alexander. *The Cabells and Their Kin.* Boston, 1895.

Brown, Robert E., and B. Katherine Brown. *Virginia, 1705-1786: Democracy or Aristocracy?* East Lansing, Mich., 1964.

Brydon, George MacLaren. *The Established Church in Virginia and the Revolution.* Richmond, 1930.

——. *Virginia's Mother Church and the Political Conditions under Which It Grew.* 2 vols. Vol. 1, Richmond, 1947. Vol. 2, Philadelphia, 1952.

Bucke, Emory Stevens, ed. *The History of American Methodism.* 3 vols. New York, 1964.

Cohen, Evelina Gleaves. *Family Facts and Fairy Tales.* Wynnewood, Pa., 1953.

Conway, Moncure D. *Omitted Chapters of History Disclosed in the Life and Papers of Edmund Randolph.* New York, 1888.

Cross, Arthur L. *The Anglican Episcopate and the American Colonies.* New York, 1902.

Davis, Richard Beale. *Intellectual Life in Jefferson's Virginia, 1790-1830.* Chapel Hill, N.C., 1964.

Des Cognets, Anna Russell. *Governor Garrard of Kentucky, His Descendants and Relatives.* Lexington, Ky., 1898.

Dunn, Joseph B. *The History of Nansemond County, Virginia.* N.p., 1907.

Eckenrode, Hamilton James. *Separation of Church and State in Virginia: A Study in the Development of the Revolution.* Rept. New York, 1971.

Foote, William Henry. *Sketches of Virginia, Historical and Biographical, First Series.* Richmond, 1850.

Gewehr, Wesley M. *The Great Awakening in Virginia, 1740-1790.* Durham, N.C., 1930.

Grigsby, Hugh Blair. *The History of the Virginia Federal Convention of 1788.* 2 vols. in 1. Rept. New York, 1970.

——. *The Virginia Convention of 1776.* Rept. New York, 1969.

Handy, Robert T. *A Christian America: Protestant Hopes and Historical Realities.* New York, 1971.

[Harrison, Fairfax]. *The Virginia Carys: An Essay in Genealogy.* New York, 1919.

Hart, Freeman H. *The Valley of Virginia in the American Revolution, 1763-1789.* New York, 1942.

Hayden, Horace Edwin. *Virginia Genealogies.* Rept. Baltimore, 1959.

Healey, Robert M. *Jefferson on Religion in Public Education.* New Haven, 1962.

Henriques, Ursula. *Religious Toleration in England, 1787-1833.* Toronto, 1961.

Henry, William Wirt. *Patrick Henry: Life, Correspondence and Speeches.* 3 vols. New York, 1891.

Howell, Robert B. *The Early Baptists of Virginia.* Rev. ed. Philadelphia, 1864.

James, Charles F. *Documentary History of the Struggle for Religious Liberty in Virginia.* Lynchburg, Va., 1900.

Johnson, Thomas Cary. *Virginia Presbyterianism and Religious Liberty in Colonial and Revolutionary Times.* Richmond, 1907.

Jones, Rufus. *The Quakers in the American Colonies.* New ed. New York, 1966.

Jordan, W. K. *The Development of Religious Toleration in England.* 4 vols. Cambridge, 1936-40.

Lee, Cazenove Gardner, Jr. *Lee Chronicle: Studies of the Early Generations of the Lees of Virginia.* Ed. Dorothy Mills Parker. New York, 1957.

Leyburn, James G. *The Scotch-Irish: A Social History.* Chapel Hill, N.C., 1962.

Little, Lewis P. *Imprisoned Preachers and Religious Liberty in Virginia.* Lynchburg, Va., 1938.

Loveland, Clara O. *The Critical Years: The Reconstruction of the Anglican Church in the United States of America.* Greenwich, Conn., 1956.

Main, Jackson Turner. *Political Parties before the Constitution.* Chapel Hill, N.C., 1973.

——. *The Upper House in Revolutionary America, 1763-1788.* Madison, Wis., 1967.

Malone, Dumas. *Jefferson and His Time.* 5 vols. to date. New York, 1948–.

May, Henry F. *The Enlightenment in America.* New York, 1976.

Mays, David John. *Edmund Pendleton, 1721-1803: A Biography.* 2 vols. Cambridge, Mass., 1952.

Mead. Sidney E. *The Lively Experiment: The Shaping of Christianity in America.* New York, 1963.

Meade, Robert Douthat. *Patrick Henry.* 2 vols. Philadelphia, 1957-69.

Meade, William. *Old Churches, Ministers, and Families of Virginia.* 2 vols. Philadelphia, 1891.

Morgan, Richard E. *The Supreme Court and Religion.* New York, 1972.

Morrison, Alfred J. *The College of Hampden Sidney: Calendar of Board Minutes, 1776-1786.* Richmond, 1912.

Morton, Richard Lee. *Colonial Virginia.* 2 vols. Chapel Hill, N.C., 1960.

Ruffin, Beverly. *Augusta Parish, Virginia, 1738-1780.* Verona, Va., 1970.

Rutland, Robert Allen. *The Birth of the Bill of Rights, 1776-1791.* Chapel Hill, N.C., 1955.

Ryland, Garnett. *The Baptists in Virginia, 1699-1926.* Richmond, 1926.

Semple, Robert B. *A History of the Rise and Progress of the Baptists in Virginia.* Richmond, 1810.

Slaughter, Philip. *A History of St. Mark's Parish, Culpeper County, Virginia.* Rept. in *Notes on Culpeper County, Virginia.* Comp. Raleigh Travers Green. Baltimore, 1958.

Smith, Elwyn A., ed. *The Religion of the Republic.* Philadelphia, 1971.

——. *Religious Liberty in the United States: The Development of Church-State Thought since the Revolutionary Era.* Philadelphia, 1972.

Stokes, Anson Phelps. *Church and State in the United States.* 3 vols. New York, 1950.

Strout, Cushing. *The New Heavens and New Earth: Political Religion in America.* New York, 1974.

Sweet, William Warren. *Methodism in American History.* Rev. ed. New York, 1961.

Swem, Earl G., and John W. Williams. *A Register of the General Assembly of Virginia, 1776-1918, and of the Constitutional Conventions.* Richmond, 1918.

Sydnor, Charles S. *Gentlemen Freeholders: Political Practices in Washington's Virginia.* Chapel Hill, N.C., 1952.

Talbert, Charles Gano. *Benjamin Logan, Kentucky Frontiersman.* Lexington, Ky., 1962.

Thompson, Ernest Trice. *The Presbyterians in the South.* 2 vols. Richmond, 1963.

Tyler, Lyon Gardiner, ed. *Encyclopedia of Virginia Biography.* 5 vols. New York, 1915.

——. *The Letters and Times of the Tylers.* 2 vols. Richmond, 1884-85.

Wallace, George Selden. *The Carters of Blenheim.* Huntington, W.Va., 1955.

Whitelaw, Ralph T. *Virginia's Eastern Shore: A History of Northhampton and Accomack Counties.* 2 vols. Gloucester, Mass., 1968.

Whitsitt, William H. *The Life and Times of Judge Caleb Wallace, Some Time a Justice of the Court of Appeals of Kentucky.* Filson Club Publications, 4. Louisville, Ky., 1888.

Wilson, Howard McKnight. *The Tinkling Spring, Headwater of Freedom: A Study of the Church and Her People, 1732-1952.* Fisherville, Va., 1954.

Wood, Gordon. *The Creation of the American Republic, 1776-1787.* Chapel Hill, N.C., 1969.

Articles

Adair, Douglass. Introduction and Notes to "The Autobiography of the Reverend Devereux Jarratt, 1732-1763." *William and Mary Quarterly,* 3d ser., 9(1952): 346-93.

Brant, Irving. "Madison: On the Separation of Church and State." *William and Mary Quarterly,* 3d ser., 8(1951): 3-24.

Brydon, George MacLaren. "David Griffith, 1742-1789: First Bishop Elect of Virginia." *Historical Magazine of the Protestant Episcopal Church* 9(1940): 194-230.

Buller, Paul F., Jr. "George Washington and Religious Liberty." *William and Mary Quarterly,* 3d ser., 17(1960): 486-506.

Butterfield, L. H. "Elder John Leland, Jeffersonian Itinerant." *Proceedings of the American Antiquarian Society* 62(1952): 155-242.

Corbin, Francis. "The Corbin Family." *Virginia Magazine of History and Biography* 30(1922): 315-18.

Crowe, Charles. "Bishop James Madison and the Republic of Virtue." *Journal of Southern History* 30(1964): 58-70.

Cushing, John D. "Notes on Disestablishment in Massachusetts, 1780-1833." *William and Mary Quarterly*, 3d ser., 26(1969): 169-90.

Goodwin, Gerald J. "The Anglican Reaction to the Great Awakening." *Historical Magazine of the Protestant Episcopal Church* 35(1966): 343-71.

Goodwin, Rutherfoord, "The Rev. John Bracken, 1745-1818: Rector of Bruton Parish and President of William and Mary College in Virginia." *Historical Magazine of the Protestant Episcopal Church* 10(1941): 354-98.

Gundersen, Joan Regner. "The Myth of the Independent Virginia Vestry," *Historical Magazine of the Protestant Episcopal Church* 44 (1975): 133-41.

Hardy, Stella Pickett. "The Pickett Family." *Fauquier Historical Society Bulletin*, 1st ser. (1921-24), 207-15.

Harrison, Lowell H. "A Young Virginian: John Breckinridge." *Virginia Magazine of History and Biography* 71(1963): 19-34.

Hood, Fred J. "Revolution and Religious Liberty: The Conservation of the Theocratic Concept in Virginia." *Church History* 40(1971): 170-81.

Hughes, N. C., Jr. "The Methodist Christmas Conference: Baltimore, Dec. 24, 1784–Jan. 2, 1785." *Maryland Historical Magazine* 54(1959): 272-92.

Hukner, Leon. "The Jews of Virginia from the Earliest Times to the Close of the Eighteenth Century." *Publications of the American Jewish Historical Society*, no. 20(1911): 100-105.

Isaac, Rhys. "Religion and Authority: Problems of the Anglican Establishment in Virginia in the Era of the Great Awakening and the Parsons' Cause." *William and Mary Quarterly*, 3d ser., 30(1973): 3-36.

Ketcham, Ralph L. "James Madison and Religion—A New Hypothesis." *Journal of the Presbyterian Historical Society* 38(1960): 65-90.

——. "James Madison at Princeton." *Princeton University Library Chronicle* 28(1966): 24-54.

"King Family of Virginia." *William and Mary Quarterly*, 1st ser., 16(1916): 105-10.

McLoughlin, William G. "Isaac Backus and the Separation of Church and State in America." *American Historical Review* 73(1968): 1392-1413.

Main, Jackson Turner. "The One Hundred." *William and Mary Quarterly*, 3d ser., 11(1954): 354-84.

Middleton, Arthur Pierce. "The Colonial Virginia Parish." *Historical Magazine of the Protestant Episcopal Church* 40(1971): 431-46.

——. "The Colonial Virginia Parson." *William and Mary Quarterly*, 3d ser., 26(1969): 425-40.

Monk, Samuel H. "Samuel S. Smith." Pp. 86-110 in *The Lives of Eighteen from Princeton*. Ed. Willard Thorp. Princeton, N.J., 1946.

Moss, Roger W., Jr. "Isaac Zane, Jr., a 'Quaker for the Times.' " *Virginia Magazine of History and Biography* 77(1969): 291-306.

Nichols, James Hastings. "John Witherspoon on Church and State." *Journal of the Presbyterian Historical Society* 42(1964): 166-74.

Risjord, Norman K., and Gordon DenBoer. "The Evolution of Political Parties in Virginia, 1782-1800." *Journal of American History* 60(1974): 961-1002.

Rivers, Mrs. Flournoy. "The Markham Family of Virginia." *Virginia Magazine of History and Biography* 5(1897): 205-6.

Ryland, Elizabeth Hawes. "Hawes Family of Caroline Co., Va." *William and Mary Quarterly,* 2d ser., 15(1935): 143-50.

Schaffer, Alan. "Virginia's 'Critical Period.' " In *The Old Dominion: Essays for Thomas Perkins Abernathy.* Ed. Darrett B. Rutman. Charlottesville, 1964.

Sellers, Charles Grier, Jr. "John Blair Smith." *Journal of the Presbyterian Historical Society* 34(1956): 201-25.

Singleton, Marvin K. "Colonial Virginia as First Amendment Matrix: Henry, Madison, and Assessment Establishment." *Journal of Church and State* 8(1966): 344-64.

Smylie, James H. "Madison and Witherspoon, Theological Roots of American Political Thought." *Princeton University Library Chronicle* 22(1961): 118-32.

Stanard, W. G. "Harrison of James River." *Virginia Magazine of History and Biography* 30-33(1922-25), passim; 36(1934): 183-87.

—. "Thornton Family." *William and Mary Quarterly,* 1st ser., 25(1916): 124-28.

Stealey, John Edmund, III. "George Clendinen and the Great Kanawha Valley Frontier: A Case Study of the Frontier Development of Virginia." *West Virginia History* 27(1966): 278-95.

Tyler, Lyon G. "Sheild Family." *William and Mary Quarterly,* 1st ser., 3(1895): 268-71.

Wright, C. Conrad. "Piety, Morality, and the Commonwealth." *Crane Review* 9(1967): 90-106.

Unpublished Works

Brown, Katherine L. "The Role of Presbyterian Dissent in Colonial and Revolutionary Virginia, 1740-1785." Ph.D. dissertation, Johns Hopkins University, 1969.

Kay, Miryam Neulander. "Separation of Church and State in Jeffersonian Virginia." Ph.D. dissertation, University of Kentucky, 1967.

Lohrenz, Otto. "The Virginia Clergy and the American Revolution, 1774-1799." Ph.D. dissertation, University of Kansas, 1970.

Maganzin, Louis. "Economic Depression in Maryland and Virginia, 1783-1787." Ph.D. dissertation, Georgetown University, 1967.

Paxton, M. W. "Zachariah Johnston of Augusta and Rockbridge and His Times." Virginia Historical Society, Richmond.

Quinlivan, Mary Elizabeth. "Ideological Controversy over Religious Establishment in Revolutionary Virginia." Ph.D. dissertation, University of Wisconsin, 1971.

Rich, Myra Lakoff. "The Experimental Years: Virginia, 1781-1789." Ph.D. dissertation, Yale University, 1966.

Robertson, Archibald G. "Judge Archibald Stuart." An address delivered at the annual meeting of the Augusta County Historical Society, May 15, 1968. Virginia Historical Society, Richmond, Va.

Index